CARSON·PIRIE·SCOTT

CHICAGO ARCHITECTURE AND URBANISM
A series edited by Robert Bruegmann, Joan Draper,
Wim de Wit, and David Van Zanten

CARSON·PIRIE·SCOTT

LOUIS SULLIVAN AND THE
CHICAGO DEPARTMENT STORE

JOSEPH SIRY

THE UNIVERSITY OF CHICAGO PRESS
CHICAGO AND LONDON

Works in Chicago Architecture and Urbanism are supported in part by funds given in memory of Ann Lorenz Van Zanten and administered by the Chicago Historical Society.

Joseph Siry is assistant professor of art at Wesleyan University.

Publication of this book has been supported by Carson Pirie Scott & Company.

The University of Chicago Press, Chicago 60637
The University of Chicago Press, Ltd., London

97 96 95 94 93 92 91 90 89 88 54321

Library of Congress Cataloging-in-Publication Data

Siry, Joseph, 1956–
    Carson Pirie Scott : Louis Sullivan and the Chicago department store / Joseph Siry.
        p. cm. — (Chicago architecture and urbanism ; v. 2)
    Bibliography: p.
    Includes index.
    ISBN 0-226-76136-3
    1. Carson Pirie Scott (Dept. store).   2. Sullivan, Louis H., 1856–1924—Criticism and interpretation.   3. Architecture—Illinois—Chicago.   4. Architecture, Modern—20th century—Illinois—Chicago.   5. Skyscrapers—Illinois—Chicago.   6. Department stores—Illinois—Chicago.   7. Chicago (Ill.)—Buildings, structures, etc.
    I. Title. II. Series.
NA6233.C4C387   1987
725'.21'0924—dc19   87-34003
                                                                 CIP

102953

CONTENTS

ACKNOWLEDGMENTS

This study began in a seminar on Chicago's architecture led by Robert Bruegmann at M.I.T. in the fall of 1981. His initial encouragement of the project, his continued interest in its development, and his detailed criticisms of the manuscript have been invaluable.

This project could not have been completed without the cooperative expertise of many individuals. In Chicago, John Vinci, A.I.A., generously permitted access to the wealth of documentation related to his restoration of the Carson Pirie Scott Building in 1979 and to the archives of the late Richard Nickel, whose able research on the building served as a foundation for my own. Timothy Samuelson of the Commission on Chicago Landmarks gladly aided this project, sharing his remarkable knowledge of his city's architecture and the works of Louis Sullivan. Katherine Walsh, director of Corporate Communications for Carson, Pirie, Scott & Co., arranged access to surviving records and to different parts of the building itself. Wim de Wit and Scott La France of the Architectural Collection at the Chicago Historical Society helped to locate valuable sources of information. Members of the families of the building's original clients, Messrs. Leopold Schlesinger and David Mayer, were ever gracious in response to my inquiries.

Barbara Ryan of Editorial Associates in Middletown, Connecticut, proved to be an invaluable resource thanks to her expertise and patience in editing and word processing several drafts of the manuscript. The assistance of Stephen Lebergott of Olin Library at Wesleyan University is gratefully acknowledged. The Department of Architecture at M.I.T. provided financial assistance for research in Chicago, and Wesleyan University's grants in support of scholarship helped to defray expenses of preparing the manuscript.

Stanford Anderson, director of the program in history, theory, and criticism of architecture at M.I.T., created a stimulating and supportive context for graduate studies and served as the reliably critical advisor for the dissertation on which this book is based. David Friedman and Henry Millon of M.I.T. read the dissertation and provided valuable criticisms. David Van Zanten of Northwestern University offered editorial guidance in preparation for publication. My colleagues and students at Wesleyan also made significant contributions toward completion of the project.

This study owes much to the inspiration of former teachers. Among these, Anthony Vidler of Princeton University provided a memorable education in historical and critical studies of architecture and urbanism. My deep gratitude goes to the late Mario J. Romanach of the University of Pennsylvania, whose special gifts as an architect and teacher brought the art to life in a unique way.

By far the author's greatest debts are those he owes to his family. Their educational support over a long period of time, their encouragement of this project, and their great patience with its demands enabled its realization. Their willingness to read many revisions of the text greatly improved the final version. In this task, their sympathy, skill, and perseverance have shown them to be true friends of the reader, and thus, of the author. Their generosity of spirit brought this book into being.

CARSON·PIRIE·SCOTT

Fig. 1. Schlesinger and Mayer Store (now Carson Pirie Scott), Chicago, 1899–1904. Louis Sullivan, architect. Reprinted from *Architectural Record* 16 (July 1904), courtesy of Architectural Record and Chicago Architectural Photographing Company.

INTRODUCTION

The Schlesinger and Mayer Store, known by the name of its present owners, Carson Pirie Scott & Co., has long been recognized as an important work in the history of architecture. The building was the last large commercial structure designed by Louis Sullivan and is thus cited as a culminating work in his career as a designer of tall buildings. The Schlesinger and Mayer Store has also been seen as a climax of efforts in Chicago in the late nineteenth century to develop an architectural expression for the steel frame. For these reasons the building is pivotal for understanding Sullivan's individual achievement and the relationship of his work to the architectural development of Chicago. Carson Pirie Scott emerged from a particular historical situation and urban context. Its design was a response to specific cultural conditions that the completed work in turn helped to define. Through this building Sullivan gave expression to notable facets of the life of Chicago in 1900. Carson Pirie Scott is thus a monument characteristic of a place and time, as well as the work of a remarkable architect.

Initial critical response to the Schlesinger and Mayer Store appeared soon after the building's opening in 1903, when the work of Sullivan and his colleagues in Chicago had already gained a reputation outside the city. Writing for the *Architectural Record* in 1904, Henry W. Desmond prefaced his criticism of the completed Schlesinger and Mayer Store stating that Sullivan at that moment occupied "something of the usually iso-

3

lated position of the prophet, the forerunner, the intensely personal force. . . . For, let it be well understood, Mr. Sullivan is really our only Modernist. . . . To say that he has invented a style would, of course, be to say too much, but he has certainly evolved and elaborated a highly artistic form of superficial decorative expression in logical connection with the American steel skeleton building."[1] Carson Pirie Scott was regarded in 1905 as a work in which Sullivan had "carried his logic to extreme lengths. It is a crystal palace of glass and masonry, and iron overwrought with ornament-like flowers and frost. Here indeed is a new architectural art, superior to *l'Art Nouveau* of Europe in that it is born of reason and not of whim."[2] In the same year another critic asserted that, "as far as architecture goes, Chicago has even created a new school, virtually a new style, 'un nouveau art,' which antedates the movement in the same direction about which so much is heard in Paris and among our German friends. Louis Sullivan was the first man—in Chicago or anywhere else—who boldly cast off the thralldom of precedent and treated the new condition of structure in a frank and artistic manner."[3] In 1906 the Schlesinger and Mayer Store was praised as evidence of the possibility that steel could be treated as an architectural material with a system of expression derived from its unique proportions and lightness. Sullivan's building in Chicago and Ernest Flagg's later first Singer Building in New York were cited as works whose architects had "not feared to discard conventional models and to make modern structures in a modern way with modern means and materials, even as the ancient Greeks and Medieval masons did, and, like them, to even found a new style in architecture, expressing the needs and taste of a nation."[4]

The Schlesinger and Mayer Building marked the culmination of the period in which Sullivan's historical position was first consolidated not only in America but in Europe. As early as 1901, A. W. Barker had asserted that "since Richardson, no American architect has attracted the interest of foreign critics to the degree that Mr. Sullivan has. Recently, a Danish reviewer, writing on the art of optimism, quoted his work to uphold his belief that Europe would ultimately have to learn architecture in America, and French and English critics in general take him much more seriously than his own countrymen."[5] In at least one instance, general European awareness of Sullivan extended to specific interest in Carson Pirie Scott. The building received close attention from Hendrik Petrus Berlage, Sullivan's exact contemporary and counterpart as a founder of a new architecture in Holland. On his visit to America and Chicago in 1911, Berlage was already familiar with the work of Sullivan and Wright. William Purcell, who escorted Berlage around the city, recalled that of all Sullivan's buildings, Berlage was particularly intrigued with Carson Pirie Scott. Berlage's "questions were very penetrating and concerned every aspect of the building—its plan, engineering, economic relations, relation to the community, what people thought about it, how the designs were produced, what was the background of the people who worked on it, the relation of Sullivan to his engineer—nothing escaped the man's examination."[6] Berlage mentioned the building in his accounts of American developments published after his return to Europe, citing it as an example of Sullivan's inclination to decorative art in all his works of architecture. In Berlage's view, Carson Pirie Scott was a building "overloaded with ornament, but nevertheless it makes a quiet and distinguished impression."[7]

American accounts of Sullivan's architecture that appeared in the 1920s included fewer references to Carson Pirie Scott. In his autobiography of 1924, Sullivan himself described the emergence of the tall steel building in Chicago as a structural novelty, a new architectural type, and a monumental form.[8] Neither Sullivan's autobiography nor his obituaries in 1924, however, referred to Carson Pirie Scott among his major works. Histories of American architecture written in the twenties tended to portray Sullivan and his followers as representing an extreme position.[9] In retrospect the work of the Chicago school around 1900 was interpreted as an anomaly unrelated to a renewed interest in eclectic historicism. In 1928, George Edgell, while acknowledging Sullivan's contribution to the form of the skyscraper, argued that structural expression was no longer the issue that should preoccupy designers. In 1922 the competition for the new Chicago Tribune Building had elicited many designs that had featured the application of historic motifs to towers of steel. Writing in the wake of this competition and the apparently successful adaptation of traditional styles to a range of contemporary types, Edgell concluded that "more classical formulae may be applied to [steel structure] without producing reactionary work."[10] In this same period the historian Fiske Kimball did mention the Schlesinger and Mayer Store in his account of American architecture, though not in relation to Sullivan's major contribution to the tall building, but as an example of his characteristic foliate ornament. The building was thus compared not with the earlier skyscrapers but with the Transportation Building of the World's Columbian Exposition of 1893.[11]

In the late 1920s European historians of the modern movement in architecture cited Carson Pirie Scott as an important work. In his book of 1927 entitled *Groszstadt Architektur*, Ludwig Hilbersheimer included an illustration of the building as a representative example of America's contribution to the new architecture. He noted that the centralization of commercial life in metropolitan areas had produced new types of buildings such as the department store. Hilbersheimer stated that these new types demanded increased illumination of their interior spaces and the possibility for modification or expansion which had led to the reduction of the traditional wall to a skeletal structure. The architectural form of such a skeletal structure could have either a vertical or a horizontal emphasis. In department stores the horizontal emphasis on division between floors clearly showed their layering one upon another. Hilbersheimer described Carson Pirie Scott as a design in which the layering of story upon story found such a clear architectural expression. He maintained that Sullivan's building could be compared in its formal horizontality to French department stores following the example of the Bon Marché in Paris begun in 1869 (Figure 2). This tradition would continue to inform later variations on the horizontal theme, such as Erich Mendelsohn's Schocken department store in Chemnitz of 1929 (Figure 3).[12] Thus, for

Fig. 2. Magasins du Bon Marché, Paris, 1869–79. A. Laplanche, L.-A. Boileau, L.-C. Boileau, and G. Eiffel, architects. Reproduced by permission of the Bibliothèque Nationale, Paris (H50912).

Fig. 3. Schocken Department Store, Chemnitz (Karl Marx Stadt), Germany, 1929.
Erich Mendelsohn, architect. Photo courtesy of the Museum of
Modern Art, New York.

Hilbersheimer, Carson Pirie Scott fit within a tradition of architectural
expression associated with department stores as a new type of commercial building in the nineteenth and twentieth centuries.

European awareness of Chicago developments as precedent for a new
architecture soon inspired their reconsideration by American historians
sympathetic to the nascent modern movement. Lewis Mumford laid the
foundation for a new historiography in a series of lectures on American
art and architecture in the late nineteenth century first published as
The Brown Decades in 1931. Focusing on the work of Richardson, Sullivan, and John Wellborn Root, Mumford asserted that "between 1880
and 1895 the task and method of modern architecture were clarified
through the example of a group of American architects whose consistent

and united efforts in this line antedated, by at least a decade, the earliest
similar innovations in Europe."[13] In making a case for the American
origins of modern architecture, Mumford discussed Carson Pirie Scott
as a precedent for architecture informed by the ideal of the *neue Sach-
lichkeit*, or the new functionalism. Echoing Hilbersheimer's account,
Mumford cited the Schlesinger and Mayer Building as a neglected mas-
terpiece. He wrote that in this design for a department store, "Sullivan
used a bold system of horizontal windows and gained a legitimate accent
at the corner by a rounded glass bay: a clean, logical solution for the problem, more decisive in every way, it seems to me, than his skyscrapers." [14]

Upon arriving in America and visiting Chicago in 1938, Walter Gro-
pius is said to have remarked that "had the *avant-garde* in Europe known
the Carson-Pirie-Scott Building, the evolution of modern architecture
there might have been accelerated by fifteen years."[15] The historian
Sigfried Giedion developed this sense of the building and Chicago's
achievement in his compendium on the sources and rationale of the
modern movement first published in 1941 as *Space, Time and Architecture*.
In identifying the zeitgeist of modernity, Giedion focused on the phenomena of science and mechanization. Giedion characterized Chicago's
architecture and urbanism as the representative crystallization of these
modern conditions. He asserted that from 1880 through 1893, the business quarter of Chicago "was the center of architectural development
not merely for the United States but for the whole world."[16] Giedion
maintained that "the importance of the [Chicago] school for the history
of architecture lies in this fact: for the first time in the nineteenth century the schism between construction and architecture, between the engineer and the architect was healed ... the Chicago School strove to
break through to pure forms, forms which would unite construction and
architecture in an identical expression."[17] Given this historiographic perspective, Giedion identified Carson Pirie Scott as a culmination of earlier
attempts in Chicago to lend expressive clarity to the steel frame. He
wrote that the building's front "is designed to fulfill its indispensable
function, the admission of light. Its basic elements are the horizontally
elongated 'Chicago windows,' admirably homogeneous and treated to
coincide with the framework of the skeleton. The whole front is executed with a strength and precision that is matched by no other building
of the period."[18]

Giedion's view of Carson Pirie Scott and the Chicago school made
these works a part of the canon of modern architecture, suggesting the
value of more detailed historical treatment. This was the task assumed
by the historian Carl Condit, whose thesis first appeared in an article of
1948 entitled "The Chicago School and the Modern Movement in Ar-

chitecture."[19] Condit characterized Chicago building as representative of science, technology, and industrialization as "the chief cultural phenomena" of modernity. He discussed a series of key works in the history of the city's commercial architecture to the turn of the century as examples of a development through which Chicago building "ceased to be a solid mass of masonry" and approached "the dissolution or dematerialization of the wall into glass."[20] Chicago innovations of the late nineteenth century could thus be understood as an antecedent of the architecture of Mies van der Rohe, whose aesthetic of steel and glass had become prevalent in Chicago, where he had built and taught since arriving from Germany in 1938. In the 1950s Ludwig Hilbersheimer, now Mies's colleague in Chicago, saw Sullivan's upper elevation as the forerunner of such designs as Mies's Lake Shore Drive Apartments of 1949–51 (Figure 4). Condit wrote that above the ornamental base of Sullivan's building, there rise "the great cellular elevations, bold and exact, dynamically and perfectly proportioned articulations of the steel and iron frame. . . . The elevations above the base have a cleanliness and precision so nearly absolute that the most minute change in proportions could be detected. There is no better revelation of the architecture of modern industry and commerce." Condit concluded that Carson Pirie Scott was "the ultimate achievement of the Chicago School and one of the great works of modern commercial architecture in the world."[21]

The assessments of Giedion and Condit fixed the historical position of Carson Pirie Scott as a work representative of Sullivan's and Chicago's contribution to the history of architecture. Their views are not the only historical or critical perspectives that have been brought to bear on this building, but their consensus established it as a key monument of international significance.[22]

This study is an attempt to clarify the origins of Carson Pirie Scott in the Chicago of the late nineteenth century. The following chapters treat the history of the building's urban setting, the story of its design and construction, its character as a department store, and Sullivan's intentions for it as a work of architecture. The attempt has been to show the significance of Sullivan's design in its historical context. The Schlesinger and Mayer Store is treated as one point of entry into broader questions about the commercial and urban development of Chicago, the culture of shopping along its major mercantile street, and the array of aspirations that Sullivan brought to his art. The aim has been to reconstruct the convergence of conditions and intentions that underlay the building's original form. From this perspective Sullivan's work emerges as a richly complex artifact whose analysis can contribute a range of insights into the character of its city and the achievement of its architect.

Fig. 4 Upper west elevation of the Carson Pirie Scott Building (*above*). Richard
Nickel Archive, courtesy of the Richard Nickel Committee, Chicago. Exterior of
860 Lake Shore Drive (*right*), Chicago, 1949–51. Ludwig Mies van der Rohe,
architect. Reproduced by permission of Hedrich-Blessing, Chicago.

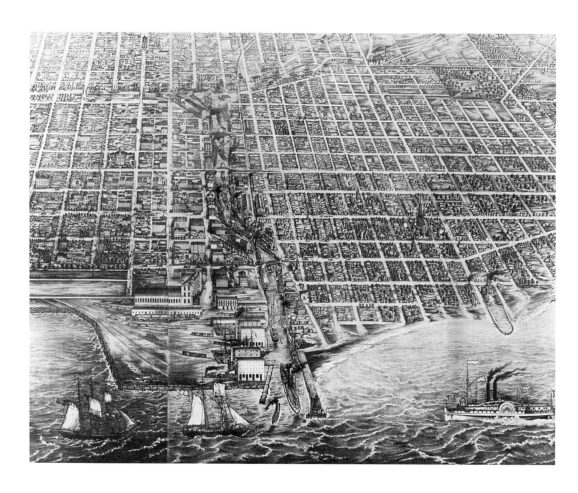

Fig. 1-1. View of Chicago, about 1857. Courtesy of the Chicago Historical Society (ICHi-17276).

I

THE DEVELOPMENT OF CHICAGO'S STATE
STREET AND ITS DEPARTMENT STORES TO 1898

The history of Chicago's mercantile culture closely parallels the development of the city itself. Since it became a town in 1833, Chicago grew as a central point of distribution for goods manufactured in the eastern United States and shipped west to supply the needs of communities on the frontier. As a settlement situated far into the hinterland of the old Northwest Territory, Chicago became a pivotal point of exchange in this transcontinental trade. A view of Chicago in 1857 emphasizes its identity as the major port on Lake Michigan at the mouth of the Chicago River (Figure I-1). At that time the commercial core of Chicago extended east to west along the main channel of the river inland from the lake. Surrounding this zone of water traffic, the street grid of the nascent town extended outward over the flat continuity of the land to the north, south, and west sides. There appears to have been no rigid distinction between the country and the city. Beyond the concentration of business along the river, the residential streets of Chicago are shown lined with trees. The street grid defined plots on which were set houses whose density dissipates into open land at a distance from the boat channels. Apart from brick commercial structures near this wharfage, buildings were predominantly of wood and the streets themselves were largely unpaved as they continued into the countryside. The inhabited blocks in the foreground extend into unbuilt plots toward the frontier suggesting the role of the grid as a basis for urban development. The view thus conveys the idea of a settlement growing over a landscape, as if the image were the pictorial equivalent of Chicago's motto, "Urbs in Horto," or the city set in a garden.

Chicago's geographic position encouraged its merchants to concentrate on wholesaling. The city's location at the convergence of water routes and rail lines had been a decisive factor in its early growth. Since 1848 the city had been a depot for transshipment of goods along the Illinois and Michigan Canal from Lake Michigan to the Mississippi Valley. By the mid 1850s Chicago had also become the focus for a network of railroads that heightened the city's identity as the principal junc-

Fig. 1-2. Lake Street, looking east from Clark Street, about 1867. Courtesy of the Chicago Historical Society (ICHi-04309).

ture between the eastern seaboard and the great northwestern region of the country. For this reason, mercantile houses which later evolved into some of the city's largest department stores had their origins as suppliers of dry goods to the population of the prairie.[1] These houses had their headquarters along Lake Street, Chicago's first commercial corridor, which ran east-west one block south of the wharves along the Chicago River (Figure I-2). Lake Street was not a boulevard or an avenue but simply a main street along which were found the city's hotels, newspaper offices, and post office.[2] Though Lake Street's dry goods houses were mainly wholesale distributors, they did maintain small retail stores on the street level of their buildings. In these stores one could buy an assortment of clothing and fabric often sold alongside groceries and household goods. All varieties of merchandise were displayed together in the manner of rural general stores. The lack of elegance and the rudimentary array of goods in Chicago's first retail stores were in keeping with the firms' primary role as suppliers of provisions to the frontier. The regional demand for basic goods had so encouraged wholesaling that Chicago itself lacked any fashionable retail houses comparable to those that had developed along Manhattan's Broadway during the first half of the nineteenth century.

The individual most responsible for the transformation of retailing in Chicago was Potter Palmer (1826–1902).[3] Palmer had begun his career as a merchant in Lockport, New York. Impressed with Chicago's potential for commercial growth, he persuaded friends of his family and other acquaintances in New York and New England to invest capital in his attempt to establish a combined wholesale and retail firm in Chicago. He migrated to Chicago in 1852 and opened a dry goods store on the first floor of one building on the north side of Lake Street. Palmer attempted to distinguish his dry goods store, specializing in clothing, materials, and fashionable items of apparel, from existing local general stores where one could buy an assortment of goods "from codfish to calico."[4] Palmer sought a spacious shop interior to differentiate his operation from older stores, which were typically small, cramped, and poorly ventilated. He stocked his store with the highest quality of imported women's fashions and introduced the locally unprecedented policies of permitting exchange of goods or their return for cash refunds. The house was selective in extending credit, though liberal with those to whom it did. The result was that Palmer cultivated a clientele attracted to a higher grade of fabrics and apparel in a store whose refined persona extended to its arrangement of shelves and its treatment of customers. Such a distinguished dry goods house was the first of its kind in the Chicago of the 1850s.

Fig. 1-3. First A. T. Stewart Store, New York, 1845–46. John B. Snook and Joseph
Trench, architects. Courtesy of the New-York Historical Society, New York City.

Palmer's original quarters were only the street level of a single building. By 1858, however, Palmer found more expansive quarters in a
newly constructed marble-fronted building on Lake Street which appears as the tallest central building in Figure I-2. The new headquarters
of P. Palmer & Co. was described as a "business palace" modeled on the
architecture of dry goods houses on New York's Broadway such as A. T.
Stewart's, whose early quarters, begun in 1845–46, had been known to
Manhattan as "the marble palace" (Figure I-3).[5] Palmer thus advertised
his new marble-faced store on Lake Street as the "A. T. Stewart of
the West."[6]

Palmer's innovations extended beyond his store to include a broader
vision of the role of his business in Chicago's urban development. In his
memoirs Palmer recalled that he invested much of his capital in real
estate and buildings in order "to form a foundation of support for my
merchandising interests."[7] He apparently viewed control of Chicago's
desirable commercial properties as a means of creating an urban environment which would enhance the success of his own retail and wholesale trade. After the Civil War, Palmer focused his interest on State
Street, which until that time had remained for most of its length an unpaved road with two-story frame buildings housing shops and trades

below living quarters.[8] From 1865 through 1867, Palmer gradually withdrew from partnership in his mercantile business, leaving his wholesale and retail operations to the direction of Marshall Field and Levi Z. Leiter. Palmer then began to concentrate his attention on the future development of State Street, buying three-fourths of a mile of its commercial frontage south of Lake Street.[9] His strategy was evidently based on the prediction that Chicago would soon grow along the lines of its new horse-car railways. The first of these had been inaugurated on State Street in 1859, linking its central commercial corridor to the fashionable residential districts developing on the city's South Side.[10] The realignment of Chicago's growth along the horse-car routes permitted Palmer to envision a new scale of projected development, improving a continuous length of properties over several blocks rather than over adjacent lots as had been the pattern in the earlier pedestrian city. Having acquired control of such substantial frontage along State Street, Palmer financed the construction of a palatial six-story dry goods store on the northeast corner of State and Washington streets into which he persuaded his former firm of Field, Leiter & Co. to move in 1868. The sudden departure from Lake Street of its largest and most prestigious merchandiser induced neighboring smaller dry goods stores to relocate on State Street. To accommodate this dramatic shift of mercantile activity, there were erected from 1869 to 1871 between thirty and forty of what were described as marble-front buildings on State Street to create the new commercial avenue of Chicago (Figure I-4).[11]

Palmer's vision of the street was evidently rooted in his familiarity with the simultaneous urban development of Paris and New York. In 1867, the year before he began to transform State Street, Palmer had taken an extended vacation in Europe, where he observed the later phase of Haussmann's rebuilding of Paris under Napoleon III. Thus, a contemporary described Palmer's program of urbanism as the "Haussmannizing of State Street."[12] He had widened the street and sought to unify its architecture in order to approximate a Parisian boulevard of the Second Empire. The effect of Palmer's initiative in creating a continuously renewed thoroughfare prompted one observer of 1870 to note that State Street "has taken the precedence over all others in point of substantial improvements, and is now the fashionable retail street—the Rue de Rivoli—of Chicago."[13] In addition to Parisian precedent, Palmer compared the architectural development of State Street to Manhattan's Broadway. A description of New York's premier retail street in 1866 noted that "the eye is greeted everywhere by long lines of marble and stone buildings, many of them of great architectural elegance."[14] When Palmer had completed his initial transformation of State Street in 1868,

Fig. 1-4. State Street, looking south from Lake Street, about 1869. Courtesy of the
Chicago Historical Society (ICHi-04738).

he thus asserted that he had intended to create "the Broadway of Chicago" whose length would be similarly graced with a continuous frontage
of ornate marble facades.[15]

The building that more than any other established the character of
commercial architecture on State Street before the Fire was the Field,
Leiter & Co. Store (Figure I-5). This structure was clad in a surface of
white Connecticut marble carved in ornate relief. Such a monumental
design was among the first of its kind in Chicago, though comparable
stores of cast iron were built in the same era in Manhattan's shopping
district. In New York the original prototype for the image of a marble
palace had been the early A. T. Stewart Store on Broadway, wherein the

first floor was devoted to retailing and the upper floors were given over
to a wholesale trade. To accommodate his expanding retail business
A. T. Stewart had built another store farther north on Broadway in
1859–62 (Figure I-6). This larger A. T. Stewart Store was famous in the
New York of its time for its extended facades of cast iron painted white
that recalled the marble architecture of the earlier store and others like
it along Broadway. The Field, Leiter Store resembled this later Stewart
Building in its show windows set within a Corinthian colonnade along
the sidewalk and in its ranges of arched windows through the upper
stories that provided light for the interior sales floors. Like the first

Fig. I-5. Field, Leiter and Co., Chicago, 1867–68. Courtesy of
the Chicago Historical Society (ICHi-01584).

Fig. 1-6. Second A. T. Stewart Store, New York, 1859–62. John Kellum & Son, architects. Courtesy of the New-York Historical Society, New York City.

A. T. Stewart Store, however, the new Field, Leiter Store was devoted to retailing on its street level with wholesale departments above. Also, like the earlier Stewart's, the new Field, Leiter Store was a true marble edifice on its exterior, though it was modeled after different stylistic sources. Like other buildings of its era, the Chicago store also featured a crown of mansard roofs that heightened its associations with Parisian precedent. When the Field, Leiter Store was completed in 1868 its grand opening was a civic event with the building festooned and lighted inside and out to receive a throng of invited patrons who arrived at its carriage entrance on Washington Street for an evening of celebration. The opening served as a theatrical inauguration not only of the building itself but of Palmer's commitment to enhance the whole of State Street with Field, Leiter & Co. as its centerpiece. As a monument keyed to a vision of the city's future, the new store was hailed as "the chief pride of Chicago's architecture."[16]

No sooner had the preeminence of State Street been established than its entire commercial corridor was destroyed in the Great Fire of 1871. The devastation of the Fire caused much speculation that Chicago could not survive and would not be rebuilt.[17] One account of the disaster's aftermath records that the day after the Fire, the city's merchants met in a local club building to discuss the situation and their options. Potter Palmer, Marshall Field, Levi Leiter, and others were present at this meeting. Some members of the group proposed that their remaining assets be assigned to creditors and that their businesses be closed. Yet the merchants reached a consensus to carry on. They resolved not to repudiate their debts and to reopen their operations and rebuild their facilities as quickly as possible.[18]

The first buildings, which literally rose from the ashes, were thus charged with meaning as the most visible symbols of the city's commitment to sustain its existence. From 1871 to 1873 the new business blocks to emerge from the desolated townscape were documented in a series of engravings and descriptions published in *The Land Owner*, a monthly journal devoted to real estate interests. Two years after the Great Fire, the wave of new and ornate building provoked the editors to assert that Chicago was then "The Paris of Western America," the center of its trade and commerce as well as its architectural capital.[19] Chicago aspired to regional dominance in all fields of economic and cultural activity comparable to the central position of the French capital in its national affairs. The choice of Paris as the city to emulate also suggests that separate structures rebuilt on scattered sites through Chicago were conceived in a spirit of a unified architectural identity for the new city comparable to Haussmann's vision of an imperial urbanism. The monuments of rebuilt Chicago were thus initial points of reference which set a standard of aspiration amid the ashes of the pre-Fire city, just as the major landmarks of the Second Empire had emerged from the flattened rubble of old Paris.

A central event in the rebuilding of Chicago was the construction of the new Palmer House as the city's leading hotel completed in 1875 (Figure I-7).[20] This new iron and brick building, designed by architect John Van Osdel, was billed as the world's first completely fireproof hotel. Its street fronts were faced with a gray granite, thereby endowing the building with an appearance of substantiality to counter the image of Chicago as the wooden frontier town consumed by the Great Fire. Within the exterior lower floors of the Palmer House there were planned separate rented quarters for specialty shops such as jewelers, tailors, confectioners, and others catering to the hotel's anticipated class of trade. These shopfronts were set within the street level and a mezzanine floor or *entresol* with plate glass windows framed in massive castings of ornamental iron. The Palmer House was one of the first major commercial buildings in Chicago to incorporate an entresol within its base. This feature of Parisian origin was to be continually reinterpreted in the later architecture of State Street.[21] The Palmer House's rounded corner and dome

Fig. 1-7. The Old Palmer House, Chicago, 1875. John Van Osdel, architect. Reprinted
from Randall, *History of the Development of Building Construction in Chicago.*

enhanced the building's identity as an architectural landmark of the rebuilt city. Van Osdel probably adapted this motif from the domed
rounded corners of Parisian apartment houses that became characteristic of the city's architecture beginning in the later years of the Second
Empire.[22] From the time of its completion until it was replaced by the
present Palmer House, designed by Holabird and Roche (1925–27),
Van Osdel's domed corner served as a visual anchor along State Street at
its intersection with Monroe, marking the southern extent of the fashionable shopping district in the post-Fire era.

The ornate commercial facades further north along State Street after
the Fire are documented in a photograph of 1878 looking north from
Madison Street (Figure I-8). The major structure in the center of the
block was the Colonnade Building completed after the Fire by architects
Wheelock and Thomas. Its street front featured superimposed colon-
nades on the upper stories and dual arched cornices with miniature spires
or finials above the names of the two owners. Along the building's base
a continuous range of plate glass display windows was set between col-
onnades. Similar variations of this motif continued up the block to define neighboring shopfronts creating a succession of show windows from
corner to corner. The strip of sidewalk nearest the buildings was raised

above the wider expanse of walkway nearer the curb to create a platform for outdoor showcases and placards flanking their entrances. The doorways themselves projected on the sidewalk with either small vestibules or generous awnings. These extensions of the shopfronts reclaimed a portion of the sidewalk to introduce and attract passersby to the merchandise inside the stores. The stores sought to initiate a psychological transaction between the passing crowds and displays of their stocks, the shopfronts forming a continuous invitation to browse and enter as people passed from window to window. The mercantile life of the street thus informed the distinctive conventions of its built environment. Above the

Fig. 1-8. State Street, looking north from Madison Street, about 1878. Courtesy of the Chicago Historical Society (ICHi-04753).

sidewalk level the carved ornament of limestone in the upper walls of the Colonnade Building established a vocabulary of surfaces characteristic of State Street's commercial architecture after the Fire. A description of this structure upon its completion in 1872 noted that "in this elaborate design Messrs. Wheelock and Thomas took a departure from anything ever introduced here. . . . In the crown of Rebuilt Chicago these buildings are the rarest gems." [23]

Just to the south of this view, the Bowen Building, predecessor of Sullivan's later Schlesinger and Mayer Store, was built on the southeast corner of State and Madison streets (Figure I-9). This structure was designed by William Boyington, one of Chicago's major commercial architects of the period before and after the Great Fire. [24] The Bowen brothers were the financiers who developed the property to house the entire operation of the clothing firm of Clement, Morton & Co. Founded in Chicago in 1865, this firm maintained a large retail trade for Chicagoans, in addition to filling orders for wholesale customers throughout the surrounding region. The upper floors of the new building were devoted to the manufacture and storage of clothing with a salesroom on the main floor nearest the street. The building was of iron construction and open floor plan to permit "a liberal extension should it be required." [25] This capability of expansion, planned in the original Bowen Building, was later utilized under the subsequent ownership of Schlesinger and Mayer, who added both upper stories and adjacent frontage to Boyington's structure. At the time of its completion in 1873 the original building was also considered a model of commercial architecture in its interior equipment, featuring both steam heat and steam-powered elevators.

On the exterior of the Bowen Building, Boyington created a variation on the elegant corner of the neighboring Palmer House then under construction one block to the south. The intersection of State and Madison streets, however, contained subtle variations in the width of the two streets across the intersection which may also have suggested the idea of adopting a rounded pavilion as the distinctive motif on the southeast corner. These variations derived from the fact that the intersection was at the juncture of four different subdivisions of the original town of Chicago in the 1830s. [26] The consequent nonalignment of State and Madison streets at their crossing was compounded by later widenings of State Street before 1871. In mappings of the intersection after the Fire, Madison Street, running west to east across State, shifts slightly to the north and increases in width (Figure I-10). About 1868 Potter Palmer had first widened State Street north of Madison by 60 feet by pushing back frontage on the west side of the street. In 1870 State Street south of Madison

Fig. 1-9. Bowen Building (originally Clement, Morton and Co.), State and Madison streets, 1873. Courtesy of the Chicago Historical Society (ICHi-01657).

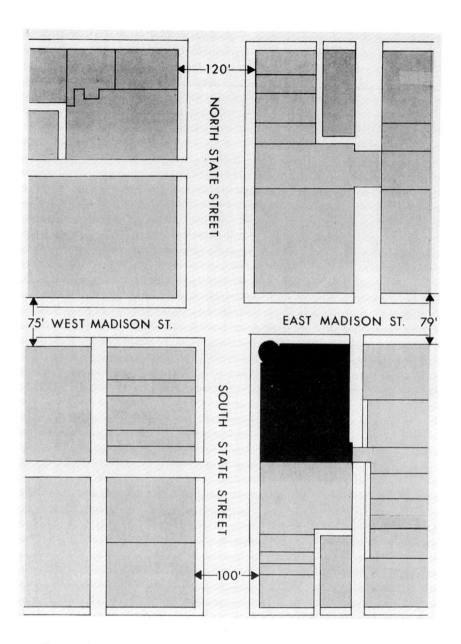

Fig. 1-10. Intersection of State and Madison streets showing width of streets and area of Sullivan's building of 1899, 1903–4 in black and width of streets and sidewalks between building fronts.

was widened 27 feet by pushing back properties on the east side of the street.[27] These improvements distinguished State Street from what was perceived as the pervasive narrowness of Chicago's streets, which had compelled architects to build structures that could not be seen to advantage along the confined corridors of the city's grid. An observer of 1879 wrote that by contrast, "the effect of large spaces upon buildings can be readily seen by anyone who visits State street at the point between Madison and Lake streets. Here is a broad street whose buildings on either side are brought into a most desirable prominence by the ample space in front of them. One gets here the full architectural effects of these massive structures through the aid of the distance from which they may be viewed."[28]

The anomalies in street width and alignment at State and Madison make the southeast corner of the intersection particularly visible when seen from the north down State Street, and when viewed from the west on Madison. This unusual condition was noted in the original description of the Bowen Building published in 1872:

From the accident of a break in Madison Street which brings this corner into prominent projection from the general line of the street, the corner doorway has a peculiarly commanding position, which has been evidently considered in the design by its accentuation. The general line of the wall front is here depressed and made a quadrant, with a large radius. Two columns, running though two stories, divide the quadrant and flank the entrance. From the columns the door is deeply recessed with side windows, thus forming a portico at once imposing from its dimensions, the architectural arrangement, and prominent position. The circular corner is continued the whole height of the building, having two orders of disengaged columns running two stories each, and surmounted with a dome. Around the base of the dome are three dormer windows, the accentuation of the center being still observed by the crowning of that dormer with a circular cornice, and broken pediment with a rich urn in the key, supported by two life-size Caryatides on moulded and panelled pedestals. The building is divided horizontally by two moulded story courses: one at the height of the store ceiling, of slight projection, and one on the second story, of bold projection, on carved medalions, forming a cornice to the large columns and pilasters. The main cornice to the front is of light proportions, as required by the second course of columns, and to bring into prominence the baluster and pedestal, and the rich dormers above. Behind the dormers is a steep French roof, crested with a role ornament and deep cresting. The ornament is continued round the dome, and a similar cresting at the flat termination forming a deck on the dome summit. We make remark that the view from the top is a most extensive one, and repays the climbing of upwards of ninety feet. The proportion of open and wall space is ex-

ceedingly pleasing, the absence of internal divisions giving a good opportunity for the exercise of good taste in this respect. The mouldings and
ornament used are of French modern character, with a good deal of Grecian severity, and the latter are but sparingly used, but where they do occur
are unusually rich and well carved.[29]

Boyington thus adapted compositional ideas and decorative motifs
from contemporary Parisian sources to create an architectural identity
for a Chicago wholesaler. Boyington's concept of commercial architecture embraced both an ornate surface as an embellishment of the street
and interior spaces whose design fulfilled utilitarian criteria. Many of
the features of the original Bowen Building became the basis for its later
expansion and renovation by architects Adler and Sullivan during the
occupancy of Schlesinger and Mayer through the 1890s. In his subsequent Schlesinger and Mayer Store of 1899–1904, Sullivan would rein-
terpret the Bowen Building's interior spatial logic, its ornamental marble
exterior, and its rounded corner to create a new mercantile house on the
same site.

The Development of Department Stores on State Street

The years 1867–73 constituted the first phase of State Street's development as Chicago's main mercantile thoroughfare. Though building was
interrupted by the Great Fire, subsequent reconstruction of the street
did not mark a great change in type, scale, or stylistic pretension of its
architecture. Throughout Chicago, rebuilding was checked by the Panic
of 1873 and the subsequent depression which deepened through 1877.
Real estate values declined sharply and a contraction of capital limited
the funds available for building. These trends did not reverse themselves
until about 1880, and it was not until 1883 that downtown land values
recovered to the level of a decade before and building activity enjoyed a
commensurate revival.[30] The depression did not destroy State Street,
whose properties, when compared to those on neighboring streets, suffered less decline in value, but it did foster the creation of the city's leading popular department stores as an alternative kind of retail business.
    The Fair was the Chicago department store that contemporary ac-
counts cited as the prototype of its kind. Founded in 1875 by the
German-born Ernest J. Lehmann, The Fair developed out of a small
shop in a one-story building with a frontage of just 16 feet on the west
side of State Street north of Adams.[31] Lehmann adopted a merchandising strategy fundamentally different from that of established dry goods
houses like Marshall Field's. First, although The Fair did eventually de-

velop a wholesale trade over time, Lehmann's was primarily a retail house. By contrast, the Field establishment was primarily a wholesale business, of which the most locally visible component was the retail store on State Street. The Fair, however, did not specialize in apparel and fabrics of a more expensive grade but instead carried a diverse inventory which included almost every conceivable item of personal and household use. From the beginning Lehmann carried less expensive jewelry, notions, pictures, china and hardware in addition to clothing of varied grades.[32] His strategy may have derived from the conditions of depression, when the lowered profitability of any single line of goods had inspired attempts by many speciality stores to branch out into other lines to sustain overall sales and thus keep their businesses alive.[33] Lehmann thus promoted his store as an attraction to a wide range of buyers because his premises were a combination of many stores offering centralized shopping under one roof. When a rival firm failed, Lehmann's practice was to buy its full range of unsold inventory regardless of its relation to his existing stock and add the acquired merchandise to his store as a new "department."[34] Throughout the early development of The Fair, Lehmann was said to have placed his faith in "the immense economic strength of sheer VOLUME."[35] Such a policy was distinct from the buying tradition of Field's where discriminating selection of items rather than varied quantity of inventory was advertised as the policy of the house. Field's reputation for quality often meant that agents of the store dictated to manufacturers the desired specifications of an item or line of items.[36] By contrast The Fair's buying and selling policies created "departments" as large, ever changing collections of wares in the spirit of an ongoing bazaar. The term "department store" in Chicago usage thus connoted a diverse multiplicity of goods which were marketed in what might later be termed a variety store. Lehmann was said to have named his store The Fair to signify "that the store was like a fair because it offered many and different things for sale at a cheap price."[37] In 1891 The Fair boasted that its assortment of stocks included children's toys, games for adults, baby carriages, furniture, kitchen equipment, sewing machines, fancy groceries and a dental parlor.[38] As early as 1881 the *Tribune* proclaimed that "what the Bon Marché is to Paris and Continental Europe, 'The Fair' is to Chicago and the Northwest."[39] The original Chicago department store was thus likened to the original French department store, both having dedicated their development to the most inclusive array of wares and the broadest class of clientele. By contrast the model for the Field store at its inception had been the marble palace of A. T. Stewart in New York as the prototype for an elegant dry goods house in the United States. Marshall Field conceived of his retail store as a dry goods house; hence its specialties had traditionally been limited to carpets, upholstery, and materials in addition to clothing. Not until the late 1880s did Field's concede the necessity of diversifying its stocks to compete with the department stores. The store did not decide to carry shoes until 1889, and Field personally opposed expansion into certain lines of merchandise which he did not consider consistent with the character of the house.[40] It is said that to the end of his life, Field denied that his establishment was a department store, even opposing the word "department" to describe any branch of its operations.[41]

The department store's ideal of a vast array of merchandise was aimed at attracting a varied clientele. The Panic of 1873 had spurred demand for a broad range of goods at reduced prices. Thus, according to The Fair's own account of its history, Lehmann, beginning in the depths of a depression, "deliberately ignored the trade of the rich and prosperous" in favor of "commerce with the common people."[42] Marshall Field consistently catered to the tastes and thereby cultivated the loyalties of a more affluent and thus more limited clientele. The Fair, however, proclaimed its mission as "retail merchandising for the millions" through provision of "Everything for Everybody."[43] The comparative result of the merchandising policies of The Fair and Marshall Field is evident in their success as retailers through the 1890s. In 1875 the retail sales of the well-established Field, Leiter & Co. amounted to $3,139,000. By 1898 these sales had more than tripled to $9,615,000.[44] But The Fair increased its sales from its inception in 1875 to a total of over $8,000,000 by 1898.[45] Thus, The Fair was not larger in the scale of its retail operations; rather its popular orientation had been rewarded with a remarkable rate of annual growth, compared with Field's steady but less dramatic increases over the same period.

The rise of stores like The Fair may be interpreted as one consequence of Chicago's extraordinary demographic expansion through the late nineteenth century. In 1850, seventeen years after it became a town, the population of Chicago was just under 30,000. By 1870, the city's population had grown by an order of magnitude to just under 300,000. By 1880 Chicago claimed just over 500,000 inhabitants, and by 1890 the city reached the size of about 1,100,000. Thus, at the time of the World's Columbian Exposition, Chicago's population had grown by more than 250 percent since the Great Fire just over twenty years before, becoming the sixth largest city in the western world and the second largest in the United States after New York.[46] The rate of increase in Chicago's population between 1850 and 1890 was a fundamental fact of the city's development that underlay its display of innovative energy in many fields. Chicago's rapid growth created a commensurate demand for goods and services of all kinds, including the provision of retail merchandise for a rapidly expanding market of newcomers. That the vast majority of these people were of modest means when they arrived in the city perhaps accounts for the extraordinary growth of stores like The Fair that were devoted to large assortments of less expensive items.

Fig. 1-11. Field, Leiter and Co. (Second Singer Building), Chicago, 1878.
E. S. Jennison, architect. Courtesy of the Chicago Historical Society (ICHi-01587).

The contrasting mercantile characters of Marshall Field's and The Fair were evident in the development of their firms' architecture. Field's conservative elegance was clearly represented in its first building, of 1868, and in its successor, the first Singer Building, completed in 1873 on the same site.[47] This structure, financed by the Singer Sewing Machine Company, housed Field's until 1878, when it was destroyed in a second fire and was replaced by the Second Singer Building, also designed in the mode of the French Second Empire (Figure I-11). Like its predecessor, Field's rebuilt dry goods house displayed an ornate fashionability as the palatial home for a clientele who typically arrived by carriage. The Singer Building conveyed an authoritative hauteur through allusion to Parisian monuments. The store's crown of domed mansard roofs and corner pavilions, as well as its sculptural program, signified Field's emulation of French standards of taste in architecture as in merchandise. As a marble palace the building was an adaptation of a clearly defined architectural type which served as an unmistakable image of Field's mercantile persona.

The Fair's phenomenal growth from its founding through the 1880s corresponded to a rapid expansion of its sales space. Lehmann's policies had included appropriation not only of the stocks but also the premises of adjoining stores as these either failed or were bought out by The Fair.[48] Lehmann's associate, Otto Young, an incorporator of The Fair in 1886, undertook a program of real estate acquisition which expanded the store's facility from the original 2000 square feet in 1875 to 286,000 square feet by 1891. The Fair's total leasehold was valued at over $3,000,000, making it the largest consolidation of downtown property achieved in Chicago up to that time.[49] By 1891 The Fair had acquired the entire southern half of the block bounded by Marshall Place and State, Adams, and Dearborn streets. Through the 1880s the store consisted of an assemblage of contiguous buildings over this property with its major front of just two stories on the north side of Adams Street between State and Dearborn. In the era before 1890, all the retail business of The Fair was conducted on the street level while its upper floors were reserved for wholesale trade. An 1885 illustration for The Fair's tenth anniversary shows the Adams Street front of the store with placards advertising its departments set above the awning over the street level, above the second story, and extending around the sides on State and Dearborn (Figure I-12). A block-wide sign three stories high proclaims the name of the store at an urban scale, announcing its location to those entering the shopping district along the cable car lines from the city's South Side on State Street depicted in the lower right. The mercantile identity of The Fair was thus communicated less through the archi-

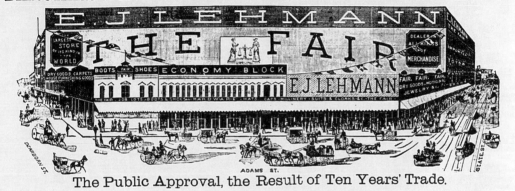

Fig. I-12. Advertisement for The Fair Store. *Chicago Tribune*, 31 May 1885.

tecture of these early buildings than by attached or painted signs. The resulting image was that of a new kind of business which would soon find architectural accommodation in a new building designed to suit the store's operation and character.

The New Architecture of State Street

The contrasting establishments of Marshall Field's and The Fair stood at opposite ends of Chicago's central shopping corridor. During the 1890s, the city's major retail stores were arrayed along the seven block segment of State Street extending from Randolph Street on the north to Congress Street on the south (Figure I-13). The more expensive and prestigious dry goods houses clustered near the north end of the street, including Marshall Field's, Carson Pirie Scott & Co., Mandel Brothers, and Schlesinger and Mayer. Field's was housed at the northeast corner of State and Washington. Starting in 1891, Carson Pirie Scott had its location diagonally opposite Field's on the southwest corner of State and

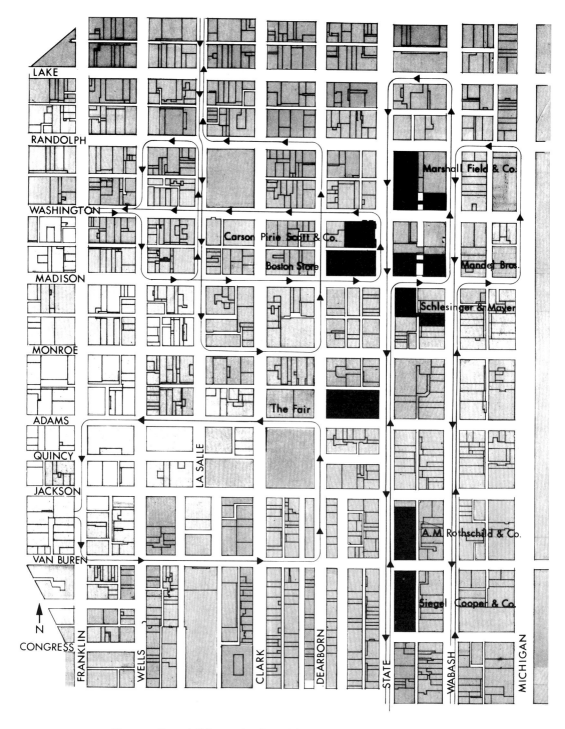

Fig. 1-13. Central Chicago, showing cable car routes and location of major
department stores on State Street, about 1903.

Washington, in the renovated First National Bank Building built in
1872. After 1895 Carson Pirie Scott had its quarters in the lower floors
of the Reliance Building and adjacent structures on the same site. Mandel Brothers' quarters since 1874 had been in the Colonnade Building
on the east side of State Street north of Madison. Like Field's, Carson
Pirie Scott and Mandel Brothers were among the most venerable firms
in Chicago, both dating their origins prior to 1871. By 1885 the concentration of elite retailers along State Street between Madison and Randolph led one observer of real estate in the shopping district to conclude
that "the east side of State street for a distance of about two blocks is
considered the choice locality of the city for a first-class dry goods business. Custom and fashion have very closely restricted the localities available for such purposes."[50] Owners of these more prestigious stores
thought that the density of shopping crowds attracted by the stores' concentration benefitted sales more than would the stores' dispersal
through other locations. Toward this end Marshall Field encouraged two
of his major competitors, Mandel Brothers in 1898 and Carson Pirie
Scott in 1904, to remain close to Field's retail store at moments when
these neighboring firms were contemplating relocation away from State
Street.[51]

The larger popular department stores, all of which dated their origins
to the years after the Great Fire, were located mainly toward the south
end of the retail corridor near The Fair. The leaders of the less expensive trade included Siegel, Cooper & Co. and Abram Rothschild. Also
serving this trade was the Boston Store, founded in 1873, with quarters
after 1894 in the lower floors of Holabird and Roche's Champlain Building on the northwest corner of State and Madison streets. Set within this
concentration of large retail stores along State Street were innumerable
smaller shops that enhanced the impression of varied commercial life
within a small district. By 1900 the street's secondary attractions included cafés, bakery-and-lunch eateries, jewelry stores for a range of
tastes and means, teahouses, bookshops, confectioners, drugstores, and
pet shops.[52] Anthologies of photographic views of Chicago from the
1870s and later typically included views of State Street looking north
from Madison as if this mercantile street were a notable public place. By
the turn of the century State Street's shopping corridor served as a linear
spine of commercial activity. The continuous fronts of its buildings defined a walled passage analogous to an arcade or a gallery of urban scale
yet without a glazed roof (Figure I-14). Thus texts from the period, following conventional usage of the time, refer to a business or individual
being "in" rather than "on" State Street.

What made State Street hum was the coming of the first cable car
"loop" to the downtown in the early 1880s (Figure I-15). The cable cars

Fig. I-14. State Street, looking north from Madison Street, about 1908. Courtesy of the Chicago Historical Society (ICHi-19268).

of this era moved by "gripping" an endless moving cable under the surface of the street. The inaugural line of cable cars in Chicago was put into State Street in 1882 by a company whose directors included Marshall Field and Levi Leiter. These and neighboring store owners foresaw the system's potential to connect their businesses with the growing residential districts of the South Side.[53] A map of the downtown cable car lines in place upon the system's completion shows State Street served directly along the entire length of its shopping corridor (Figure I-13). The cable cars ran north to Madison, turned east to Wabash, turned north, and continued to Lake Street, where they turned west and proceeded one block to State Street, turning south for their return trip. The actual loop of moving cable within the surface of the street needed to accommodate the circuit of the cars' path is thought to be the origin of the term Loop as a general name for Chicago's central business district at the north head of the South Side.[54] State Street merchants were soon also linked to the city's outlying districts on the West Side by the cable system, which brought shoppers in along Madison Street as well, returning them via Washington Street.

The intersection of State and Madison thus retained its focal position from the horse-car days when the major lines had also crossed there. In 1885, when the cable car system was nearing completion, properties at the intersection were appraised as the most valuable real estate in Chicago.[55] The daily influx of commuters from the cable cars, combined with the density of State Street's shopping attractions, produced an extraordinary number of people on its sidewalks. So great were the numbers of pedestrians and so frequent their clashes with vehicular traffic that from the mid 1890s there appeared a series of proposals to erect an elevated moving sidewalk to alleviate crowding and danger at curbside.[56] In 1890, at the time of the completion of the main cable car routes to the downtown, it was estimated that 100,000 people passed the display windows along the shopping corridor each day.[57] In the same year actual counts of pedestrians confirmed that more than 7,500 people passed hourly along State Street from Madison to Monroe.[58] State and Madison streets' crucial location within the city's system of transportation was probably the origin of the intersection's popular characterization as "The World's Busiest Corner." Remarking on the commercial properties

Fig. 1-15. A State Street cable car of the 1880s. Courtesy of the Chicago Historical Society (ICHi-05489).

Fig. 1-16. The Bee Hive, on State Street, after remodeling by Adler and Sullivan, *Chicago Tribune*, 4 August 1895.

around this site, one observer of 1890 noted that "with the West Side cable forcing its hundreds of thousands into the throng, already dense, of North and South Side shoppers, the limit of rental values is governed only by the profit on the trade of the number of people who can be accommodated in a given space in a given time. In comparison with similar centers Chicago largely leads. In New York shopping hours are confined to the late forenoon and afternoon and early evening. Here, from early morning until dark, there seems no halt in the procession."[59]

Typical development on State Street before 1890 included the renovation of the lower floors of post-Fire buildings to improve stores' capacities to accommodate the shopping crowds.[60] One of these was a remodeling project designed by Adler and Sullivan for a retail store known as the Bee Hive, on the west side of State south of Monroe in 1885.[61] The Bee Hive dry goods store began in 1883 as a popular merchandiser devoted to the type of low-priced retailing characteristic of The Fair. The Bee Hive advertised a wide range of inexpensively acquired inventory sold in high volumes at bargain prices, with its name suggesting the resultant intensity of sales activity within its walls. By 1886 the store controlled a continuous frontage that included two adjacent post-Fire buildings along State Street whose different yet contiguous elevations are shown in an advertisement of 1895 (Figure I-16). Adler and Sullivan connected the interiors of these two structures across the party wall that had formerly separated them. On the exterior the architects extended a crowning cornice over the southernmost or left-hand building identical to that of its northern neighbor. At street level the two buildings were given a common identity as one store through the creation of a continuous front of display windows with a new entrance set at the center of the renovated structures. Over this doorway there appeared a large flattened representation of a beehive as an emblem of the house. As a memorable, popularly legible image, this motif symbolically linked the bustle of the sidewalk with the pace of activity inside the store, both being the realm of swarming shopping crowds that passed in and out through the doorway. It is not known whether Adler and Sullivan were responsible for this motif, but Sullivan's later design for the base of the nearby Schlesinger and Mayer Store can be seen as an architecturally developed response to the same issues of visual effect and signification along the street evident in the renovated Bee Hive.

Adler and Sullivan's renovation of the Bee Hive exemplifies the fact that State Street through the late 1880s had not yet felt the full force of new possibilities in construction being explored elsewhere in the city's commercial architecture. Before 1890 there were no tall steel frame buildings along the entire length of the shopping corridor. The first

structures of this kind had been developed elsewhere in downtown Chicago on Dearborn and LaSalle streets, the city's financial corridors one
and three blocks to the west of State. These works included Jenney's
Home Insurance Building (1884–85) and Holabird and Roche's Tacoma
Building (1887–89). Such office buildings depended for their successful
operation on the speed and capacity of elevators to connect the street
level with the uppermost floors. Once the feasibility of the new construction had been demonstrated for office buildings, owners of choice properties on State Street exerted pressure on their mercantile tenants to use
the upper floors of buildings for retailing, thereby insuring the highest
possible rate of return on the city's most valuable land. Building owners
suggested to retailers that the elevator made it simpler for shoppers,
once in the retailing district, to go to the upper stories of nearby buildings than to travel by streetcar to a location several blocks away. This
idea, however, was slow to find acceptance among shop owners, who felt
that public habit still preferred stores on or nearest to the street level.[62]
For this reason, properties along State Street derived their high land
values from intensive use of the ground floor which had direct access to
the crowds passing along the sidewalk.[63] Thus, up to 1890, retailing
along State Street was still accommodated in combined and renovated
post-Fire buildings of limited height whose architecture did not yet correspond to the intensity of innovation evident in the businesses themselves. In February 1890 the Chicago *Economist* assessed the situation on
State Street as follows:

> There is one class of structures in respect to which capitalists and builders
> of this city seem to have been blind not only to their own opportunities but
> to the crying needs of trade. Office buildings the best that ingenuity and
> money can produce, and wholesale houses combining all the conveniences
> and elegancies known Chicago has in abundance, but retail stores possess-
> ing the conveniences and attractions which modern art produces so easily
> and at such moderate expense are entirely lacking. It may be truly stated
> that there is not a first-class retail store in Chicago. This is no reflection on
> those famous stores on State street and elsewhere which command the
> trade of the public to such an enormous extent and which compare favor-
> ably with the best mercantile houses of that class in the world. It is simply
> saying that retail construction has not kept pace with office, wholesale, ho-
> tel, and other business construction. There has been no radical change in
> retail stores for a generation, whereas office buildings have changed so
> rapidly that a structure erected five years ago is already out of the category
> of first-class buildings. The retail stores of State street are an aggregation
> of old patched up structures which have been remodeled little by little in
> a makeshift way as the business of their occupants required.[64]

Within days of this assessment, Congress officially decided that Chicago would be the site of the World's Columbian Exposition of 1893, although the location of this event in Chicago had been anticipated months before. The presence of a commercial world's fair would mean a large influx of visitors to the city's shopping district, further enhancing the prospect of profitable development of its properties. In this climate of heightened expectations and rising land values, there were initiated four separate projects for tall buildings along State Street to commence construction in the spring of 1890. These structures were the Second Leiter Building and The Fair Store, both by William Le Baron Jenney with William Mundie, and the Masonic Temple and Reliance Building, both begun by Burnham and Root, with the latter building completed by Charles Atwood of D. H. Burnham & Co. The early nineties also marked the beginning of Holabird and Roche's activity on State Street; their first works within the shopping district included the Venetian, Champlain, and State Safety buildings. These projects gave a wholly new scale to State Street as a built environment. They constituted the first attempts to apply the new architectural technology of the iron and steel frame to large facilities for retailing.[65]

The first large steel building on State Street was envisioned as early as the spring of 1889. At that time Levi Z. Leiter had contemplated the construction of a new mercantile building on the east side of the block between Van Buren and Congress streets. During the summer of 1889 Leiter commissioned William Le Baron Jenney to design a vast new building intended for retailing. The structure was to be eight stories above the street with an unprecedented floor area of fifteen acres. It was envisioned that the entire building could serve as one great retail store or, if such a tenant could not be found, the building was planned so that it could be divided into as many as nine stores along State Street, each with its own entrance. The completed structure, known as the Second Leiter Building, has been described as Jenney's most important contribution to an architecture expressive of the steel and iron frame as a new means of construction (Figure I-17). At the same time the design has been interpreted as an adaptation of formal qualities evident in Richardson's earlier Marshall Field Wholesale Store of 1885–87. Jenney's building is thus viewed as both a precedent for later architecture of metal and as a response to traditions of masonry architecture.[66]

A primary functional criterion of Jenney's elevation was that it be a wall opened to daylight, hence the building's ranges of windows fill almost the whole surface of the exterior. On each floor there were originally four windows between the major vertical piers. The colonnettes between the windows were rounded to enhance the passage of light into

Fig. 1-17. Second Leiter Building (originally Siegel, Cooper and Co.), Chicago,
1889–91. W. L. Jenney and W. B. Mundie, architects. Courtesy of
the Chicago Historical Society (ICHi-19297).

the building. The idea of the wall reduced to its material minimum was
also invoked by Jenney as a principle of structural design in Chicago,
where weight on foundations had to be minimized because of the relatively poor condition of the soil for bearing. In his writings on new commercial buildings of steel Jenney had focused on their dual requirements
of maximum light and minimum weight, and earlier in his career he had
been drawn to the Gothic style as the historic example of an architecture
based on skeletal construction and traceried windows.[67] In his design for
the Second Leiter Building the style of the architecture was to be "old
English Gothic and the openings will be square. Special provisions are

made in the plans for an abundance of light all through the building."[68] In view of his earlier work this phrase suggests that perhaps Jenney conceived of the Second Leiter's exterior like a Gothic wall, with the elevations as built featuring colonnettes framing multiple windows set within each structural bay.

At the same time, the Second Leiter Building exhibits a classical character in its material and composition. In an original rendering of the design the State Street elevation is shown as a system of surfaces in dressed and carved stone overlaid onto the metal structure (Figure I-18). The street fronts of the building are faced with a light gray Maine granite as a protection for the outermost columns of the iron and steel cage, thereby suggesting the complete fireproofing of the skeleton. Jenney was concerned that the place of origin, geologic properties, and the working qualities of a stone enhance the identity of his commercial buildings as contributions to the city's architecture.[69] The ability of local builders to import large quantities of a pure crystalline granite from remote New England quarries signified Chicago's development from its origins as a wooden town into a city of lithic monumentality. The building's length of 402 feet along State Street is visually divided into nine

Fig. I-18. Rendering of the Second Leiter Building. Reprinted from *Architectural Reviewer* (Chicago) 1 (February 1897).

Fig. 1-19. Recent views of details of the west elevation of the Second Leiter
Building showing groups of colonnettes and remodeled fenestration.
Barbara Crane, photographer, for the Commission on Chicago Landmarks.

major sections by vertical piers that resemble elongated classical pilasters. These vertical piers and the groups of rounded colonnettes halfway
between them mark the position of structural steel columns (Figure 1-19).
Thicker piers bound the composition at its corners, while the whole
design is crowned with a massive cornice. This major horizontal line is
echoed in the lintels that mark the third and sixth floors below. The
elevation thus exhibits gradations of scale and relief characteristic of a
building conceived as an edifice of masonry.

This formal quality as counterweight to the openness of the wall gives
the Second Leiter Building an architectural presence which contemporary observers saw as appropriate for a structure of its type. The description of Jenney's building in *Industrial Chicago* published in 1891
characterized it as severely plain on the exterior yet grand in its proportions, with "great corner piers of granite carried up to a chaste cornice,

the central piers of the same material, the beautifully capped capitals dividing the windows, the carved granite cornice, all in perfect accord with the commercial style."[70] In this sense Jenney's structure may have reflected concern not only with the problem of structural expression, but also with the task of expressing a general ideal of commercial character in architectural form. In the Chicago of 1890 one building that exemplified this ideal in the eyes of contemporaries was Richardson's Marshall Field Wholesale Store (Figure I-20). In his tribute to this structure Louis Sullivan wrote of its design on one level as an example of expression

Fig. I-20. Marshall Field and Co. Wholesale Store, Chicago, 1885–87. H. H. Richardson, architect. Courtesy of the Chicago Historical Society (ICHi-01688).

keyed to purpose, characterizing it as "a monument to trade, to the organized commercial spirit, to the power and progress of the age," as well as to the individual achievement and character of Marshall Field.[71] Sullivan was not alone in his appreciation of Richardson's building. Another visitor to Chicago in 1888 wrote of the city's business center on the south side as "the miracle of the time, the solid creation of energy and capital since the fire." After describing the metropolitan pandemonium of Chicago's streets during the working week, this observer wrote:

> On a Sunday, when business gives place to amusement and religion, the stately city is seen in all its fine proportions. No other city in the Union can show business warehouses and offices of more architectural nobility. The mind inevitably goes to Florence for comparison with the structures of the Medicean merchant princes. One might name the Pullman Building for offices as an example, and the wholesale warehouse of Marshall Field, the work of that truly American architect, Richardson, which in massiveness, simplicity of lines, and admirable blending of artistic beauty with adaptability to its purpose, seems to me unrivalled in this country. A few of these buildings are exceptions to the general style of architecture, which is only good of its utilitarian American kind, but they give distinction to the town, and I am sure are prophetic of the concrete form the wealth of the city will take.[72]

Jenney's building conveys a similar sense of the authoritative role of mercantile activity in the life of the city, and of the building's association with an individual client, Leiter, whose name is carved into the cornice in Roman lettering, along with the date of its completion (1891). In the Chicago of that year Leiter's new structure may have been perceived in part as a response to the monumentality of Field's wholesale store, as if the architectural identity of the two buildings testified to the independent success of each of the two former partners who had gone their separate ways ten years earlier. Upon its completion in 1891 the Second Leiter Building was rented to Siegel, Cooper & Co., a department store established in 1887. Henry Siegel and Frank H. Cooper had developed their retailing operation along much the same lines as The Fair, with both stores catering to a less expensive trade.[73]

The building most similar in type and style to the Second Leiter Building was The Fair's new store, designed by Jenney and Mundie in 1890 (Figure I-21). The building was to be "the largest in Chicago and much the largest structure in the world devoted to similar purposes on the basis of the amount of floor space, far exceeding in extent the famous Bon Marché of Paris, which has only four floors."[74] By the time construction of The Fair began, the project had grown to a seventeen-story building depicted in a rendering published in February 1892 (Fig-

Fig. 1-21. Advertisement for The Fair Store, Chicago, 1892–97. W. L. Jenney and W. B. Mundie, architects. *Chicago Tribune*, 10 June 1897.

Fig. I-22. Project for The Fair Store as envisioned in 1892. Reprinted from
Inland Architect and News Record 19 (February 1892).

ure I-22). The eventual projected height of the building was to have
accommodated the activities of The Fair on its lower floors, with the
upper stories to be rented as office space. The new building was to be
entirely of steel construction, to be erected in sections while the business
of the store continued in remaining parts of the older building and
partially completed sections of the new structure.[75] The design of the
seventeen-story project had to combine expressive treatment appropriate for both an office building above and a department store below. The
exterior scheme as a whole adapted the general idea of an expansive
commercial palace to accommodate both functions, with its parts differ-
entiated to suggest different uses. Along the main front on Adams Street
the new Fair building would appear as a pair of tower blocks of offices
set atop a six-story base articulated with horizontal belt courses. The
treatment of the corners as rusticated piers, and the crowning of the

whole building with an overhanging cornice are formal conventions of a traditional building of masonry applied to a skeleton of steel. The frame was to be clad on the exterior in brick and terra cotta whose ornamental treatment would convey festive associations appropriate to the mercantile persona of The Fair.

The original design for a seventeen-story building clarifies the exterior form of The Fair as actually built to 1897. At that time the whole of the new building was devoted to the uses of the store. The horizontal belt courses, originally intended to crown the base of the twin tower scheme, fell at the midsection of the building completed to nine stories. Hence the major lines of the built block recall an unrealized ambition for a much taller structure proposed in the original design. The image of masonry overlaid onto The Fair's upper exterior contrasts with the filigree of metalwork and glass along its base. This treatment of the base was an architectural feature that clearly identified the building as a department store, and Jenney's design for the lower two floors of ornamental metalwork may have alluded to such Parisian precedents as the Bon Marché, to which The Fair compared itself. The delicacy of surface relief in the decorative frames surrounding the glass corresponded to the character of the goods displayed in the windows. The most ornate motifs along the base were the arched doorways on State Street, which adapted the Richardsonian arched entrance of Chicago office buildings, yet rendered it here not in rusticated stone but in cast iron (Figure I-23). Inside, the new Fair, when completed, was perceived to be a definitive example of the department store as a new type of building in Chicago. Jenney's interior featured large light courts and aisles of unprecedented width which convey the impression that the store's spaciousness could accommodate the crowds that came through its doors.

In the architecture of State Street the adaptation of historic styles to commercial buildings was pronounced in projects directly associated with the World's Columbian Exposition of 1893. The anticipated influx of foreign visitors to Chicago for the World's Fair inspired characterization of State Street as a thoroughfare comparable to the great boulevards of the world (Figure I-24). One guidebook concluded that:

> If you are from Paris, State Street will remind you of Avenue de l'Opéra, or the Avenue Malesherbes, from the steps of the Madeleine; if from Berlin, Friederich Strasse or Leipziger Strasse will be recalled to your mind; if from Vienna, you will see a resemblance to some sections of the Ring Strasse; if from London, Regent Street may be suggested; if from Dublin, a part of Sackville Street, although you will miss the Nelson Monument. All of the great streets of the world to-day bear a strong resemblance to each other, although there is in reality a vast difference between them.[76]

Fig. 1-23. State Street entrance (above) and jewelry department (right) of The Fair
Store. Reprinted from Forrest Crissey, *Since Forty Years Ago: An Account of the Origin
and Growth of Chicago and Its First Department Store* (Chicago, 1915).

One work of commercial architecture closely and intentionally associated with the exposition was the Marshall Field Annex, designed by
D. H. Burnham and Co. (Figure I-25) in the spring of 1892 for the
northwest corner of Washington Street and Wabash Avenue. The architect of this building was Charles Atwood, who had replaced John Root
as Burnham's partner for design in 1891. Atwood played an important
role in the World's Columbian Exposition as architect of the Fine Arts
Building, the most celebrated example of neoclassical architecture at the
fair. The Marshall Field Annex, made ready for opening in August 1893
during the exposition, was intended to be in keeping with the spirit of

Fig. 1-24. Dedication Day Parade of the World's Columbian Exposition, State
Street, looking north from Madison Street, 21 October 1892. Photo by
J. W. Taylor. Courtesy of the David Phillips Photographic Collection, Chicago.

Field's as the host city's leading commercial institution. The lower three stories of the annex were occupied by the retail store and tearoom of Marshall Field's. The central three were workrooms connected with their business, while the uppermost three were rented as professional offices around a central light court. The interior structure was a steel frame, but the vertical supports around the periphery of the building were masonry piers whose thickness was apparent in the floor plans (Figure I-26).[77] The visible exterior walls were faced with different materials through successive floors. In the lower three stories the Field Annex was clad with a light-colored granite whose piers and arches framed the display windows of the street and mezzanine levels. The central three stories were faced in a light-colored terra cotta, elaborately modeled to resemble carved stone. The seventh and eighth stories were of brick and terra cotta, with the attic story and cornice faced entirely with decorative terra cotta.

The Annex's exterior was treated as a variation on a Renaissance palazzo similar in style to such works of McKim, Mead, and White as the Hotel Imperial of 1891 on 32nd Street and Broadway in New York (Figure I-27). Atwood had been familiar with such urbane designs during his years as an architect in New York before joining Burnham's office in Chicago. Like the Fine Arts Building, the Field Annex in its time was praised as proof of Atwood's ability to work with the subtleties of a renewed classical vocabulary then fashionable in the East. The style of the building was said to be that of the Spanish Renaissance, in keeping with the Columbian Exposition's commemoration of Columbus' voyage to America under the sponsorship of Spain.[78] Although generally regarded as successful on its own terms as an adaptation of historical forms to a contemporary building, the Field Annex was presumably the work that Louis Sullivan criticized in Kindergarten Chat V as a structure that did not clearly communicate its particular commercial function. When Sullivan wrote the *Kindergarten Chats* in 1900–1901, the first section of his Schlesinger and Mayer Store had been completed a few blocks away. He thus presented Atwood's building as distinct from his own solution to a similar architectural problem. He implied that the Field Annex's purpose as a mercantile building, and thus its identity as an architectural type, could not be well distinguished from the design for the Imperial Hotel as a building wherein similar historical motifs clad a structure built for a different purpose. Atwood's Field Annex was thus, in Sullivan's view, the opposite of Richardson's Field Wholesale Store. For Sullivan, Richardson's building conveyed an architectural character appropriate to its use. He praised it as an architectural statement of the identity of

Fig. 1-25. Marshall Field and Co. Annex, Chicago, 1892–93. D. H. Burnham and
Co. (Charles B. Atwood), architect. Photo courtesy of Marshall Field and Co.

Fig. 1-26. Plans of first and typical upper floors of Marshall Field and Co. Annex. Reprinted from
Prominent Buildings Erected by the George A. Fuller Co. (Chicago, 1904).

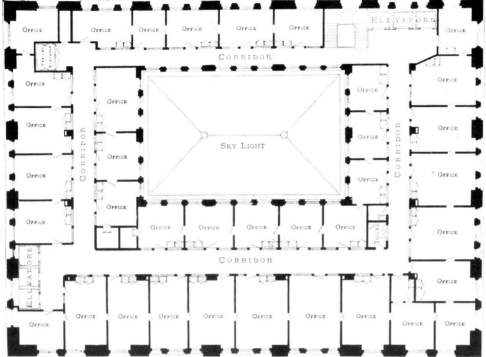

OFFICE · OFFICE · OFFICE · OFFICE · OFFICE · OFFICE · ELEVATORS · OFFICE

CORRIDOR

OFFICE

OFFICE

OFFICE

OFFICE

OFFICE · CORRIDOR

OFFICE

OFFICE

OFFICE

SKY LIGHT

OFFICE

CORRIDOR

OFFICE

OFFICE

OFFICE

OFFICE · OFFICE · OFFICE · OFFICE · OFFICE · TOILET

ELEVATORS

CORRIDOR

OFFICE

OFFICE · OFFICE · OFFICE · OFFICE · OFFICE · OFFICE · OFFICE · OFFICE · OFFICE

Typical Floor Plan.

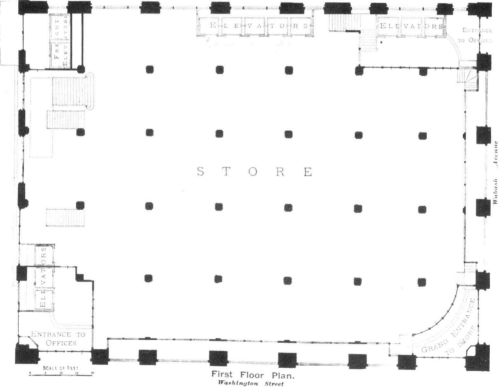

FREIGHT ELEVATOR · ELEVATORS · ELEVATORS · ENTRANCE TO OFFICES

S T O R E

Wabash Avenue

ELEVATORS

ENTRANCE TO OFFICES

GRAND ENTRANCE TO STORE

SCALE OF FEET

First Floor Plan.
Washington Street

an institution as well as an index of Richardson's powers of mind as an artist. Yet in assessing Atwood's design for the Field Annex, Sullivan wrote that

> Surely, if it were a department store, all masonry would be reduced to a minimum, and there would be an expanse of glass for light and display. If you doubt it, there are several department store buildings hereabout that will serve to illustrate my meaning. . . .
>
> [This structure] stands, for our purpose, as the type of a large class of structures, fortunately, for us, more rampant in the East than in the West, which represent what I might denominate the current jargon of architecture: the incapacity . . . to express in simple well-chosen language the casual, current experiences of life.[79]

In fairness Atwood's design may be said to convey festive and commemorative associations appropriate to a building conceived as an extension of the World's Columbian Exposition. The choice of a Spanish Renaissance style for the building may have been intended to signify the role of Marshall Field as one of the mercantile supporters of the fair. Atwood's tripartite scheme may also reflect the original three-part division of the building's function as department store, rooms for Marshall Field & Co., and rental space above. The design's allusion to a palatial type was thus made to serve as a shell for different interior uses. Atwood may also have conceived of his annex as the urbane counterpart of Richardson's wholesale store. In its major motif of tall arched openings over several central floors surrounded with rusticated surfaces and a gradation of scale and materials through its height, Atwood's building is not without formal similarity to Richardson's. The differences between the two designs, such as Atwood's treatment of the base and his greater use of ornamental enrichment above, may be logically ascribed to the different associations of his building as a center for retail trade near State Street, hence distinct from the character of Richardson's monument, keyed as it was to the different architectural context of the city's wholesale district. In this way Atwood's and Richardson's buildings together would have defined the architectural persona of different facets of the Field enterprise across the city. Hence they might be read as symbolically linked rather than conceptually antithetical.

Sullivan was averse to the adaptation of historical styles in architecture of his time. Instead he advocated new formal solutions suited to new architectural types. Sullivan's assertion that there were "several department store buildings hereabout" that illustrated a correspondence of form to use suggests his sympathetic familiarity with other works on State Street. In the 1890s, architects Holabird and Roche designed a

Fig. 1-27. Hotel Imperial, New York, 1889–91. McKim, Mead and White, architects. Reprinted from *American Architect and Building News* 30 (25 October 1890). Photo courtesy of Leland M. Roth.

number of commercial structures along the shopping corridor that exhibited a notable clarity of expression in exterior design. Among the most short-lived of these was the State Safety Building, completed in 1894 at the northeast corner of State Street at its intersection with the new elevated line of commuter trains along Van Buren Street. (Figure I-28).[80]

Being only seven stories above grade the State Safety Building was of

Fig. I-28. State Safety Building (A. M. Rothschild and Co. Store), Chicago, 1894. Holabird and Roche, architects. Reprinted from *Prominent Buildings Erected by the George A. Fuller Co.* (Chicago, 1904).

semi-mill construction, meaning columns of cast iron and floors of heavy timber. An early description of the project stressed that as much glass as possible would be used on the exterior to light the depth of floor area.[81] The State Safety was the only major new building erected on State Street during the 1890s with a cast iron front. The relative lightness of the cast iron had encouraged its use as a facing for new upper stories added to renovated post-Fire buildings throughout the city's center during this period. Like the exteriors of these renovated structures the State Safety's cast iron facade was painted white to convey an appearance of washable cleanliness in the notoriously smoky atmosphere of central Chicago at this time.[82] The architects designed the corner as a projecting circular bay from the second through the seventh stories accented by a columnar emblem with a crowning sphere and eagle. A. M. Rothschild & Co. leased the entire State Safety Building while it was under construction. This firm was newly organized in 1894 specifically to create a retail business to occupy the new building.[83] In the lines of its upper elevation the design of the State Safety Building closely followed the rectangular bays of its skeletal structure. The metal facing on the exterior featured a scheme of ornamental detail in cast iron with delicate colonnettes set between the windows on the top floor. Holabird and Roche's design of this building, with its horizontal extension of bays anchored by the rounded corner, anticipated Sullivan's solution for the upper stories of the Schlesinger and Mayer Store.

The final project that immediately preceded Sullivan's intervention on State Street was the expansion and renovation of the Mandel Brothers Store in 1897–98, located in the southern half of the Colonnade Building in the block north of Madison, near Schlesinger and Mayer's. Mandel Brothers had occupied the site since 1874, and they later rented the adjacent structure south of the Colonnade Building. In 1897 the Mandels commissioned Jenney and Mundie to remodel the base and roof of their quarters (Figure I-29).[84] The original colonnade along the sidewalk was removed and replaced with plate glass and ornamental iron show windows two stories high whose bays projected onto the sidewalk like enlarged versions of the showcases formerly placed in front of the store. The style of the ironwork was described as Louis XV with some of the decorative relief in the patterns of Persian arabesque whose moldings were "small and delicately modeled, producing a pleasing sense of scale so often missed."[85] The counterparts of such show windows were said to be "only found in the big stores of Paris, [Mandel Bros.] being the first to use this style in America."[86] The upper lights of these show windows were fitted with prismatic Luxfer glass, which refracted sunlight into the building to illuminate the interior depth of the lower floor salesrooms.

Fig. 1-29. Initial renovation of southern half of Colonnade Building (left) and
adjacent structure (right) for Mandel Brothers Store on State Street, 1897. W. L.
Jenney and W. B. Mundie, architects. *Chicago Inter Ocean*, 19 September 1897.

The completed renovation was thus described as one of the handsomest improvements that had been made on State Street in years.

Mandel Brothers' remodeling of the Colonnade Building was the first step in a transformation of their older facility. In 1896 the store had acquired the adjacent building on the northeast corner of State and Madison streets.[87] Early in 1898, they extended the new base of show windows around their entire State and Madison street frontage (Figure

Fig. 1-30. Mandel Brothers Store as expanded and renovated, 1898. Reprinted from *Inland Architect and News Record* 32 (September 1898).

I-30). The renovation entailed the removal of existing supports around the periphery of the corner building and the insertion of a steel frame to permit the largest possible expanses of glass along the sidewalk. Two additional stories were added to the whole facility. These stories replicated the older structure's motif of the Venetian arcade, substituting cast iron for marble, and the whole exterior was repainted white. The windows above the base were fitted with new plate glass like that of the show windows below. Thus, "above the lower stories the structural iron effect, with large plate glass windows, will be carried to the top of the building."[88] The initial transformation of the show windows along the sidewalk thus became the inspiration for the architectural renewal of the whole building. In an account for the *Inland Architect*, a contemporary observer characterized the emergence of this aesthetic as the gradual development of a new architectural style along State Street. Writing in the manner of a student of the history of architecture in the tradition of rational thinkers through the nineteenth century, this observer perceived past styles as emerging logically from the material needs and resources of a civilization. He thus saw in the commercial environment of Chicago a contemporary reenactment of what some theorists of his era believed to have occurred in earlier times:

> Chicago streets are undergoing a change. . . . In place of crude stone carvings of "after-the-Fire" architecture appears a style of architecture entirely American and of commercial origin. The style was invented by necessity. The demand of the window dresser—an artist of recent development—was constantly for a more showy place in which to exhibit his goods; and the buyers demanded more light. The style had small beginnings. First, the glass was moved to the outside of the deep reveals. The muntins began to disappear and the pieces of glass became larger.
>
> The woodwork was next removed and the glass placed close to the stone or brick, with only a stop to hold it in place. Some of the piers and columns were then removed and their places spanned by rolled iron beams, which took the place of the cast-iron lintels. Finally, the old work was removed complete and new steel columns, with steel lintels of long span, formed a frame for immense pieces of plate glass.
>
> Still there was call for more light, and the Luxfer prisms, filling the upper portion and sending the surface rays to the rear of the store, seem to complete the development of a new style in commercial architecture.[89]

On Memorial Day weekend in May 1898, when Mandel Brothers formally opened their remodeled store to the public, Schlesinger and Mayer published the first announcement of their engagement of Louis Sullivan to rebuild their store on the adjacent southeast corner of State and Madison. Sullivan's design of the lower stories of the Schlesinger and

Mayer Store thus had an immediate precedent in Jenney and Mundie's renovation of a store of comparable character. In developing his design, Sullivan's challenge was first to perceive the aesthetic possibilities inherent in the surrounding built environment and then to create a work of architecture that gave his clients a unique identity among their neighbors on State Street.

Fig. II-1. Interior of Synagogue of Chicago Sinai Congregation, as remodeled by
Adler and Sullivan, 1892. Reprinted from *Reform Advocate* 36 (30 January 1909).
Photo courtesy of the Chicago Historical Society.

II

A CHRONOLOGY OF THE
SCHLESINGER AND MAYER STORE

Sullivan's new structure for the Schlesinger and Mayer Store, completed in 1904, can be understood as the culmination of a continuous process of construction on one site. Sullivan's final building for this mercantile house emerged from a series of earlier renovations of its facilities. These renovations, designed by Adler and Sullivan, began as early as 1885 and continued through 1897, when Sullivan alone was responsible for alterations to Schlesinger and Mayer's store. Sullivan's project for the new building in 1898 and the subsequent history of its construction from 1899 to 1904 responded to the character of the store's preexisting quarters as well as to the architectural initiatives of Schlesinger and Mayer's competitors. In this light Sullivan's landmark appears not only as a statement of his intentions in architecture, but also as a work that gave visible expression to Schlesinger and Mayer's aspirations for their particular enterprise.

Leopold Schlesinger (1843–1914) and David Mayer (1851–1920) both immigrated to the United States from Bavaria in the 1850s and had begun their partnership in February 1872 after the Great Fire.[1] At this moment it was thought that with the fire's destruction of the old retail corridor on State Street, new stores west of the downtown would obtain a share of the city's dry goods trade. For this reason Schlesinger and Mayer located their original store at 136 West Madison Street, within the shopping district of Chicago's West Side along the city's main east-west horse-car line. However, the resurgence of State Street after the depression of the 1870s reaffirmed its desirability as a central location. In April 1881, therefore, Schlesinger and Mayer moved their principal store from the West Side to the Bowen Building at the southeast corner of State and Madison streets. There they secured a lease on half of the ground floor and "consolidated their interests, desiring and intending to confine themselves to building up a mammoth business in one spot."[2] Schlesinger and Mayer undoubtedly chose to relocate at State and Madison streets because of the intersection's position at the crux of the cable car lines. By 1890 dry goods merchants in Chicago estimated that this intersection was "perhaps the greatest retail trade center in America. . . . The success of branch establishments has not been such as to encourage further enterprise in that direction. The people have come to recognize one point as pivotal and can not be changed from their conclusion. While extension must come, it will be from this point as a center."[3] Schlesinger and Mayer's relocation to State Street also signified their intention to enhance their store's position among the retail houses of Chicago. The house of Schlesinger and Mayer from then on would be measured against the city's leading emporia whose metropolitan clientele corresponded to their central location.

The existing Bowen Building handsomely defined Schlesinger and Mayer's location and cultivated the popular perception of the store as a landmark on State Street. The firm promoted the emblematic quality of its corner in advertising through the 1880s. Unlike other major neighboring dry goods houses Schlesinger and Mayer was at first devoted exclusively to retailing. The original occupant of the Bowen Building, Clement, Morton & Co., was primarily a wholesale firm, manufacturing and storing clothes on the upper floors and displaying their stocks for local and out-of-town buyers on the street level. At first Schlesinger and Mayer appropriated only this street level for what was at that time a wholly retail business. The growth of their trade through the 1880s enabled the house to acquire leases to the upper floors, which were converted from manufacturing and storage lofts to sales floors, creating a wholly retail facility.

The Parisian imagery of the Bowen Building served well as a symbol for a firm which grew to promote itself as an importer catering to a predominantly fashionable clientele. Catalogues of the store noted buying offices in New York and Paris by 1887, with additional addresses for the firm in London, Vienna, and Berlin listed by 1889. Thus, on one hand, Schlesinger and Mayer aspired to create a cosmopolitan image comparable to that of the most esteemed dry goods houses in Chicago. David Mayer described his ambition for his store at a time of expansion in 1891, asserting that "the house's pride is to have the most extensive exclusive dry goods establishment in the city, and with room ahead we will succeed. We are not branching out into any experimental lines but will carry on a strictly dry goods business."[4] On the other hand, Schlesinger and Mayer's advertising through the 1880s presented the house as a less expensive alternative comparable to State Street's department stores. Schlesinger and Mayer followed the example of these emporia in their willingness to run large newspaper advertisements highlighting bargains and low prices as characteristic of their house. By 1886 Mayer attributed his success in part to truthful advertising which demanded a monthly investment of many thousands of dollars. The store owners "spare[d] no pains or expense to inform the public of the many advantages they have to offer."[5] Thus Schlesinger and Mayer apparently tried to attract patronage from both ends of State Street, emphasizing their devotion to a high grade of imported wares and their simultaneous leadership in popular prices. The store promoted itself with both the prestige of a dry goods house and the populism of a department store, just as its building on State Street stood between Marshall Field's to the north and The Fair to the south.

The identity of Schlesinger and Mayer relative to neighboring establishments on State Street may be inferred from reference to the store in Theodore Dreiser's novel *Sister Carrie*, written in 1899–1900, whose early chapters are set in the Chicago of 1889. As a close observer of the American urban experience, Dreiser sought in this and other works to portray its human realities in poignantly specific terms comparable to the portrayals of Paris in the writings of Balzac and Zola. In *Sister Carrie*, Dreiser begins by describing Carrie's arrival in Chicago as a young woman from a small Wisconsin town. In her first weeks in the city she is confronted with a new urban environment that is both threatening and alluring. Her early attempt to find a first position leads her to Chicago's department stores as likely employers. The first store Carrie encounters and the one where she most wants to work is The Fair, for she is dazzled by the glittering array of goods on display in a quantity and variety she had never seen before. Carrie is not successful at finding work there and is soon befriended by her first suitor in Chicago, the traveling salesman Drouet. As a representative for a Chicago clothing manufacturer, Drouet knows the full variety and gradation of the city's mercantile institutions, as well as its restaurants and theaters. He is portrayed as a moderately successful but not overly tasteful fellow who loved "fine clothes, good eating, and the company of successful men."[6] He delighted in the display of a new suit, shined shoes, or a stylish watch, just as he enjoyed an eating and drinking establishment which featured "its polished marble walls and floor, its profusion of lights, its show of china and silverware, and above all its reputation as a resort for actors and professional men."[7] He frequented places where he thought it proper for a successful man to be seen. Drouet appeared generous, assured, and affectionate. When he initiates involvement with Carrie, he gives her money and encourages her to buy a new set of clothes. Carrie at first hesitates about accepting the offer, yet goes to The Fair, lingering over its garments on display and eyeing a particular fall jacket. She purchases nothing, however, and goes to rendezvous with Drouet downtown. Learning of her hesitancy, Drouet takes her to lunch at "one of the very nicely furnished restaurants off State Street, in Monroe."[8] Afterwards he suggests that they go to Schlesinger and Mayer's, where Carrie is to pick out what she wants in the way of a new jacket. In that store "they found that shine and rustle of new things which immediately laid hold of Carrie's heart. . . . She looked about and picked a jacket like the one which she had admired at The Fair."[9] The jacket in hand, a saleswoman helped Carrie on with it. Carrie admired herself in a mirror and decided to keep the jacket as the first piece of clothing she bought in Chicago. It was thus at Schlesinger and Mayer's that Dreiser's famous character began her transformation from a plainly clothed country girl into an attractively outfitted urbanite. In his attempt to impress Carrie, Drouet took her to a store whose location and cachet presumably distinguished it from The Fair, where the array of goods had so impressed the newly arrived Carrie. As one who knew State Street Drouet took Carrie to Schlesinger and Mayer's as a store whose service and atmosphere he deemed sufficiently enhanced to represent his taste and munificence.

Schlesinger and Mayer's early development of their business through the 1880s coincided with their other activities and associations, which may have brought them in contact with architects Adler and Sullivan. For many years Leopold Schlesinger was involved in charitable work as one of the directors of the Jewish Training School for vocational education, an institution founded by members of Chicago Sinai Congregation.[10] Sinai Congregation's synagogue at Indiana Avenue and 21st Street had been built in 1875–76 by the firm of Burling and Adler, with Dankmar Adler as chief designer and supervisor of construction. The interior of this early synagogue for Sinai Congregation was renowned for "its brilliant and unique ornamentation" by Louis Sullivan, who had served as designer of the interiors in the winter of 1875/76 while he was employed by the firm of Johnston and Edelmann.[11] The home for Sinai Congregation thus marked the inaugural collaboration of Adler and Sullivan, who, during their later partnership, were responsible for remodeling the interior of the same building in 1891–92. The renovated sanctuary for Sinai Congregation was an architectural design whose surfaces featured polychrome ornamentation to create an embellished setting for worship (Figure II-1).[12] Familiarity with the original and remodeled interiors of Sinai would have given both Schlesinger and Mayer a personal appreciation of Sullivan's special abilities as a decorative artist. Schlesinger's awareness of Adler and Sullivan's work at Sinai may have led him to commission these architects in 1884 to design a house for himself on South Michigan Avenue.[13] Schlesinger was also a member of the Standard Club, whose building at the southwest corner of Michigan Avenue and 24th Street was also designed by Adler and Sullivan in 1887–88.[14] Finally, Schlesinger may have been among the members of Sinai Congregation who commissioned Adler and Sullivan to design the building for the Jewish Training School located at 554 West 12th Place in 1889–90. Thus Schlesinger had seen evidence of the architectural capabilities of Adler and Sullivan in the design of religious, domestic, social, and educational buildings with which he was intimately familiar.

Schlesinger and Mayer commissioned a series of remodelings of their old store building from 1885 to 1897. During these years the house underwent a growth in its volume of trade remarkable even by Chicago's standards. The store consequently expanded through a series of property acquisitions adjacent to the original Bowen Building (Figure II-2). Schlesinger and Mayer's first architectural initiative was a three-bay expansion of their store to the south in 1885, when the firm acquired the lease on adjacent frontage at 133–35 State Street immediately south of the old Bowen Building.[15] A rendering of the store building in the firm's 1889 catalogue shows an extension of the Bowen Building's elevation three bays south of the original structure (Figure II-3). In 1890 Schlesinger and Mayer commissioned Adler and Sullivan to renovate their facility.[16] The original corner dome and fifth-floor mansard roof of the Bowen Building were removed. Two stories were then added to the structure including its three additional bays to create a six-story facility with a flat roof marked by a decorative cornice. The fronts of the added upper floors were made of galvanized cast iron and the whole facade was painted white. The design of the cast iron fronts of the new added fifth and sixth floors adapted the motifs of the old marble facade below. This renovated Bowen Building can be seen as the building numbered 12 in Figure II-4.

Schlesinger and Mayer acquired control over two additional adjacent buildings at 137–39 State Street in 1890 and at Nos. 141–43 in 1891, extending the store's total holdings through 180 feet south of Madison Street (Figure II-2).[17] As seen in Figure II-4, these two adjacent buildings were four stories, each with a different facade. A proposed project

for an expanded Schlesinger and Mayer Store incorporating only Nos.
137–39 appeared in a rendering published in May 1890 (Figure II-5).
This project shows a six-story facility whose elevation would be extended
in repeated bays down State and Madison streets. It was reported that
Schlesinger and Mayer "intended to change the various facades into
one . . . building similar in style to the corner building."[18] A version of

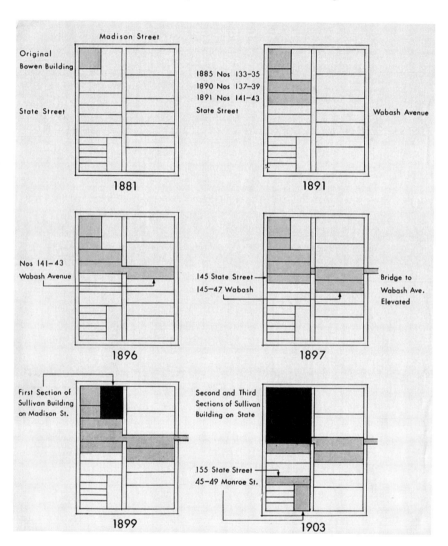

Fig. II-2. Property acquisitions of Schlesinger and Mayer on State Street, Madison
Street, Monroe Street, and Wabash Avenue, 1881–1904.

Fig. II-3. The Bowen Building (old Schlesinger and Mayer Store) as expanded
through 133–35 State Street in 1885. Reprinted from
Schlesinger and Mayer catalogue, spring and summer, 1889. Courtesy of
the Chicago Historical Society (ICHi-20180).

Fig. II-4. Bird's-eye view of Chicago from Adams Street looking north
on Dearborn, about 1892, showing old Schlesinger and Mayer Store through
133–35 State Street after remodeling in 1890 (number 12) with adjacent buildings
at 137–39 and 141–43 State Street. Reprinted from Rand McNally and Co.,
Bird's Eye-Views and Guide to Chicago (Chicago, 1893).

this project was carried out in 1897, as shown in a rendering of the actual building published the following year (Figure II-6).[19] The drawing shows Schlesinger and Mayer in comparison with the other principal stores on State Street. The architectural distinction of Schlesinger and Mayer's rounded corner as the formal anchor of an extended frontage along Madison Street and down State Street is accentuated by horizontal cornices above the second, fourth, and sixth floors. The topmost cornice features an ornamental frieze of cast iron as a horizontal band running around the upper edge of the building. Through this exterior motif, all of Schlesinger and Mayer's properties on Madison Street and those extending nearly one-half the block on the east side of State Street from Madison south toward Monroe were given a unified architectural image.

The transformation of the original Bowen Building to accommodate Schlesinger and Mayer's growth was based largely on the need to maximize return on valuable land. By 1890 Schlesinger and Mayer's real estate was among the most expensive in Chicago, with an annual rent of

THIS BUILDING (NINE (9) YEARS' GROWTH) FORCI- BLY TYPIFIES THE WON- DROUS POWER OF LOW PRICES.

MORE COMPLETELY EQUIPPED—IN EVERY ATTRIBUTE—THAN EVER BEFORE—IN OUR HISTO- RY—OF CONSTANTLY INCREASING SUCCESS.

"AS IT WILL BE"—SEPT. 1, 1890.

SCHLESINGER AND MAYER.

IMPORTING RETAILERS.

"THE MOST AGGRESSIVELY PROGRESSIVE HOUSE IN CHICAGO— IN AMERICA."

"GIVING THE PUBLIC THE BEST—AND THE MOST FOR THE LEAST—THE TRUE TOUCHSTONE OF OUR SUCCESS."

YOU ARE INVITED MON- DAY AND TUESDAY, MAY 5TH - 6TH, TO THE NINTH "STORE BIRTHDAY," AND THE OPENING OF OUR NEW ANNEX, 137-139 STATE-ST.

YOU ARE ALSO INVITED TO A FIRST VIEW OF OUR "ALL-THE-YEAR- ROUND BARGAIN BASEMENT."

TO COMMEMORATE THE EVENT — INNUMERABLE ATTRACTIONS — THROUGHOUT THE STORE—IN EVERY DE- PARTMENT—WILL BE OFFERED.

Fig. II-5. Expansion and renovation of the old Schlesinger and Mayer Store as envisioned in 1890. *Chicago Tribune*, 4 May 1890.

Fig. 11-6. Major department stores of Chicago on State Street showing the old Schlesinger and Mayer Store as renovated through 137–43 State Street in 1897. Reprinted from *Chicago Dry Goods Reporter* 28 (January 1898).

$3,000 per front foot. The addition of upper stories to Schlesinger and Mayer's older facility expanded the building's floor area to six stories and one basement, enabling the store to generate greater sales revenue. The building's capacity to produce rental income was thus increased to better approximate the value of the corner on which it stood. However, in 1891, one observer noted that the properties around the four corners of State and Madison were experiencing a rise in value "so rapid that a new building each year would have been required to keep pace with it."[20] The suggestion is that theoretically a new taller building would have had to be built on the same ground area every year to generate enough additional rental income to reflect the ever increasing value of the land.

In 1896–97, Schlesinger and Mayer acquired control of 80 feet of frontage on the west side of Wabash Avenue at Nos. 141–47 to the east of their State Street holdings (Figure II-2). The firm's decision to expand to the adjacent north-south street followed similar moves by their neighbors, the Mandel Brothers and Marshall Field. These firms had looked to Wabash Avenue both as an alternative to lack of space along State Street and in anticipation of the new elevated railroad to be built on

Wabash as part of the completion of the Union Elevated Loop in 1897.[21] It was estimated that the elevated trains would carry several hundred thousand people a day to Chicago's commercial core. Thus Schlesinger and Mayer contemplated expansion to Wabash Avenue as a means of connecting their sales floors with the expected crowds of commuting shoppers who would arrive downtown at a station stop on Wabash Avenue just south of Madison. In 1896 Schlesinger and Mayer had first acquired a post-Fire four-story building at 141–43 on Wabash facing this station and commissioned Sullivan to reconstruct its lower two floors.[22] The stone face of the existing building was to be "transformed into a very ornate combination of glass and ornamental iron. The entire first and second stories of the front will be removed and replaced with broad, high plate glass windows held in place by an ornamental iron frame."[23] Completed during the summer of 1896, this glass and iron front is visible in the lower right of Figure II-9, and can still be seen today in altered form along Wabash Avenue. It is the only fragment of Sullivan's architecture for Schlesinger and Mayer that remains from the renovations of the store's facilities before 1898. The design was perceived in its time as an elegant novelty in the commercial architecture of the shopping district. The *Economist* noted that "the value of apparent massiveness, the richness of plate glass and white paint[ed cast iron] are unquestionably emphasized in this front, and few people pass without noticing it as it is in wide contrast with anything in that immediate vicinity."[24]

In July 1896, Schlesinger and Mayer announced their intent to rebuild the existing building on Wabash Avenue above Sullivan's renovated front as a new ten-story structure.[25] This unrealized project called for a two-bay building of steel skeleton and plate glass as a vertical extension of the renovated front of the lower floors (Figure II-7). From the rendering it appears that the frames of the upper story windows would have continued the cast iron of the renovated lower floors. Comparison of this unbuilt ten-story project with the executed renovation of the first and second floors suggests that Sullivan planned to extend the show window upward from its conventional role along the sidewalk to become the thematic element of the whole elevation. A drawing published in 1897 shows this ten-story design extended eight bays or about 160 feet over additional properties along Wabash Avenue (Figure II-8).[26] This illustration shows that the 1896 two-bay project was designed with a repeatable bay to permit the widening of the elevation over adjacent properties at an indefinite time in the future. In this image the horizontally proportioned bays and the continuous horizontal sills of the projected elevation follow the sweep of the train tracks below to suggest an association be-

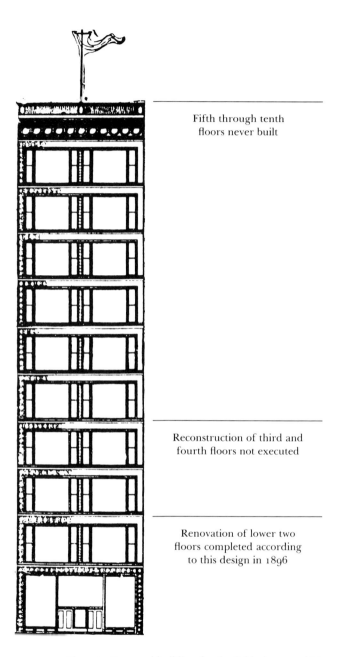

Fifth through tenth
floors never built

Reconstruction of third and
fourth floors not executed

Renovation of lower two
floors completed according
to this design in 1896

Fig. II-7. Proposed building for the Schlesinger and Mayer Store at
141–43 Wabash Avenue, showing lower two stories as remodeled in 1896.
Chicago Tribune, 5 July 1896.

1872

SCHLESINGER AND MAYER

1897

State, Madison, Through to Wabash—8 Store Entrances and Special Union Loop Entrance.

The S. & M. Anniversary Mile Stone
A quarter of a century old 1872 1897.

We congratulate The Chicago Tribune
on the fiftieth anniversary of such
continued prosperity.

A Great and Growing Store.

In 1872 this store contained 2,500 square feet of selling space. In 1881, 32,000 square feet. In 1885, 60,000 square feet. In 1890, 90,000 square feet. In 1892, 120,000 square feet. In 1897-8 this Store will contain 300,000 square feet—with more to follow.

Fig. II-8. Proposed expansion of the Schlesinger and Mayer Store into projected building on Wabash Avenue (*left*) and renovated building on State Street (*right*), 1897. *Chicago Tribune*, 10 June 1897. Photo © copyright 1897, Chicago Tribune Company, all rights reserved, used with permission.

tween the lines of this innovative architecture and the line of the new elevated railroad.

The proposed ten-story structure for Wabash Avenue was never actually built. But to facilitate a continuous flow of shoppers from the new train platform, Schlesinger and Mayer did commission Sullivan to design a pedestrian bridge linking the elevated station with the second level of their renovated front on Wabash (Figures II-9 and II-10). Opened in time for the Christmas shopping season of 1897, this connecting bridge featured steel girders spanning from platform to storefront above and below a glazed passageway with slender mullions. Projecting ornamental motifs were set atop these mullions between electric lights along the uppermost girders. The metalwork was painted white with an amber glaze to match the lower iron window frames and upper stone wall of

the renovated storefront. The roof of the bridge was a continuous sky-
light. The bridge's festive cadence of ornament similarly harmonized
with Sullivan's decorative metalwork around the building's base, and with
the column capitals and carved surfaces of the post-Fire facade above.
In the context of Schlesinger and Mayer's plans for Wabash Avenue,
their bridge's white color and ornamental distinction made it an unmistakable sign of the store's location when seen from the passing trains.
Sullivan's walkway has been compared to *passerelles* or elevated pedestrian bridges characteristic of Paris in the late nineteenth century.[27] One

Fig. 11-9. Pedestrian bridge from Schlesinger and Mayer Store to the Wabash Avenue elevated looking south, showing renovation of lower floors of 141–43 Wabash
Avenue in lower right. Courtesy of the Chicago Architectural Photographing Co.

Fig. II-10. Pedestrian bridge from Schlesinger and Mayer Store to the Wabash Avenue elevated looking north, 1897. Reprinted from *Inland Architect and News Record* 31 (April 1898).

notable Parisian counterpart of Sullivan's bridge was meant for people walking from a railway station to a hotel, moving from an elevated platform to elevated entrance without descending to the street. As a similarly distinctive passage, Schlesinger and Mayer's bridge may have conveyed the idea that those who entered the store from the train were being received in a special way.

Sullivan's Project for the New Schlesinger and Mayer Store

Schlesinger and Mayer pursued their program of assimilating properties and gradually improving their old facilities to compete with neighboring stores' architectural improvements on State Street. The most immediate of these was Mandel Brothers' acquisition of the neighboring northeast corner of State and Madison streets and their extensive renovation of their store's exterior. This architectural renewal gave Mandel Brothers a facility with a distinctive presence along the sidewalk enhancing the display of goods for the eyes of the passing public. During these years of intensive growth, the State Street stores' continuing transformations of their physical premises were well-publicized indices of their commercial success. Any announced changes in architecture served to keep a department store continually in the public mind by emphasizing a graphic correspondence between growing sales and expanding facilities. Schlesinger and Mayer's situation in the spring of 1898 resembled those of its neighbors. The department stores, which usually leased the ground and buildings in which they carried on their operations, typically paid high annual rents which were based on the total value of the property. If they chose to rebuild, the stores as leaseholders incurred the financial burdens of construction. The decision to rebuild was thus a considerable risk; yet the stores were compelled to maintain their competitive position along State Street by improving the capacity and attractiveness of their facilities.

Mandel Brothers' newly remodeled building encouraged Schlesinger and Mayer to rethink the future of their neighboring quarters. In April 1898 Leopold Schlesinger approached his landlord, Levi Z. Leiter, to negotiate a long-term lease for his store's properties at State and Madison streets with the intention of covering the corner with modern buildings, to be financed by Schlesinger and Mayer. Leiter had owned the corner property since 1878 as one of numerous pieces of real estate he had acquired in downtown Chicago. An observer of 1898 wrote that "Schlesinger and Mayer were moved to the necessity of this measure by the very superior advantages as to street frontage and external appearance, which the present changes being made by Mandel Brothers, would give [Mandel Brothers]. S. & M. are thoroughly stirred up by these moves and regard it as a prime necessity to make a corresponding one."[28] The new lease with Leiter specified that Schlesinger and Mayer's new facility was to be a "first class, fireproof building or buildings, not less than eight stories in height, of steel and iron construction, covering the whole of [the] premises, as nearly uniform in external appearance as practicable, upon plans to be approved in writing by myself, the said Levi Z. Leiter, or other party or parties who may stand in the place of myself as lessor in said lease." The new structure was to be completed no later than 1 July 1908.[29]

Given the close relation between architectural distinction and commercial identity along State Street, Schlesinger and Mayer's choice of a designer for their new building was an important decision for the future of the house. This decision had been somewhat complicated by the dissolution of the firm of Adler and Sullivan. The onset of a national depression in 1893 had greatly decreased new construction and Adler and Sullivan lacked business. Adler then took a position as an associate of the Crane Elevator Company in July 1895 and his partnership with Sullivan was dissolved. Six months later, however, Adler left his new position and returned to the practice of architecture in partnership with his sons. Adler and Sullivan each continued their individual practices separately after January 1896, yet sources indicate that David Mayer of Schlesinger and Mayer chose to retain Sullivan as the store's architect. Frank Lloyd Wright left this account of the situation in Sullivan's office after Adler's departure: "As a matter of course the clientele had been mostly Adler's as Sullivan now had reason to know. Louis H. Sullivan, Architect, so faced the fact that he must take what was left to him from the Adler connection and start to build a practice for himself. Only one Adler and Sullivan client stayed on with lonely Sullivan: Mayer of Schlesinger and Mayer. Dave Mayer employed him to design his new retail store building on State Street, Chicago."[30] In an account of the building after its completion in 1904, the *Economist* also noted that the new store "was designed and constructed after plans by Louis H. Sullivan who had given the subject the most thorough consideration. . . . The construction of the building had been given the closest attention upon the part of David Mayer of the firm of Schlesinger and Mayer, every detail having been gone into in the most thorough manner."[31]

Like his partner, David Mayer had devoted his primary energies to the development of the Schlesinger and Mayer Store since his youth. Apart from his immersion in business, however, Mayer, as early as 1886, was said to be "popularly known in social as well as commercial circles."[32] He held a membership in the civic-minded Union League Club, to which Leopold Schlesinger also belonged.[33] David Mayer's wife, Florence Blum Mayer, had been educated in France at the Sorbonne, had travelled extensively in Europe, and maintained a strong interest in music.[34] Like Sullivan, Mayer himself was known to be avidly interested and involved in music, particularly opera, whose home in Chicago was Adler and Sullivan's Auditorium.[35] Thus David Mayer would have been particularly familiar with this civic landmark as the most noted work of its architects, and the building in which Adler and Sullivan, and later Sullivan alone, had their architectural offices.

Mayer's distinctive interest in music was a characteristic he shared with the early domestic clients of Frank Lloyd Wright in suburban Chicago.[36] In fact Mayer had the distinction of being one of the individuals to have

commissioned designs from both Wright and Sullivan. In 1905 he joined
with a group of New York and Chicago capitalists in commissioning
Wright to prepare a design for a large amusement park on acreage just
south of Jackson Park, the site of the World's Columbian Exposition. The
unexecuted project called for "the construction of a number of buildings, widening the beach and beautifying the tract with landscape gardens."[37] Mayer's partners modeled the project on amusement parks
developed near Manhattan during the previous decade. After his departure from State Street retailing, Mayer embarked on a second career as
investor and developer of Chicago commercial properties. He focused
his attention on the central city, commissioning a series of projects for
the renovation or new construction of office buildings between 1905 and
1913. For these speculative buildings Mayer relied consistently on D. H.
Burnham & Co. as his architects.[38]

For the building of his new department store in 1898 Mayer did not
select Burnham as architect, although according to Wright, Burnham
did solicit the job.[39] As a dry goods house, Schlesinger and Mayer had
enjoyed a distinction on State Street by virtue of its older building, whose
curved corner and ornamental surfaces bespoke an elegant establishment comparable to the Palmer House one block to the south and Marshall Field's one block to the north. In contemplating the rebuilding of
his store, Mayer would logically have sought to maintain and heighten,
if possible, the particular architectural distinction of the house. By virtue
of his association with Adler and Sullivan over many years and his personal familiarity with their buildings, Mayer would have known of Sullivan's capacities as a designer of national prominence since the completion of the Chicago Auditorium. Mayer may thus have retained Sullivan
to give Schlesinger and Mayer's new building an architectural persona
that would lend a special presence to the store among its neighbors along
State Street. While the completed structure has traditionally been
praised for the clarity with which the typical condition of the steel frame
is expressed in its upper elevation, the original clients may have wanted
Sullivan because his skill as a designer of ornamental exteriors would
make their store a unique work of architecture in a competitive visual
environment.

Published accounts of the new Schlesinger and Mayer Store suggest
the significance that the owners attached to the aesthetic distinction of
their house. Announcements of the forthcoming project in 1898 noted
that "it is expected that the building when completed will be unique
among structures of its kind."[40] It was not proposed that the new em-
porium "rival other institutions of like character, but the aim is that it
shall surpass in beauty of design, the material used in construction and

embellishment, anything that has heretofore been attempted."[41] The employment of Sullivan as architect was announced as if to certify to the public that such architectural aspirations would be realized in the new building. Sullivan was identified in press notices not as an architect with considerable experience in the design of commercial buildings, but rather as "the architect who, in conjunction with Dankmar Adler, designed the Auditorium."[42] By implication Schlesinger and Mayer's new building would thus be a worthy successor to the most notable work of architecture in Chicago's recent history. The constructive skill and decorative artistry that had made the Auditorium famous as an achievement of its city would now be brought to bear on their mercantile house as a commercial building with a civic presence. Sullivan was known as the architect whose ornamental skills were evident on the Auditorium's interiors. He had more recently designed "the ornate exteriors of all the Schlesinger and Mayer extensions." Because "his success in that direction has attracted wide attention," it was logical that "his master hand will be employed" in the design for the new store.[43]

Sullivan's retention by Schlesinger and Mayer may be compared with Sullivan's commission to design the facade of the Gage Brothers' new building on Michigan Avenue in 1898. The Gage project was developed in Sullivan's office in the same period as the original scheme for the Schlesinger and Mayer Store. The Gage's comparable purpose as a commercial building and its proximity in Chicago to State Street make its design a companion to that of the Schlesinger and Mayer Store in Sullivan's oeuvre. Sullivan published renderings of these two works together in the spring of 1899 as representative of his recent production. The Gage facade was part of a larger building project initiated by Stanley R. McCormick, son of Cyrus McCormick, who had assembled a continuous frontage of 168 feet of property along the west side of Michigan Avenue between Madison and Monroe streets.[44] McCormick developed an agreement with three of the leading houses of Chicago's wholesale millinery trade, Gage Bros. & Co., Theodore Ascher & Co., and Edson Keith & Co., whereby he would construct three contiguous buildings for their use on this property. This plan to create a distinctive wholesale millinery district along one of the most attractive thoroughfares of the city was comparable to the development of State Street as the avenue of fashionable retailing.

McCormick commissioned architects Holabird and Roche for the planning and construction of all three buildings in the summer of 1898 (Figure II-11). The project as first built included adjacent six-, seven-, and eight-story buildings for the three firms. The tallest and northernmost structure was to be occupied by Gage Brothers & Co., the city's

leading supplier of imported women's hats, bonnets, and headdresses of
all trims. With buyers annually sent to Europe and representatives in
New York, Gage Brothers' semi-annual exhibitions were comparable to
the openings of the State Street department stores.[45] Gage Brothers may
thus have sought an ornamental facade as the architectural emblem of
their leadership in the presentation of fashionable styles of ornate millinery. To this end, Elmslie recalled that McCormick requested that the
Gage facade was to be designed by Louis Sullivan.[46] As McCormick's
prime tenant the Gage firm paid rent to him as financier and owner of
their building, and they offered to pay additional rent to McCormick to
cover the additional cost of employing Sullivan and erecting the special

Fig. II-11. The Gage Group as originally built on Michigan Avenue, Chicago,
1898–99. Holabird and Roche, architects; Louis Sullivan, architect for Gage
facade, at right. Courtesy of the Chicago Architectural Photographing Co.

front he designed. An editorial commented that Gage Brothers "did so because they thought it would benefit their business in an equal degree. They put an exact commercial value on Mr. Sullivan's art, otherwise he would not have been called in."[47]

The story of the Gage commission resembles that of Schlesinger and Mayer in that both clients may have sought Sullivan's artistry as a means to enhance the public face of their mercantile houses. Yet, in the case of the State Street building, Sullivan was not only the architect of a single exterior, but was responsible for the whole of a large and complex commercial structure. When Mandel Brothers celebrated the opening of their renovated store with illustrated advertisements on Memorial Day in May 1898, Schlesinger and Mayer countered with the announcement of their plans to build a $1,000,000 marble building to be designed by Sullivan on the southeast corner of State and Madison streets.[48] The following description of their project appeared in the city's newspapers on the weekend of May 28–29:

Schlesinger and Mayer will erect on the site of their present store a twelve story building of steel construction, with exterior of marble and bronze at a cost estimated at $1,000,000. The size of the structure cannot be definitely stated; nor the day when work will commence. . . .

Louis H. Sullivan has been selected as the architect. He has planned fronts that are of simple lines, leaving the beauty of the material to show for itself. The design represents the highest and most completely matured architectural thought of the day, in a type of what the modern mercantile structure should be. A union of the strictly utilitarian with the artistic; in short, a distinctively American product, a proper housing of a great enterprise, a blending of the genius of art with the genius of commerce. The two lower stories will consist of two-story bay-window showrooms, a grand display of plate glass framed in statuary bronze work of unique and exquisite design, wrought into original elaborations of rare and delicate beauty. From this to the top of the cornice, the fabric will be pure white marble from the Georgia quarries, the same material that has been chosen, with successful results, for the Corcoran Art gallery in Washington and the Rhode Island statehouse at Providence. This material will be treated with a smooth surface, combined with a fine simplicity of line and molding. The main frieze, under the solid marble cornice, will receive effective enrichment in flowing lines, accented by high points in the carving. On the Madison street front will be installed a spacious porte cochere and carriage court or rotunda, so arranged that patrons may drive directly to special elevators. All interior finish will be in bronze and San Domingo mahogany. The store will be equipped with twenty-four elevators, and the stairways will be so located as to insure facility and comfort of egress.

The construction will be thoroughly fireproof throughout, with a spacious arrangement of the columns of the interior. The structural frame will be entirely of steel, surmounted by a non-combustible covering, and every appliance known to modern science will be availed of to make the structure safe, sound, and enduring. It will be the effort of Messrs. Schlesinger and Mayer and their architect to make of this building, in every particular of design, arrangement, construction, finish, and equipment, the most complete structure of its class in the world.[49]

A presentation rendering of Sullivan's original project appeared in the catalogue of the Twelfth Annual Exhibition of the Chicago Architectural Club published in the spring of 1899 (Figure II-12). The drawing depicts a commercial building of monumental pretensions in both its scale and materials. The structure rises twelve full stories above the sidewalk, as if it were to emerge phoenix-like as the rebirth of Schlesinger and Mayer. The drawing shows the structure extending nine bays to either side of the rounded corner along both State and Madison streets, giving the project an idealized symmetry and suggesting its potential for expansion. The design as published may thus have represented the beginnings of a building that in the minds of both owners and architect could be indefinitely extended in either direction from the anchoring rounded corner. At the moment the scheme was announced, Schlesinger and Mayer were continuing negotiations for properties at 50–56 Madison Street east of their existing building with the intention of eventually acquiring the entire block front on the south side of Madison between State and Wabash Avenue.[50] The firm had also acquired the lease to an adjacent 30 feet of frontage at 145 State Street south of their store in 1897 (Figure II-2).[51] Schlesinger and Mayer continually sought to extend their control over neighboring properties on State Street and Wabash Avenue, "with no indications as to exactly where they [had] placed the limit of their desires."[52]

Schlesinger and Mayer's original design was so extravagant that its announcement met with skepticism in real estate and construction circles.[53] In consolidating their position in preparation for building, Schlesinger and Mayer's most important step before the announcement of the project in late May 1898 had been their negotiation with their landlord Levi Leiter for a long-term lease for the corner property on which the building would stand. However, shortly afterward, Leiter was compelled to sell the land to Marshall Field because of other financial difficulties. Marshall Field bought from Levi Leiter the title to Schlesinger and Mayer's corner property in July 1898. Before the sale Field had encouraged Schlesinger and Mayer's successful negotiation of the long-term lease on the property with Leiter that would enable them to go ahead with their new store building. These events were consistent with Field's policy of encouraging his rivals to maintain locations on State Street to concentrate the city's retailing near his own store. In July 1898 the terms of Schlesinger and Mayer's agreement with Marshall Field were disclosed to reveal that Schlesinger and Mayer were to pay an annual rent of $112,000 for the plots now owned by Field and extending 180 feet on State Street by 144 on Madison. This figure implied that the total property was worth approximately $2,135,000, making it the most expensive piece of real estate in Chicago with a rental value unprecedented in the city's history. The terms of the agreement with Field required that the

Fig. II-12. Rendering of the original project for a new building for Schlesinger and Mayer, 1898. Reprinted from Chicago Architectural Club, *Twelfth Annual Exhibition Catalogue* (Chicago, 1899).

new building would cost at least $600,000. According to Schlesinger and
Mayer's earlier lease with Levi Leiter, Marshall Field as their new lessor
would approve the plans for their new bulding. The announcement of
Field's acquisition of the property and the terms of his agreement with
Schlesinger and Mayer served to lend further credence to their plans.[54]

Sullivan's project of 1898 for the new Schlesinger and Mayer Store
included a rounded corner as a memorable vestige of the existing building that contrasts with the flanking fronts on State and Madison. George
Elmslie, Sullivan's principal assistant at the time, recalled that the inclusion of the corner was not part of Sullivan's earliest unrecorded designs,
asserting that

> he [Elmslie] was responsible for the curved corner at Carson's (S&M). The
> building was originally laid out in a perfect rectangle. Elmslie remembered
> that the earlier [Schlesinger and Mayer] store on the site had a curved
> corner and that it looked especially pleasing in some lights of the day. He
> suggested a curved corner to Sullivan, who approved tentatively and con-
> tacted the owner then in [New York City] who gave Sullivan the go ahead.[55]

Whether or not Elmslie was in fact responsible for the corner, his
account does imply that Sullivan's first intentions for the new store were
even more a departure from the preexisting building than was the executed scheme. A suggestion of Sullivan's original rectilinear treatment of
the corner appears in a newspaper illustration of the project published
in November 1898 a few days after a building permit was obtained (Figure II-13). In this drawing, the project has been reduced to nine stories
and the crowning marble attic has been removed. The overhanging cornice is extended to form a right angle above the rounded corner. The
squared edge of the roof as shown here subsumes the curvature of the
corner tower within a rectilinear profile for the whole building established by the lines of the steel frame. The rounded corner appears like
a motif from the old building incorporated into the new as a formal
anchor for the scheme.

The original scheme featured a continuous base of projecting glass
display windows described as bay window showrooms. These appear in
the presentation rendering as an architectural adaptation of the earlier
idea of the sidewalk showcase, which served to display wares to passersby
forward of the shop front. Sullivan's design incorporates this principle
into the base of the building, making the projecting display and entrance
bays part of the permanent structure. Around the perimeter of the
building, the entrance and display bays were on city property forward
of the building line to engage shoppers' attention. Only one such projecting bay of show windows was built on the first section of the new store

Fig. II-13. Schlesinger and Mayer's proposed new building. *Chicago Tribune,*
6 November 1898.

facing Madison Street completed in 1899. Schlesinger and Mayer paid
the city of Chicago a fee of $500 for a permit for this bay as construction
progressed in July of that year.[56] According to a city ordinance of December 1898, Schlesinger and Mayer were required to pay a tax of one
dollar per annum on each square foot of show window area extending
onto municipal property forward of the building line.[57] This ordinance
was one event in the city's ongoing campaign intended to inhibit encroachments of State Street department stores onto the public sidewalk
to enhance the promotional value of their frontage. The incremental
financial burden of projecting show windows under this city ordinance
probably discouraged Sullivan's continuation of this feature on the State
Street sections of the building redesigned and built in 1902–3.

The description of the original project noted that statuary bronze was
to be used for the frames of the show windows along the base and for
the window frames in the upper stories. This initial account may not
have been referring to the use of solid bronze, but rather to the use of

bronze-plated cast iron. Later in 1898 Sullivan specified that the metal-work of the base was to be iron "duplex electroplated in Copper Bronze," meaning that the iron would be immersed in an acid bath for 36 hours more than the standard 22 hours used for electroplating interior metalwork.[58] The aim of this process was to create an exterior surface whose thickness and durability would be equal to that of a sheet copper overlaid onto the cast iron. The appearance of bronze as the visible finish for the base may have been linked to its use in contemporary neoclassical architecture in Chicago and on the East Coast. Ornamental surfaces of bronze combined with cast iron also adorned the exterior of such Parisian department stores as Le Printemps. Yet Sullivan's design would have been an unconventional treatment of this material as a surface rendered in his unique system of architectural ornament. As the most permanent and durable of metals used for architectural hardware, bronze was originally envisioned for the base of the Schlesinger and Mayer Store because it suggested the idea of a fireproof building faced with a material renowned for its resistance to heat and flame.[59] The nature of cast bronze as a molten material would be heightened by the intricacy of the ornament to be wrought from its surface, as if the decorative forms were conceived as exquisite elaborations of the metal itself at the same time that they exhibited a personal style of expression.

The upper exterior of Sullivan's original design of 1898 may be understood as both a vivid contrast and sympathetic complement to the building's base. The upper wall was first envisioned as a white marble cladding the steel frame and its clay tile fireproofing. Sullivan's early preference for a white marble veneer may be attributed to the use of such a stone for the elevation of the preexisting Schlesinger and Mayer Store, or more generally to the use of white marble for the palatial exteriors of department stores elsewhere through the late nineteenth century. However, the description of the 1898 project emphasizes that no ornament was to be used over the upper wall except for carving confined to the cornice. The fronts were to be of simple lines leaving the beauty of the stone to show for itself. The treatment of the marble in this design was to be consistent with a formal clarity and precision associated with the steel frame. Sullivan specified that the cutting of the marble must be accurate and exact, with individual blocks of marble to be sawed so evenly that no joints would be more than 3/16 of an inch. He prescribed that "all plane surfaces must be true, and out of wind; all mouldings true to line and section, and all angles clean cut. All marble work must be so cut as to adapt itself to the structural steel supports."[60] Sullivan thus proposed to treat the stone as a curtain wall whose elegance of detail would enhance the presentation of the building as tectonic form. The crystalline blocks of marble would appear as piers and lintels as if to suggest a purely trabeated construction in stone associated with the columns and beams of the steel frame behind.

Like the bronze, marble suggests resistance to fire, and its disposition along the lines of the steel advertises the fireproof encasing of the structural metal. The choice of marble with bronze reveals an affinity between Sullivan's design and contemporary classical architecture in the East. His original description of the upper stories had noted that the stone for the new Schlesinger and Mayer Store was to be pure white marble from the Georgia quarries, the same material that had been successfully used for the Corcoran Art Gallery in Washington and the Rhode Island State Capitol at Providence. The choice of this particular stone had been a much discussed question among the New York architects who designed such civic neoclassical buildings. The exterior of McKim, Mead, and White's Rhode Island State Capitol shows the importance of this choice of material for the visual effect of the built design (Figure II-14). Henry-Russell Hitchcock noted that "the massing of its series of crisp rectangular blocks made it appear to have been sliced from the stone itself."[61] The architects had selected this stone over New England marbles because, as Mead recalled, Richard Morris Hunt had recommended that its chemical composition was "almost exactly like that of the famous Grecian marbles."[62] Similar reverence for Georgian marble, both because of its natural beauty and its resemblance to the most celebrated stone of antiquity, is evident in Ernest Flagg's handling of the material in his Corcoran Art Gallery completed in 1897 (Figure II-15).[63] Published photographs of Flagg's building highlighted the coursing scheme developed for this particular marble, whose urbane refinement of surface complemented the bronze doors, window grilles, and statuary around the main entrance to the building.

The original project for the new Schlesinger and Mayer Store exhibits a classical character not unlike that which was then being realized in great civic buildings of Chicago as well as those of the East Coast. By 1898 Chicago had committed itself anew to a classical public architecture in projects such as Henry Ives Cobb's Federal Post Office and Customs House (1896) and Shepley, Rutan, and Coolidge's Art Institute (1893) and Public Library (1897). Sullivan may thus have conceived of the Schlesinger and Mayer Store as a commercial building with civic associations that would rival his city's other new institutional monuments. In contrast to these contemporary neoclassical works, however, Sullivan's original project for the Schlesinger and Mayer Store eschews literal imitation of motifs from antiquity. Instead the first design for the building

in 1898 calls to mind the tradition of classical architecture without bor-
rowing its forms. It is as if Sullivan sought to evoke an aura of monumentality appropriate to a building of his own time. He specified marble
and bronze as a means of suggesting an ideal of grandeur associated
with those materials. Thus, out of the commission for a State Street
department store, Sullivan may have hoped to create yet one more testimony to his ability as architect of major landmarks in the heart of
Chicago. In sending plans for the new Schlesinger and Mayer Store
to Marshall Field as the owner of the property on which it would be
built, Sullivan wrote that "the plans and specifications in their present
form call for a high grade, thoroughly sound building; one that will be a
credit to the City and one with which I believe you will be abundantly
satisfied."[64]

Fig. II-14. Rhode Island State Capitol, Providence, 1891–1903. McKim, Mead and
White, architects. Photo by Leland M. Roth.

Fig. II-15. Detail of the main entrance to the Corcoran Gallery of Art,
Washington, D.C., 1892–97. Ernest Flagg, architect. Reprinted from
Architectural Record 11 (April 1902), courtesy of Architectural Record.

The Construction of the New Schlesinger and Mayer Store

Construction of the new Schlesinger and Mayer Store began in the
spring of 1899. By this time the original project of the previous year had
been considerably revised, as shown in a rendering published in April
1899 (Figure II-16). Sullivan was forced to decrease the number of stories from twelve to nine to comply with the city's legal height limit of 130
feet set in 1893. The number of bays along State and Madison streets
was reduced to conform to the extent of the properties that Schlesinger
and Mayer actually succeeded in acquiring to that time. The revised
building was expected to cost $600,000 instead of the $1,000,000 estimated for the original project.[65] Construction of the new Schlesinger
and Mayer Store was to be undertaken in stages to permit continued
operation of parts of the old Bowen Building. The first section was begun on 1 May 1899 with the destruction of a storefront at 50–56 East

Madison Street whose lease Schlesinger and Mayer had acquired from
that date (Figure II-2).[66]

One important limiting condition on the process of construction was
the need for speed. All decisions about the sequence of building were
subject to the overriding demand for enclosing sales space as quickly as
possible to offset the continuing burden of high property rentals. So

Fig. II-16. Schlesinger and Mayer's proposed new building. Reprinted from
Architectural Record 8 (April 1899), courtesy of Architectural Record.

severe were pressures of time that an observer of 1889 had noted that reconstruction of mercantile buildings along State Street would have proceeded years before, but properties had been so valuable that merchants had hesitated to rebuild because of the loss of their sites' use during construction. In the case of Schlesinger and Mayer's new building on Madison Street, the steel skeleton was erected through the ninth story by October 1899, with the interior and exterior finishes rushed to completion for opening on the first Monday in December in time for the peak of the Christmas shopping season.[67]

Through 1898–99 Schlesinger and Mayer had engaged both Sullivan and Dankmar Adler in complementary capacities to develop their building. In June 1898 they had formally contracted with Sullivan as architect to design and supervise construction of the main store building. At the same time Schlesinger and Mayer contracted separately with Dankmar Adler to design the store's power plant.[68] The expense account of Schlesinger and Mayer for construction in 1899, before Adler's death in April 1900, lists payments to him as mechanical engineer, with payments noted for Sullivan as the architect.[69] Thus Sullivan prepared a set of specifications for the new Schlesinger and Mayer Store building in December 1898 whose 136 pages of text are written in a style of prose characteristic of his literary works. This document deals with the constructive and decorative features of the building from foundations to roof, including the structural steel and iron work, and its fireproofing. However, Sullivan wrote that "for plans and specifications of the power plant, heating, plumbing, elevators, electric lighting, ventilating, water supply and waste, automatic sprinkler system, etc., reference is made to the office of D. Adler, Engineer, Room 64, Auditorium Building, by whom the same have been prepared."[70] Thus the first phase of design and construction of the new Schlesinger and Mayer Store brought the two former partners close together again in one last collaborative effort.

Upon its completion the three-bay front of the Schlesinger and Mayer Store was cited as representative of a new commercial architecture emerging within Chicago's shopping district (Figures II-17 and II-18). The larger scale and open quality of the new building, with its wide structural bays filled with plate glass, contrasted with the traditional fenestration of the adjacent renovated Bowen Building. The first part of the Madison Street front to be completed was the base, and by October 1899 passersby began to see the realization of a design anticipated for eighteen months. In these lower stories they "will at once recognize the work of Louis H. Sullivan," in the creation of ornamental surfaces "of an extremely unique design, the windows being broad and low, the whole presenting a very ornate appearance."[71] Schlesinger and Mayer

Fig. 11-17. First section of the new Schlesinger and Mayer Store on Madison Street, as completed in 1899. Reprinted from *Inland Architect and News Record* 34 (January 1900).

thus would henceforth be identified in the public mind as the department store around whose windows one could see a permanent exhibition
of decorative art created by a renowned Chicago architect. The metalwork surrounding the show windows on the lower stories was described
when completed as "ornamental iron in imitation of bronze," the less
expensive metal having been substituted for bronze as part of the revi-
sion of the original project. The overall architectural effect of the first
section was described by one observer as a distinctively appropriate expression for a building devoted to the retailing of dry goods, as if this
assessment were echoing Sullivan's own statement of his intentions.[72]

The upper floors of the new section were faced with white enamelled
terra cotta in place of the white Georgia marble originally envisioned.
The decision to face the upper stories with terra cotta in place of marble
may have resulted from a stonecutters' strike in Chicago during the summer of 1898. This event was one of a series of related job actions that

Fig. 11-18. Detail of the lower stories of the first section of the new Schlesinger and
Mayer Store on Madison Street. Reprinted from *Inland Architect and News Record* 34
(January 1900).

culminated in a general strike of the city's building trades in 1900. One major grievance of the stonecutters was the trend toward substitution of their numbers with mechanized equipment for dressing stone in the yards after its arrival from the quarries. One reason for stone companies' having turned to finishing machines was that their lower cost would enable stone companies to compete more successfully with the local terra cotta industry.[73] The lightness and lower cost of clay recommended it as a facing material for large commercial buildings, and Sullivan had used this material as the facing for his tall steel structures throughout the 1890s. In the first section of Schlesinger and Mayer's the finish and joining of the white enamelled terra cotta resembled the marble originally planned. The terra cotta was given a matt glazed finish as distinct from a highly glazed finish, perhaps to suggest the quality of the clay as akin to a natural stone rather than making it appear similar to an artificial tile. The alternating thin and thick courses of the terra cotta similarly recall the coursing scheme detailed for the original design in marble. One description of the building in construction identified the terra cotta as stone, stating that the material "had a pure and beautiful appearance as if it were marble."[74]

The crowning ninth story of the section built in 1899 shows a significant modification of the original 1898 design in that a classical motif was adapted to conform to functional logic. The windows are set back behind round freestanding columns crowned with a flat projecting cornice. The crowning story thus has the quality of a loggia or belvedere in place of the solid frieze envisioned in the original project. The built solution permitted daylight to enter the topmost floor, while the colonnade and recessed windows still provide the elevation with a terminal attic story. For the original marble project, Sullivan had specified that "the use of carving will be confined to the columns and piers in the Ninth story. . . . There will be no other ornamentation except the beading details and paneling, and sub-paneling of the cornice."[75] Ornamental treatment of these surfaces also appears in the built design of terra cotta. However, with the substitution of the clay, new bands of ornament were introduced in the upper wall running along the horizontal lintels between stories and within the reveals of the windows. Hence the appearance of ornament in the upper stories below the cornice was linked to the nature of terra cotta as a new material for a surface first conceived in stone.

After completion of the first section on Madison Street in 1899, the project for the new Schlesinger and Mayer Store lay dormant until the spring of 1902. Until that time the cost of additional construction may have been too great for the client firm whose total capital funds were estimated at $1,000,000. The first section at 50–56 Madison Street alone had cost upwards of $330,000.[76] However, early in 1902, Henry Siegel, of Siegel, Cooper & Co., began negotiating with Schlesinger and Mayer for acquisition of partial ownership of their firm. In addition to his interest in Siegel, Cooper & Co. in Chicago, Siegel from 1896 was active in developing the firm's large department store in New York, where he had also bought the older, more established dry goods house of Simpson, Crawford, and Simpson.[77] In June 1902, Siegel bought Schlesinger's half interest in Schlesinger and Mayer. Schlesinger retired from the business and the corporation was restructured with David Mayer remaining as president and executive head of the Chicago operations and Siegel as vice-president and chief investor. The firm was to continue under the old name of Schlesinger and Mayer, without merger with Siegel, Cooper & Co. The new arrangement increased Schlesinger and Mayer's capitalization to over $6,500,000. This influx of resources enabled the building project for State Street to resume.

As principal financier Siegel was ambitious to reorganize Schlesinger and Mayer, merging its buying operation in Europe and its general sales strategies with those of Simpson, Crawford, and Simpson, which commanded a prestigious corps of buyers on the Continent for its New York clientele. Siegel proclaimed of Schlesinger and Mayer that he and David Mayer intended "to make this house even of a higher grade than it is at present," dealing "only in the medium and the best" grades of merchandise. He stated upon closing the deal that the "present company will be reorganized. New blood, new methods, and new ideas will take the place of the old."[78] Siegel announced simultaneously with his acquisition that the older existing store buildings on both State and Wabash would be torn down and replaced with a new twelve-story structure.[79] Schlesinger and Mayer may have been prompted to renew rebuilding at this time by the activities of neighboring stores. Mandel Brothers had completed a large new annex across Madison Street in 1901 while Marshall Field's completed the first section of its new twelve-story facility in 1902. The popular Boston Store was also then contemplating a greatly enlarged facility to be built on the northwest corner of State and Madison streets diagonally across from Schlesinger and Mayer. Even before the official change in ownership, Schlesinger and Mayer had consequently pushed ahead with plans to revive the building campaign, evidently in anticipation of Siegel's capital. In March 1902 the firm had petitioned the city council to permit construction of a twenty-story building 280 feet tall at State and Madison. The council had recently passed an ordinance changing the old height limit of 130 feet to 260 feet. The council thus declined the petition and instead issued a permit for reconstruction not to exceed the height of 260 feet.[80] Within days after Siegel's official entry

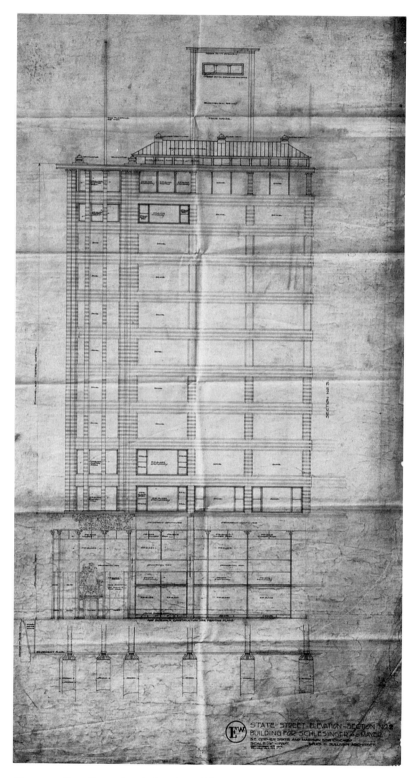

Fig. 11-19. State Street (west) elevation of the second section of the new Schlesinger and Mayer Building, 1902. Richard Nickel Archive, courtesy of the Richard Nickel Committee, Chicago.

into partnership in August 1902, Sullivan's office was at work on drawings for a twelve-story building at State and Madison to be constructed
adjacent to the first nine-story section of the new building.[81]

The design for the expansion of 1902 shows changes based on Siegel's
and Mayer's new aspirations for the store as a revitalized enterprise. The
exterior as built is documented in a working drawing of the corner and
first three bays of the State Street elevation, which would compose the
second section to be built (Figure II-19). This elevation shows the same
treatment of the upper and lower stories on State Street as on the first-
built section around the corner on Madison Street. The heights of the
added tenth, eleventh, and twelfth stories were reduced relative to that
of the floors below, perhaps because of their probable use as work and
storage space. On the roofscape of the building a 40-foot tall tower was
added to house a water tank which supplied the store's enlarged sprinkler system. The size of the tank was based on the amount needed for
the sprinkler system which, according to Sullivan, had become a focus
for the obsession of fire insurance companies that underwrote department stores.[82] The tower encasing the water tank recalls a miniature version of the Auditorium Tower as if Sullivan had sought a means to give
architectural presence to a utilitarian element.

The most important change in the design visible in the 1902 drawing
was the insertion of a circular entrance at the base of the rounded corner, in place of the multifaceted show window envisioned for this position in the earlier projects of 1898 and 1899. Such a window had been a
notable feature of the preexisting Schlesinger and Mayer Store as remodeled to 1897, though the original Bowen Building had had a corner
doorway. An early photograph shows the corner entrance to the new
building with arched doorways set in each of five curved sections of
decorative metalwork (Figure II-20). The design of Schlesinger and
Mayer's remodeled corner has been compared to the semicircular bays
at the corners of the Magasins du Printemps, one of the most prominent
Parisian department stores, designed by Paul Sedille beginning in 1882.
This was the Parisian store in which the characteristic architectural features of earlier department stores were brought together to create a
model of the type. The design of Le Printemps became the basis for the
architecture of numerous department stores elsewhere in Europe toward the end of the nineteenth century.[83] Le Printemps was the major
Parisian department store closest to Schlesinger and Mayer's buying office several blocks away on the rue d'Hauteville. Sedille's round bays
turned all four corners of the irregular site of Le Printemps. Two such corners flanked the store's main three-arched entrance on the facade along
the rue du Havre shown in Figure II-21. At the base of these rounded

Fig. II-20. Corner entrance to the Schlesinger and Mayer Store. Reprinted from
Architectural Record 16 (July 1904), courtesy of Architectural Record.

Fig. II-21. Magasins du Printemps, Paris, 1882–85. Paul Sedille, architect. Reproduced by permission of the Bibliothèque Nationale, Paris (HB66500).

corners were tall windows separated by pilasters and surmounted by
rondels. Above these the corner base was crowned by a cornice with a
smooth fascia. On the opposite side of Sedille's building, not shown in
the photograph, there were two other rounded corners whose bases did
serve as entrances. These faced in the direction of the buying office of
Schlesinger and Mayer. Sedille employed a classical vocabulary of lithic
forms to make the rounded corners a continuation of the marble facing
of the exterior. By contrast, Sullivan's entrance is a celebration of the
lightness and delicacy of cast iron rendered as ornament. The corner
doorways of Le Printemps may have served as a partial model for that
of the Schlesinger and Mayer Building because of their appeal as an
architectural emblem associated with one of the best-known department
stores of Paris, a reference consistent with Siegel and Mayer's avowed
intent of presenting the cachet of their store as an importer of fine dry
goods. Sullivan's design of doorways set between colonnettes also helped
to unify the rounded entrance with the tower above which featured a
comparable arrangement of windows between slender columnar forms.
The new entrance may have been conceived as a vivid reinterpretation
of the corner doorway of the original Bowen Building, just as the
rounded tower in Sullivan's design could be understood as a variation on
that found in the preexisting structure.

Construction of the twelve-story corner of the Schlesinger and Mayer
Store began in October 1902. The general contractor for this phase of
rebuilding was the George A. Fuller Company.[84] The laying of the foundations for the corner section was the first major feat of construction
which Sullivan supervised after the death of Dankmar Adler, who is
thought to have been primarily responsible for overseeing construction
during their partnership. Throughout the final building campaign, the
preeminent criteria were rapid assembly and minimal disruption of
store operations during construction. Thus, to preserve sales space for
as much continued use as possible, it was decided to build the new foundations beneath the existing corner store building.[85] This operation entailed shoring up the old structure on temporary foundations. Shafts or
caissons were excavated 60–90 feet underneath the existing building as
foundations for the columns of the new building. The use of concrete
caissons sunk to bedrock was not unprecedented in Chicago. However,
their emplacement beneath an existing building and the speed with
which the work was accomplished were without parallel in the building
industry up to that time. This method was more costly than sinking the
caissons on a cleared site, yet the extra cost entailed by working underneath the existing store was estimated to be far outweighed by the value
of the use of the old building during the fall shopping season of 1902.

The contractors did their work so well that the additional cost of preparing the foundations below the old store was thought to be only about $8,000 more than the price of doing the work on a cleared site. Nearly the complete grid of some 59 caissons for the new structure was in place by January 1903. Sullivan wrote an article on the foundation's construction for the *Engineering Record* as the only published account of the Schlesinger and Mayer Building that he authored under his own name.[86] The article's tone bespeaks Sullivan's pride in this achievement as unprecedented in the history of Chicago building, suggesting how at that moment in his career he wished to proclaim his competence as a building architect as a complement to his reputation as an ornamentalist.

The rebuilding of the corner site above ground began in January 1903 after the Christmas shopping season. The wrecking of the old corner was advertised as symbolic of the store's commitment to revitalize all facets of business during the process of rebuilding. The retail operations were then continued in the 1899 nine-story section on Madison Street and the old six-story section on State. David Mayer had hoped to begin selling in the lower floors of the new corner section as early as May 1903.[87] With this deadline in mind, its assembly proceeded at a record pace through the winter and spring. Steel girders and beams were used as the horizontal members of the structural frame. The demand for rapid assembly, however, had dictated the substitution of cast iron columns in place of steel columns because the latter could not be procured from the rolling mills by the January commencement.[88]

The pace of construction of the corner section of the building is documented in a series of photographs shown as Figures II-22, II-23, and II-24. The first shows the iron and steel frame erected through the tenth story. One week later the frame had been completed to the roof, five stories of white enamelled terra cotta had been set onto the frame below, as well as nearly all of the ornamental ironwork on the first and second floors. Setting of terra cotta was completed to the upper cornice in the following week, along with the completion of all the fireproof flooring, and the finished plastered ceiling on five floors. From 6 to 13 April, the exterior cornice was completed and glass partly set from sidewalk to roof. The corner section of the building was thus ready to open for business on 11 May 1903.[89] As architect, Sullivan was justifiably proud of the pace of construction as testimony to his ability in coordinating innumerable details of the work in association with the builder of this section, George A. Fuller Co. In May 1903, Sullivan received an inquiry from Carson Pirie Scott & Co. regarding his availability for designing a new wholesale store. In reply Sullivan asserted his abilities as a constructor, noting that:

Fig. II-22. Second section of Schlesinger and Mayer's new building during construction, 23 March 1903. Reprinted from *Brickbuilder* 12 (May 1903).

Fig. II-23. Second section of Schlesinger and Mayer's new building during construction, 31 March 1903. Reprinted from *Brickbuilder* 12 (May 1903).

Fig. II-24. Second section of Schlesinger and Mayer's new building during construction, 13 April 1903. Reprinted from *Brickbuilder* 12 (May 1903).

I believe that there is an impression abroad that I deal only with the more ornate forms of architectural construction. This is an error for I have done a great deal of work in heavy construction, plain factory buildings, machine shops, etc. . . . As to my general ability etc. I will gladly refer you to any officer of Schlesinger and Mayer whose new retail store I am erecting. I believe the time record made thus speaks for itself; and you know well enough that no contractor however capable would make such a record were not the architect's drawings and specifications well-nigh perfect, and every contingency discounted by him.[90]

The destruction of the last section of the old Schlesinger and Mayer Store south of the corner section of the new building began in May 1903. The steel frame for the new section was erected by the end of July and the outer walls were completed from sidewalk to cornice by late August. The entire effort culminated in the formal grand opening of the building during the week of 10 October 1903 in time for the height of the autumn shopping season.[91] The anticipated Schlesinger and Mayer Store was portrayed in a rendering of 1902 by Albert François Fleury (1848–1924), a Chicago artist and longtime associate of Sullivan who specialized in renditions of the cityscape (Figure II-25).[92] The view depicts the building as it was envisioned before construction began in 1903, relinquishing the portrayal of a symmetrical design as projected in 1898. Instead Fleury shows Sullivan's building as a strikingly novel structure within the context of State Street. Schlesinger and Mayer's new facility towers to more than twice the height of its neighbors, and the breadth of its fenestration is emphasized in contrast to the narrow facades of the adjacent older stores, as if a new architecture had risen above the post-Fire streetscape. Fleury was known for his paintings of the picturesque effects of the profiles of Chicago's new tall buildings among their neighbors. He thus portrayed the irregular outline of the Schlesinger and Mayer Store as finally built with the projecting cornices of its sections and the flagpole and towers on its roof, thereby accentuating the building's varied silhouette as if to announce its arrival on the city's skyline.

The Schlesinger and Mayer Store Becomes Carson Pirie Scott

Even as the advertising surrounding the October opening stressed the permanence and elegance of the new house of Schlesinger and Mayer, the financial condition of the firm throughout 1903 had worsened. Since March, even as the new frame was rising, David Mayer had been engaged in intensive negotiations to save his business with new sources of capital and purchasing power. Several related circumstances had combined to compel Mayer to act. The first of these was the cost of the new structure itself, which had surpassed the original extravagant estimates of $1,000,000. The total building effort by October 1903 had cost upwards of $1,650,000 with additional interior work still to be done. The figure struck at least one of Mayer's contemporaries as surprising, amounting to the extraordinarily high ratio of 31 cents per cubic foot.[93] Because of the disruption of business and temporarily reduced sales during the rebuilding process, the continuing annual property rental of $112,000 had become an exorbitant burden. Total losses in sales during construction from January through May of 1903 had approached $300,000, a figure that would only be recovered after six or

Fig. II-25. Rendering of the new Schlesinger and Mayer Store as envisioned in 1902, by Albert Fleury. Reprinted from *Inland Architect and News Record* 41 (June 1903).

more months in operation in the new facility. The loss of sales revenues was particularly burdensome because Schlesinger and Mayer, unlike some of their principal competitors, had remained primarily a retail operation dependent for inventory on outside manufacturers and whole-salers. In the spring of 1895 the store had expanded to include a whole-sale department devoted to the sale of foreign silks and dress goods.[94] Yet quick and profitable turnover of goods was probably more of a con-cern for Schlesinger and Mayer than for firms like Field's where a large wholesale division supplied the retail store whose occasional losses could thus be adjusted in house.

Mayer pursued a range of alternatives to try to alleviate his situation. He first sought additional capital and help in managing debts from Henry Siegel and his New York partners. Siegel was at first reluctant because his earlier 1902 investment had not yet shown dividends. Under these circumstances, in March 1903, Mayer approached Carson Pirie Scott about the possibility of their merging with Schlesinger and Mayer.[95] Carson's since 1902 had been searching for new and expanded quarters on State Street because their lease to properties in and adjacent to the Reliance Building was soon to expire and would not be renewed. David Mayer thus proposed to Carson Pirie Scott that they share Sulli-van's building as cotenants under a new firm name such as "Carson, Pi-rie, Mayer and Company."[96]

These negotiations for the fate of Schlesinger and Mayer's building did not immediately come to fruition. However, during the same months as he sought new sources of capital and means of financing to sustain his business, David Mayer negotiated for control of properties adjacent to Sullivan's building to facilitate its continuing expansion. The inten-sity with which he pursued control of adjoining frontage suggests that he considered its acquisition essential to the future of the firm. Only through a dramatic increase in floor area could Schlesinger and Mayer generate income enough to overcome the combined pressures of prop-erty rents, building costs, and decline in sales during construction. By the summer of 1903, Mayer had leased additional frontage at 45–49 Monroe Street and a lot farther south of the new building at 155 State Street (Figure II-2).[97] But even this new property may not have been enough, and there was speculation that Mayer sought to buy the entire block front south from Madison to Monroe. Otto Young, however, had recently acquired long-term leases to the properties south of Mayer's on the northeast corner of State and Monroe. Mayer negotiated with Young for this frontage, agreeing at one point to pay the exorbitant annual rent of $18,000 per front foot. Negotiations between Mayer and Young broke off in August 1903, however, when an "insurmountable difference" arose between them "regarding the building to be erected on the property."[98]

Late in the winter of 1904, Mayer discontinued attempts to expand and instead began to negotiate with Young to have him purchase Schlesinger and Mayer's building as well as their lease on the corner property that was still owned by Marshall Field. At this time another party stepped in to buy out both the business and the building of Schlesinger and Mayer. The purchaser, Harry Gordon Selfridge, was one of the most colorful and successful figures on State Street. For eighteen years Selfridge had been the highly successful head of Marshall Field's retail division, yet he now sought to go into business for himself. When Selfridge heard of Mayer's determination to sell, he arranged to purchase the building, its leaseholds, and the business itself for upwards of $5,000,000. Sullivan's building from June 1904 was to be known as quarters for H. G. Selfridge and Company, the newly created firm to devote itself to elegant retailing.[99] Mayer offered only a short statement at the time of Selfridge's purchase. At the age of fifty-three, he said, "I have for some time been considering the matter of retiring from active work. I have been hard at work since 1872 without a rest of any kind. The size of Mr. Selfridge's offer was inviting, and the desire on my part for a long vacation became so keen that my associates and myself finally consented."[100] After Selfridge bought out Schlesinger and Mayer's business, he then turned the financial responsibility for the building itself over to Otto Young. Later in June, Selfridge sold to Young the building and its leaseholds for $1,485,000. Marshall Field retained title to the land itself which was bequeathed to the Field Museum after his death in 1906.[101]

The disappearance of the firm of Schlesinger and Mayer marks the end of the original client's control over Sullivan's building, the completion of whose interiors had continued through the spring of 1904. Selfridge opened his new store in the building with a theatrical flourish in June. At first he sought to set up his new retail house on the model of Marshall Field's, but Selfridge was soon not happy competing with his former colleagues at Field's. He also became discouraged over the condition of the business he had acquired.[102] Accordingly late in the summer of 1904 he made his feelings known to Carson Pirie Scott, who had remained interested in the fate of the building. Selfridge thus sold his business to Carson Pirie Scott in August 1904 two years before Carson's was to lose its lease on its existing quarters in the Reliance Building. Selfridge reported that Carson's offered him "a large bonus over and above what I paid for the business about eight weeks ago." He turned over the store building to its new occupants in time for the fall shopping season of 1904.[103]

Fig. II-26. Construction of the 1906 addition to the Carson Pirie Scott Store (formerly Schlesinger
and Mayer). D. H. Burnham and Co., architect. Photo by Thompson-Starrett Company. Richard
Nickel Archive, courtesy of the Richard Nickel Committee, Chicago.

Fig. II-27. Advertisement for opening of Carson Pirie Scott's expanded store building, 1907. *Chicago Tribune,* 1 October 1907.

Carson Pirie Scott's occupancy of Sullivan's building must have been considered a coup for the firm after several years of uncertainty regarding its future location. Their relocation in the structure coincided with the fiftieth anniversary of the house and a general reorganization of its operations. In December 1904, Carson's commissioned D. H. Burnham & Co., their architects for the Reliance Building, to add a section to Sullivan's structure to extend 104 feet or five bays south along State Street (Figure II-26).[104] From the beginning it was understood that the addition would conform to Sullivan's design for the earlier section, the fireproof steel frame of twelve stories faced with ornamental iron on the lower floors and white terra cotta above. However, not all the details of the corner building were retained in Burnham's addition. The most visible changes were the elimination of the colonnade along the top story in favor of a continuation of the fenestration below, and the lack of ornamentation in the upper window reveals. The overall adherence of Burnham's addition to Sullivan's building testified to Carson's admiration for the original design. In a recommendation for Sullivan written in 1906, Carson Pirie Scott wrote of their new facility:

> The high taste and skill of Mr. Louis H. Sullivan, its architect, are well expressed in the beautiful design and general style of this structure, and our occupancy of it for these two years enables us to form an intelligent judgment upon its excellence as a structure as well as its adaptation for retail mercantile purposes. No more beautiful corner entrance of its kind is, so far as we know, in existence in this country; and the whole is a fine illustration of what Mr. Sullivan can design in the way of a retail business building. We learn from Messrs. Schlesinger and Mayer that their transactions with Mr. Sullivan were perfectly satisfactory, and gladly add our words of approval to his skill and success as an architect.[105]

When the expanded building was first opened in 1907, Carson's advertised it as the headquarters of a rejuvenated enterprise of distinction, whose stocks of linens, silks, and velvets exhibited "materials and styles which embody exclusiveness as the keynote of their attractiveness."[106] An illustrated advertisement for this opening (Figure II-27) shows a graphic border whose imagery of cornucopia and harvested abundance recalls the forms of Sullivan's ornamental surrounds for the exterior windows. Carson's perhaps sought to identify its renewal as a merchandiser with the ornate elegance popularly perceived as a chief characteristic of Sullivan's architecture.

The present condition of the Carson Pirie Scott Building reveals a series of modifications to the Sullivan and Burnham building. In 1927, Carson's expanded their facility elsewhere on the block with the construction of a fifteen-story structure on the northwest corner of Wabash

Avenue and Monroe Street designed by Daniel Burnham's Sons, whose elevation followed the scheme of the State Street fronts.[107] In 1940, Louis Kroman designed an adjacent ten-story building on Monroe Street which was incorporated into Carson Pirie Scott in 1950.[108] In 1948 the cornice and colonnade atop Sullivan's section was replaced by a parapet or low wall atop the twelfth story at the roof (Figure II-28). In 1955 Carson Pirie Scott acquired their building from Otto Young's estate, and in 1959 the structure was first designated a Chicago Landmark, a status reaffirmed in 1970. In 1960–61 Holabird and Root designed an eight-story addition adjoining the Burnham bays to the south on State Street. In 1970 the Carson Pirie Scott Building was added to the National Reg-

Fig. II-28. Carson Pirie Scott Building after removal of original cornice.
Photograph by Cervin Robinson © 1988.

ister of Historic Places and in 1975 it was designated a National Historic Landmark.[109]

In 1978, Carson Pirie Scott finally bought the land on which their building stood from the Field Museum of Natural History. The store then commissioned a partial restoration of their landmark.[110] The exterior terra cotta was cleaned and damaged pieces replaced, while the cast iron base was repainted to approximate Sullivan's original treatment of the metal. The corner vestibule was also remodeled to recall Sullivan's original designs for its surfaces and fixtures. Thus, though the present building contains alterations, Sullivan's structure survives today much as it appeared when first completed at the turn of the century.

Fig. III-1. Manufactures and Liberal Arts Building, at the World's
Columbian Exposition, Chicago, 1893. George B. Post, architect. Courtesy of
the Chicago Historical Society (ICHi-18015).

III

SULLIVAN'S DEPARTMENT STORE
ON STATE STREET

Sullivan's contemporaries recognized the department store as one of the most representative developments of their era. They saw in the scale and vitality of these new businesses evidence of distinctively modern conditions of civilization. One observer of the State Street scene wrote early in 1898 that "one never loses the feeling in walking through a department store that he is in the presence of one of the great achievements of the age. . . . As one of the chief industrial facts of the closing years of the century it commends itself to the careful study of all who would learn something of the tendencies of the times."[1] In their organization and development department stores were a new phenomenon, whose methods as commercial enterprises were thought to be the forerunner of the economic order of the twentieth century.[2] The stores' continuous and often burgeoning growth through the turn of the century attested to their popularity as unprecedented means for retail distribution.

When given the opportunity to design a department store in the heart of Chicago, Sullivan would characteristically have devoted attention to its nature as an architectural problem representative of his time. He was notably acute in his assertion that buildings were a testimony to the values of the society that created them, and he inherited the conviction from earlier thinkers of the nineteenth century that works of architecture were the expression of a people's particular way of life. In 1901 Sullivan asserted that "the critical study of architecture is in fact a study of the social conditions producing it."[3] In his essay "The Tall Office Building Artistically Considered," Sullivan had similarly identified that building type as "an evolution and integration of social conditions" which had found their convergence in the need for a new kind of structure.[4] The problem of making a work of architecture out of such commercial conditions challenged Sullivan to rethink the tall office building's relation to the history of his art. He asserted that the architectural art had persisted through the ages because of the power of individual artists to interpret the life and character of their society in its buildings. Hence Sullivan viewed the Parthenon, for example, as a symbol of the essence of Greek civilization, a monument created by a designer who had experienced his society's realities and knew its ideals.[5] Such a building's eloquence as the interpretation of a culture gave it significance as a work of art. In this way Sullivan sought to sustain architecture in his own time by creating buildings whose vitality of expression would derive from new conditions of society. Such works would emulate those historic monuments that were living symbols of an era. Sullivan believed that such a vital work of architecture would emerge as "a serious attempt, by a serious architect, to make a building grow naturally out of all its conditions, logically and poetically."[6] Such an attempt would give the building a truthfulness to its historical situation which would render it equivalent to the representative monuments of the past. With function accepted as a basis for expression, Sullivan argued, "the design of the tall office building takes its place with all other architectural types made when architecture, as has happened once in many years, was a living art. Witness the Greek temple, the Gothic cathedral, the medieval fortress."[7]

Sullivan brought these convictions to the design of the department store as a building type comparable in its significance for his time. The department store was a differentiation of the commercial problem, akin to, yet distinct from, the tall office building. In the design of both kinds of buildings, Sullivan saw himself as developing a definitive architectural form for a new order of commercial activity. Sullivan was thus to make of the Schlesinger and Mayer commission a building that would be an authentic interpretation of its purpose by an artist who was immersed in the life of his place and time. The completed building would be a significant work of architecture to the degree that it was a vivid record of those conditions from which it emerged, and which it in turn helped to define.

The department stores of Chicago had a range of attributes that informed their architecture. Criteria for their design included both functional requirements to insure the business' efficiency and symbolic associations to identify the stores' character as institutions in the life of the city. As showcases for merchandise and centers for its distribution, department stores on State Street were not unlike the exhibition halls of the Columbian Exposition. The exposition was decisive for the development of the city's mercantile life through the 1890s, and Chicago's department stores, including Schlesinger and Mayer, continually sought to associate their palatial establishments with the imagery and spirit of the World's Fair. Thus Sullivan's new building and its neighbors along State Street were promoted as permanent expositions of merchandise, buildings that continued to perform a function akin to that of the temporary pavilions of the Columbian Exposition, since torn down.[8] The greatest of these had been the Manufactures and Liberal Arts Building designed by George B. Post (Figure III-1). This structure was conceived as Chicago's answer to the mammoth Palais des Machines at the Paris Exposition of 1889. The Chicago building's 1200-foot-long main hall provided space for exhibiting a range of manufactured goods from all countries of the world.[9] The vast floor area was allocated into sections for neighboring national displays of furniture, decorative objects, and myriad representative products (Figure III-2). The array of displays within the open space of the exposition hall was analogous to the assortment of merchandise arranged over the floors of a department store. The stores promoted themselves as comparable to the great exposition halls, serving Chicago as importing retailers offering a wide range of stock. The completed Schlesinger and Mayer Store was thus described as a place wherein "most important of all to the shopper, one may wander at will through a permanent international exposition of the earth's choicest products in fabric and handicraft."[10] Individual departments used the same implicit comparison to the World's Fair to promote the "exposition of Oriental rugs" and "the largest and richest exhibit of model hats and gowns ever assembled in Chicago."[11] Like the Columbian Exposition, the Schlesinger and Mayer Store boasted of the number of visitors to its opening, especially those who had come from a distance beyond Chicago for the event. The opening was extended through a full week to enable as large a proportion as possible of the area's population of 2,000,000 to tour Sullivan's building. Schlesinger and Mayer's opening in October 1903 coincided with other grand openings along State Street to commemorate the centennial of the first built settlement of Chicago at Fort Dearborn in 1803. The stores of State Street thus became a focus for civic celebration just as had the pavilions of the Columbian Exposition. In 1899 the shopping corridor was decorated throughout its length as a replica of the 1893 Court of Honor, which had been the exposition's central space. The street's department stores were bedecked with temporary festoons of electric lights to become the counterpart of the fair's

Fig. III-2. Manufactures and Liberal Arts Building interior. Courtesy of the
Chicago Historical Society (ICHi-17532).

pavilions. Large temporary triumphal arches were set up at the north
and south end of the group, while at night the whole corridor was illuminated to imitate an evening at the World's Fair.[12] It is thus not surprising that Sullivan's original design for the Schlesinger and Mayer Store
recalled the neoclassical ideal of the Columbian Exposition whose
memory was associated with Chicago's department stores as a permanent
commercial exhibition.

The exteriors of the large retail houses of State Street resembled exposition palaces, but inside the stores were planned as machinelike systems for the distribution of merchandise. Their buildings were houses
of exchange, where the output of the world's manufacturers was traded

for the income of Chicago's urban consumers. Thus Harry Gordon Selfridge proposed that an alternative name for department stores which
more accurately described their role in the commercial life of the world
would be "distributing houses."[13] In a review of the completed Schlesinger and Mayer Store, Lyndon Smith described the functional ideal of
a department store as "an establishment where goods of many kinds
may be retailed to many people and so displayed over large floor areas,
that ease of examination and accessibility to products may be speedily
achieved."[14] On one hand, the department stores were selling agents for
the manufacturers of the lines of merchandise they carried. On the
other hand, the stores were purchasing agents for their customers, pre-
selecting from among the world's goods those that were thought most
likely to correspond to popular needs and tastes.[15] The stores' buildings
thus housed the process of trade at the critical juncture where great
quantities of merchandise passed from maker to user or from factory to
home. The importance of this process for the economic well-being of
Chicago gave department stores a powerful role in the life of the city. As
building types the great retail emporia were comparable to other monuments of commercial civilization such as wholesale stores, grain elevators, and railroad stations. All of these signified the ordering of the
material life of urban society. Descriptions of the completed Schlesinger
and Mayer Store in 1903 thus stressed the building's architectural novelty as evidence of the store's operational modernity as a distributor of
manufactured goods:

> Because we strive for progress, we shall open next Monday a magnificent
> new building of the most modern construction and equipment. If all were
> content to do the same old thing in the same way, the world would still be
> riding in stage coaches, reading by the light of tallow dips, and wearing
> homespun, but the world must advance. That which was new yesterday is
> old today, and will be obsolete tomorrow. Each day brings forth something
> new, something better than the day before could yield, some addition to
> the joys and comforts of life which needs only to be brought to the user
> to be enjoyed. To meet this necessity, our new store has been compre-
> hensively planned and constructed to serve as the connecting link between
> the people of Chicago and the best factories, workshops, and markets of
> the world.[16]

As distributors of unprecedented size the department stores of State
Street stressed their role as suppliers of needed merchandise to the city's
entire population. An advertisement for Marshall Field's in 1903 solic-
ited suggestions from its clientele for improvement of its inventory and
operation, asserting that "this store belongs to the great buying public—it is their downtown home. It is an important factor in the lives of

almost every family in and around Chicago."[17] The sense of the stores
as inclusively democratic institutions enmeshed in the life of the city was
considered to be a hallmark of American retailing. The American department store was thought to represent an advance over the traditional
atmosphere of shops in such European capitals as London and Vienna
which sustained rigid distinctions between selected patrons and the general public.[18] Chicago merchandisers proclaimed that their facilities were
accessible to all. The delights of wandering through the sales floors of
State Street were "free to the public, with no regard to rank or station,
the millionaire's wife or the workingman's."[19] Within these buildings
"each and every feature is entirely and absolutely for the convenience of
the shopping public, and as such free to all the people."[20]

   The department stores of Chicago advertised themselves as democratic commercial institutions in part because of their close association
with the ready-made or ready-to-wear clothing industry. Ready-made
clothing was a phenomenon of the nineteenth century when people
came to buy complete items of apparel made in a factory, not by an
individual tailor or by the family at home. As late as 1880, less than half
of all men's clothing in the United States was purchased as ready-to-wear.
But by 1900 estimates concurred that about nine-tenths of all clothing
worn by men and boys in the United States was ready-to-wear.[21] Continuing advances in cutting and sewing techniques through the late
nineteenth century made clothes produced in factories available to
the general population thereby encouraging a national tendency toward
equality in dress as a distinguishing characteristic of American life.[22] The
department stores could claim to be a democratic alternative in shopping
because of their role as the chief means of distribution for ready-to-wear
clothes. The stores promoted themselves as aiding in the process of social assimilation by providing immigrant Americans with the opportunity to dress in the manner of established natives. Thus one department
store owner spoke in 1900 for the merchant-clothiers who had founded
the great department stores, claiming that "We have provided not alone
abundant clothing at a moderate cost for all classes of citizens, but we
have given them at the same time that style and character in dress that
is essential to the self-respect of a free democratic people."[23] That the
Schlesinger and Mayer Store considered itself such a clothier for the public is suggested in an advertising rendering which focused on the corner
entrance (Figure III-3). At the base of the building are shown men and
women all dressed in urbane attire. The advertisement stresses that the
buying agents of Schlesinger and Mayer's international organization had
provided fashionable clothing, presumably like that worn by the people
in front of the building.[24] A comparable image is presented in the photo-

Fig. III-3. Advertisement for the opening of the new Schlesinger and Mayer Store. *Chicago Record-Herald*, 9 October 1903.

graph of the store's corner entrance chosen for publication in the *Inland Architect* in 1903, where the ornamental iron base serves as a backdrop for a well-clothed sidewalk crowd (Figure III-4). Like neighboring dry goods houses along State Street the Schlesinger and Mayer Store served the shopping public conceived as a democractic clientele, yet at the same time the store's architecture conveyed an image of elegance associated with a high grade of merchandise.

As facilities for merchandising to the whole of a shopping public,

Fig. III-4. View of the corner entrance of the Schlesinger and Mayer Store.
Reprinted from *Inland Architect and News Record* 41 (June 1903).

Chicago's department stores employed sizable staffs and accommodated large numbers of daily visitors. In 1904 Marshall Field's, in addition to its work force of more than 8,000, accommodated as many as 250,000 customers a day.[25] In 1898 The Fair employed about 2,500 people working in 100 different departments.[26] When they first moved to State Street in 1881 the Schlesinger and Mayer Store employed about 200 people. By 1891 the business had grown threefold to require a staff of between 700 and 800, and the store had more than a thousand employees in 1898, before it occupied Sullivan's building.[27] The unprecedented concentration of shoppers along State Street demanded that its stores develop their facilities with the daily flow of customers ever in mind. Sullivan's building, when sold to H. G. Selfridge in 1904, was described as a model of department store design because the structure was "equipped with every labor and time saving device for handling the State Street crowds."[28]

While appealing to the broadest range of potential customers, the Chicago department stores, like their counterparts in New York and Europe, aspired to create a distinctive atmosphere to enhance the experience of shopping. The great stores competed intensively in their provision of amenities to foster a stable clientele.[29] In 1906, Benjamin Schlesinger, brother of Leopold and the superintendent of Carson Pirie Scott's retail store, stated that "we draw people to our store through *conveniences* and *accommodations*" meaning "properly arranged telephone booths, tea tables, cafe, and similar service; next, the intelligent and tasteful floor walkers and salesmen-managers."[30] Typical advertisements stressed the stores as simulating the range of services and special rooms found in a social club with its residential atmosphere. Thus shoppers at Marshall Field's in 1898 were offered

> the many spacious floors of this great retail store as the "downtown headquarters" for all residents of Chicago and vicinity and for all visitors to the city. The waiting and resting rooms, the tea room, the many correspondence desks, the check room, the hundreds of conveniences—make this store, to those who know of them, almost as homelike as home itself.[31]

One perception governing the development of stores' services, special facilities, and decor was that the majority of shoppers were thought to be women. A characteristic observation of the time was that ninety-nine of every hundred purchases on State Street were made by ladies.[32] The shopping corridor was thus known as "the Women's Street of Chicago."[33] The model department store on State Street in 1898 was thought to be "a palace with every convenience and beauty that money can provide. . . . Being to so large an extent patronized by women, [the modern merchant] takes this into account, and surrounds the shoppers with an atmosphere of elegance and refinement, and provides every convenience for a woman's comfort and pleasure."[34] Sullivan incorporated this idea of architectural character into the design of the Schlesinger and Mayer Store. According to the assumptions of the day, the department stores' associations contrasted with those of office buildings, such as Adler and Sullivan's earlier Guaranty Building in Buffalo, whose character as an architectural type in 1900 was considered masculine. Sullivan's colleague, Lyndon Smith, asserted that the Guaranty was a type of commercial structure "dominated by men and devoted to the transaction of their business . . .—the elements of activity, ambition and directness of purpose, are all shown thereby in the architectural forms."[35] By contrast the treatment of ornamental detail in the Schlesinger and Mayer Store was thought to be "essentially appealing in its quality to femininity. It is sensitive to a high degree, delicately pleasing to the sympathetic eye and with fine feeling and movement permeating its most incidental ramification."[36] The association of the store's new architecture with a clientele of women appears in another advertisement for the 1903 opening whose graphic design pairs a typical shopper in the upper left with a perspective of the building in the lower right (Figure III-5). These images are linked with a branch of oak leaves which recalls the actual ornament rendered in cast iron along the base of the building.

The Show Window in the Shopping Culture of State Street

Among the most characteristic features of the department store as an architectural type at the turn of the century was the show window. Display windows set within the street front of smaller retail stores had been a familiar element of commercial architecture in London and Paris since the early nineteenth century.[37] These windows were confined to the width of the traditional shop along the sidewalk and were set within the wall plane of the building. The window area itself was often framed in decorative iron, though the small size and expense of panes of plate glass had limited the development of the show windows. In the United States the show window developed in conjunction with Manhattan's earliest department stores on lower Broadway. Of these, A. T. Stewart's apparently established the convention of large sheets of imported plate glass set between columnar supports across the length of the storefront at the sidewalk (Figure I-3). Stewart's windows were an adaptation of the shop windows of London's Regent Street. This tradition of show window design was imported by Potter Palmer to his Lake Street store in the 1850s and extended to the store of Field, Leiter & Co. and other commercial fronts on State Street built prior to the Great Fire of 1871.[38]

Schlesinger & Mayer

IN FIVE DAYS ANOTHER GREAT STORE.

The world moves every day. Men and institutions must keep step with it to attain success. The laggard stumbles down the road to failure. This thought has been constantly before the builders of the beautiful new Schlesinger & Mayer building, which will be formally opened next Monday, October 12th.

In striving for the highest success in store building, they have drawn to the limit on experience, skill, enterprise, and great resources. We believe the results have never been surpassed. The general public is invited to inspect the new building, with its exposition display of merchandise from all parts of the habitable globe, during the grand opening days, Monday, Tuesday and Wednesday, October 12th, 13th and 14th.

G.A.RIEMAN. 03

Marked features of new building.

The corner circular entrance.
The mahogany and marble fixtures.
New combination arc and incandescent lights.
Largest and finest display windows in the world.
The restaurant, grill and tea room.
The reading, writing and rest rooms.

Telephone booths.
The emergency medical aid room.
The unique French lingerie room.
The spacious art galleries.
The brilliant cut-glass room.
The great fabric room.
Another "largest" basement salesroom
Guides, etc.

Fig. III-5. Advertisement for the opening of the new Schlesinger and Mayer Store. *Chicago Inter Ocean,* 7 October 1903.

In this same period after the Civil War the art of window trimming,
or the design of decorative displays within windows, developed as an
artistic feature of stores on Broadway. The displays were set in continuous projecting bays of show windows along the base of the store buildings. Among the first stores in Manhattan to develop show windows as a
distinctive means of advertising its merchandise was R. H. Macy's, whose
annual Christmas window arrangements of dolls and mechanical toys
along its Sixth Avenue front became popular downtown attractions.[39]
Such windows were featured in views of Manhattan street life in the city's
illustrated newspapers. Because the major department stores of both
New York and Chicago were importing retailers, it is likely that they were
aware of the role of show windows in European department stores. The
new quarters for the Bon Marché, the prototypical Parisian department
store, included a two-story base of show windows or *vitrines* framed in
cast iron, and similar treatments at the street level were characteristic of
other Parisian stores during this same period. Individual shop fronts
with show windows surrounding their entrances also developed as a
genre of architectural design in tandem with the creation of Haussmann's new boulevards. Louis Sullivan recalled his enjoyment of window
shopping along the rue de la Paix in Paris during his student days at the
Ecole des Beaux-Arts in 1874–75, when he delighted in the cosmopolitan vitality of the city represented in part by its shop fronts.[40] Sullivan's
contemporaries regarded European techniques of mercantile display as
a source of instruction for American department stores. One account of
Manhattan developments noted that "window dressing in the 80s was
just becoming a profession. The more important dry goods concerns
were sending men to Europe for the express purpose of studying this
art, and soon a school of these artists was established in New York and
Chicago who excelled the old masters of Vienna and Paris."[41]

The number and concentration of large department stores on State
Street encouraged the intensive development of the show window as both
a form of decorative art and as a chief means of advertising. The direct
display of carefully and attractively arranged merchandise along the
sidewalk was developed as a primary method of drawing shoppers into
the store. As a medium for advertising, the show window displays were
closely related to the stores' illustrated newspaper advertisements.[42] The
full-page, persuasively written, and graphically effective advertising copy
supplied by the State Street stores to Chicago's dailies was a first means
of reaching the shopping public throughout a metropolitan area. Chicagoans bought a range of newspapers, and stores' advertising managers
were careful to supply different information to different papers, seeking
through each to reach a different class of clientele. The stores assumed

that shoppers became familiar with their lines of goods in each department through daily perusal of the newspapers. This initial invitation was intended to draw shoppers downtown, where they would encounter show window displays that would correspond to their memory of the newspaper illustrations. Given the proximity of the major stores, all of which placed comparable advertising in the newspapers, a shopper's decision to enter a particular house would be influenced by the attractiveness of show window displays. A close resemblance between the layout of the graphic advertisement and the arrangement of the displays within the windows was conceived as an important step in establishing a store's daily credibility. The turn of the century store manager was thus instructed to "strive to make his window displays accord with, or even excel his newspaper descriptions of the goods he has upon his shelves."[43] The window displays would carry out this policy of the store "by thus confirming the statements in the newspaper and furnishing a panoramic view of goods for sale within the store announced in the advertisements."[44] Poster size reproductions of the newspaper advertisements were often placed in the windows, with their illustrations set next to the real articles.[45] The displays were also changed several times per week to synchronize with daily change in the advertising copy.[46]

The individual bays of display windows were conceived as showrooms analogous to the chambers of an art gallery. The succession of windows constituted an ongoing exhibition of objects displayed in sequence along the base of the building. A professor of fine arts at the new University of Chicago recommended the windows of Marshall Field's as examples of decorative design, where artists designed displays and directed their execution by the window dressers.[47] He concluded that the window displays served to elevate public taste through exposure to motifs from the historic styles of art as well as natural forms:

> In view of this systematic art treatment, it is only fair to admit that these displays are powerfully co-operant even with the Art Institute in arousing the dormant art sense of this Philistine city. Here is an arts and crafts exhibition, not once a year but once a day, drawn not from Chicago and vicinity, but from Japan, India, Turkey, Austria, Italy, France, Germany, and England, all which countries are regularly visited by buyers to secure the best they afford.[48]

Contemporaries believed that department stores' window displays contributed to the cultural life of Chicago, enhancing the popular experience of its main street. An observer of the shopping corridor wrote in October 1903 that when merchants and trimmers sought to draw attention to goods for sale within their stores, they did also "aid in beautify-

Saturday, last day of grand opening, will be set apart for a childrens' carnival and fete day. Decorations, music, etc.

Schlesinger & Mayer

Grand opening days.

A population of two millions cannot see a great new store in three days. We have been requested, and have therefore decided, to continue our grand opening throughout the week. A very large portion of Chicago's population has visited us. Thousands have personally expressed their appreciation and approval, but have regretted the brevity of the festal season as fixed in our opening announcements. Three more days will give all Chicago an opportunity to see the opening of this great new store.

Special feature..restaurant, grill and tea room.
Our restaurant, grill and tea room is beautiful, perfectly equipped and unique in style. It occupies the entire 8th floor. Service in every detail from kitchen to table is the best to be had.

Great selling days.

Selling days, coincident with the formal opening of our new store, demonstrate that we have been successful in meeting the shopping wants of the people as well as in providing for their comfort. Commanding great resources and free range of the markets of the world, our buyers were able to assemble for this occasion a complete merchandise exposition on terms highly advantageous to shoppers. Their work has contributed to make this opening of another great store an event notable for the values offered.

Special feature..popular millinery, main floor.
The popular millinery section on the new main floor is a feature we are able to provide for the convenience of shoppers in our new building. It will be found complete and satisfactory in every respect.

Knit underwear
Third floor.

ECONOMICAL purchasers will recognize these as unusual bargains. An opportunity at the beginning instead of end of winter season.

$2.10 for silk union suits.

$1.25 for union suits.

75c for wool vests and drawers.

Novelty hosiery
Main floor—center.

SEVENTY distinct styles in hosiery.

50c for fine lisle hosiery.

Important waist event.
New waist section—third floor.

EXQUISITELY dainty and pretty are these evening waists of fluffy chiffon, lace and silk.

Corset specials at $5.
Third floor—center.

THE same careful attention is given to the correct fitting of these medium-priced corsets by our scientific corsetieres as is given to our finest French models.

$5 for "Valois D," the S. & M. special.

Novelty dress trimings
Main floor—center.

ALMOST every day brings some pretty new conceit in trimming novelties for this new section.

A sale of smart suits and coats.
New coat and costume section—fourth floor.

IT would be difficult—impossible, we believe—to find elsewhere so many clever styles as we now show at popular prices.

New zibeline suits, $45.

Handsome fall suit, $35.

Military suit, $35.

New military long coats, $25.

New raincoats, $20.

Cravenette coats, $25.

New fall suits, $25.

French robes..sacques.
New lingerie section—third floor.

ALMOST every foreign idea, including the notably beautiful Parisian novelties, will be found in this representative collection.

$5.75 for silk dressing sacques.

$2.95 for lounging robes.

$3.75 for albatross dressing sacques.

$5.95 for cashmere tea gowns.

$5 for lounging robes.

The annual glove sale.
Main floor—center.

THE unqualified success of our great annual glove sale.

$1 for women's mannish street gloves.

Lace novelties.
Main floor—north aisle.

ALL of the newest and prettiest of the season's styles are now displayed in the new section.

French lace novelties, silk.

Black silk lace galloons.

Curtains, portieres, tapestries.
New drapery section, sixth floor.

One of the special advantages of this large new section is the perfect north light in which all colors can be seen and estimated from an artist's point of view.

Cluny lace curtains.

Arabian lace curtains.

Renaissance lace curtains.

Tapestries and damasks.

L'art berbers portieres.

Saxony Brussels lace curtains.

Tapestry couch covers.

Window shades.

Black crepe de chine.
New fabric section—second floor.

DOUBLE width, rich black, all-silk crepe de chine at the lowest price ever quoted for these qualities of this, the season's most popular black silk favorite.

Double width, rich black, all-silk crepe de chine, $1.25
Double width, superior black, all-silk crepe de chine, $1.55

The new broadcloths
New fabric section—second floor.

SHIPMENTS are arriving daily. Scarcely a rare shade, tint or color that cannot be found in our new cloth section.

Silk petticoats.
Third floor.

PETTICOAT "special" of unusual merit which will further acquaint our customers with the superior qualities that are offered at very moderate prices in this new section.

$4.75 for silk petticoats.

$5 for silk petticoats.

$5.95 for silk petticoats.

Bohemian glassware...dinnerware
New art and china section, fifth floor.

One of the delightful surprises awaiting visitors to our great china section, now such a marvel of attractiveness, is the new display of beautiful white and gold Bohemian glass.

$1 for Bohemian glass nappies.
$1.25 for Bohemian glass nappies.
$2.50 for Bohemian glass small bowls.

Haviland dinner sets at special prices.
Special offering of Haviland dinner sets.

Three special lots: Lot 1, $35. Lot 2, $37.50. Lot 3, $40.

Fig. III-6. Advertisement for the opening of the new Schlesinger and Mayer Store.
Chicago Daily News, 14 October 1903.

ing and adorning the business thoroughfares and thus relieving them of much that is coarse and repellent. Through their efforts the streets and avenues become vistas of attractiveness, delightful to the stranger within the gates."[49] The accessibility of the displays to all classes of people reinforced the image of the stores as democratic institutions that sought to appeal to the widest possible shopping clientele. A daily scene on a commercial street at the turn of the century would include children "looking at toys, women at cravats or shirt-waists, while the day-laborer with his tin pail stops at sundown to study great paintings."[50] The windows were thought to be a form of cultural outreach to passersby which would engage their imagination and curiosity as a medium of decorative art.

In the case of the Schlesinger and Mayer Store, the show windows' distinctive architectural frames became incorporated into the graphic design of newspaper advertisements. The ornamental surrounds for the great sheets of plate glass on State Street were easily adapted as the masthead and border for full-page advertisements of the opening of the store. The interplay between the architecture and advertising graphics helped cultivate readers' image of the store in the printed medium in anticipation of the experience of the building itself. In one full-page advertisement for the store's opening, the upper border is a representation of the ornamental frieze which runs continuously over the second-story show windows along State and Madison streets (Figure III-6).[51] In the upper center of the sheet is drawn the round corner entrance to the store with its decorative crown extended to either side. Along the upper left and right sides of the page are vertical motifs that resemble the mullions between the show windows in the actual building. This representation of ornamental elements of the architecture along the top of the sheet serves to introduce the descriptions and illustrations of merchandise that continue down the page. In the real building, these items would be displayed within the frame of the show window as an introduction to their availability inside the store.

The pivotal role of the show window in the process of drawing customers into the stores lent importance to the development of their decorative trimming. The decorative art of the displays was the province of the window trimmer, a full-time designer and manager of the rotating arrangements of merchandise in all the sidewalk windows of the large department store. The occupation of window trimming developed into one of the more highly regarded and artistic specialties of store management, on a par with the advertising manager.[52] The simultaneous development of this novel field in Chicago and New York led to the founding of a trade organization, the National Association of Window Trimmers of America, in 1898, the year after the first publication of a trade jour-

nal, *The Show Window*. The National Association also began a series of
annual conventions, designed to promote the trimmers' line of work as
a newly established profession.[53] The trimmers of the State Street department stores were evidently a moving force behind the association, as
its journal's editorial offices in Chicago closely followed local developments. The association held its 1899 convention in Chicago, the central
event of which was a walking tour of the show windows on State Street
where many special displays were made by local trimmers for the occasion. The visitors' consensus following the inspection was that "Chicago
led the world in originality of window display, as well as in the number
of large and well arranged windows."[54]

The window trimmers' essential task was to attract attention. One
measure of a trimmer's success was the size of the crowds that formed in
front of his windows when new displays were periodically unveiled for
inspection. The designs had to contain unusual and distinctive features
to catch the eye and arrest the attention of busy people as they hurried
along the street. When shoppers' interest was aroused to the degree that
they would stop and gaze, only then would they notice the excellence of
the goods and desire to purchase them. For this purpose State Street
stores employed window gazers, or attractive, well-dressed men and
women whose role was to stroll along the street and appear to stop and
window shop in front of their employers' windows. Their fixed stare
and pretense of enrapt attention would attract a crowd of other passersby
who would also stop to study the same displays.[55]

The attractiveness of a display depended on the artistry of its background. Within the depth of the show window the trimmer was charged
with the creation of a scenic world in which elaborate, decorative backdrops filled the full width and height of the window area. These larger
backdrops framed an array of mannequins and smaller objects on which
the goods were arranged in the foreground. The background display
when first seen from a distance would attract passersby to the window,
where an individual's attention would shift to the apparel or other goods
positioned for intimate inspection just inside the glass. The art of the
trimmer lay in his ability to achieve this complementarity of effect
whereby the background would enhance but not overwhelm the merchandise itself.[56] One of Marshall Field's windows of 1904 displaying elegant women's costumes exemplifies this technique with a background of
mirrored panels framing a foreground of dressed mannequins (Figure
III-7).

Among the devices trimmers habitually used to achieve a balance between the display of the merchandise and the decoration of the whole
window were curved forms of backdrop framing displays of folded

drapery. The curvilinear lines of such temporary backdrops were typically designed as decorative contrast to the rectangular boundary of the window frame.[57] Backgrounds used to achieve this effect sometimes included motifs from the French Art Nouveau. Variations of this style of contemporary European decorative art appeared on State Street in the windows of Marshall Field's. In one of Field's windows from the fall sea-

Fig. III-7. Window display for Marshall Field and Co., 1904. Reprinted from *Merchants Record and Show Window* 15 (November 1904).

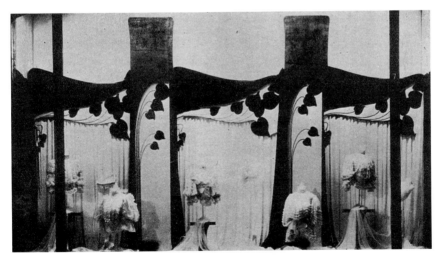

Fig. III-8. Window display for Marshall Field and Co., 1904. Reprinted from *Merchants Record and Show Window* 15 (November 1904).

son of 1904, backdrops of sawed wood were silhouetted against white
crepe creating a graphic effect to draw attention to a display of blouses
and shirtwaists (Figure III-8). Such adaptation of current Parisian decorative art to the trimming of Field's show windows may have been intended to signify the store's link to Continental modes of merchandise.
Variations on the motifs of Art Nouveau in the design of State Street's
window displays corresponded to the role of department stores not only
as importers of fine dry goods but also as showcases of current international trends in the arts. The stores thus became analogous to museums
specializing in exhibitions of decorative and applied arts, educating and
shaping the tastes of Chicago's shoppers. One notable instance of this
function at Field's was its exhibition of William Morris textile and carpet
designs in 1890, which helped to stimulate local interest in the English
Arts and Crafts Movement.[58]

The use of artificial and natural foliage was a convention of window
trimming. Floral embellishment as a tradition in display was related to
the imagery of fashion. Women's styles at the turn of the century featured intricate decorative patterns of imported laces derived from floral
forms, while trim on dresses and hats consisted of arrays of flowers and
blossoms. The popularity of floral decoration made from crepe, papier-
mâché, silk, linen, and ribbon developed as an extension of the use of
these materials within the garments themselves. In windows exhibiting ornate apparel trimmers fashioned these same materials into backgrounds that featured artificial vines, leaves, wreathes, garlands, boughs,
whole plants, or flowers such as roses, irises, and carnations. Companies
that surveyed the use of plant materials in European show windows sold
comparable artificial foliage to Chicago stores, enabling them to adapt
Continental modes of trimming to State Street.[59] Window trimmers were
advised that when their budget was limited, they might go out into the
woods surrounding their towns during autumn to gather colorful clus-
ters of real leaves as decorative material for their displays.[60] In other
cases the trimmers created backgrounds consisting of hundreds of artificial, handmade blossoms that gave a floral texture to entire window
scenes (Figure III-9).

The omnipresence of foliage as a decorative theme in window trimming corresponded to its use throughout the interiors of department
stores. Continual alteration of decor inside the buildings was closely co-
ordinated with the rotation of displays in the show windows. Semi-
annual openings at the onset of the fall and spring shopping seasons
inspired the temporary transformation of sales floors into autumnal
woodlands or celebrations of Easter.[61] The use of flowers for these oc-
casions accentuated the seasonal nature of shopping, as the periodic

Fig. III-9. Window display for Charles A. Stevens and Bros. Reprinted from
Merchants Record and Show Window 10 (May 1902).

transformation of interior decor announced the arrival of new stocks
of merchandise throughout the course of the year. An instructional
manual for trimmers first published in 1903 noted that such decor
should serve to induce a particular mood appropriate to the calendar.[62]
Schlesinger and Mayer adopted a floral theme for their grand opening
in the fall of 1903, when their building was "bedecked with flowers and
full of music, light and color," while the sales floors were arrayed with
some 15,000 chrysanthemums, the state flower of Illinois. Festoons of
artificial flowers were illuminated by electric bulbs in each blossom, the
colors of which varied from floor to floor.[63]

Fig. III-10. Carson Pirie Scott and Co. Cover design for *Chicago Dry Goods Reporter* 28 (23 July 1898).

The seasonal cycle of retail trade in Chicago corresponded to that of the agricultural economy of the Midwest. The fall openings of the major State Street stores coincided with the influx of clothing merchants who came from surrounding states to buy from the city's wholesalers. In this way Chicago's emporia played a pivotal role in the regional dry goods trade. Each year merchants came to the city after the harvest season on the prairies, planning to select a stock of the season's latest fashions and ship the goods to their local stores in time to meet the farming community's desire for new clothes after their harvest had been sent to market. An abundant harvest meant that the dry goods trade throughout the Midwest would prosper, resulting in a more successful year for Chicago's wholesalers and retailers.[64] Part of the ritual of these merchants' visits to Chicago was to inspect the latest trends in goods and retailing on State Street as a guide to their buying from the city's wholesale houses for their own stores at home.[65] During the fall shopping season the city's department stores thus served as showcases not only for fashions, but also for sales and display techniques that would be imitated by these merchants throughout the surrounding states.

The relationship of Chicago's retail and wholesale trade to the seasonal cycle of agriculture was the theme of a cover design commissioned by Carson Pirie Scott for the *Chicago Dry Goods Reporter* in 1898 (Figure III-10). The cover featured an image of Ceres, the classical goddess of the harvest and symbol of agricultural abundance. In one hand Ceres holds sheaves of rye and wheat, the two principal grains of the prairies, while in the other she holds a horn of plenty from which she scatters gold and silver coins over representations of the retail trade in the lower left and the wholesale trade in the lower right. Another image of Ceres appeared in a newspaper advertisement for the opening of the Schlesinger and Mayer Store (Figure III-11). The goddess stands atop a pedestal in the upper left of the page holding the fruits of the harvest in her apron, suggesting that the store building to the right was similarly filled to overflowing with an abundance of goods. The house would offer the public a newly replenished inventory like the harvest of a prosperous crop. The State Street stores thus appropriated the imagery of the bounties of nature as metaphor for the fullness of their stocks, their commercial success going hand in hand with agricultural prosperity.

The Design for the Base of the Schlesinger and Mayer Store

The role of the show windows in the mercantile life of State Street made their design a central programmatic issue in Sullivan's scheme for the Schlesinger and Mayer Store. The importance of this part of the old

Fig. III-11. Advertisement for the opening of the new Schlesinger and Mayer Store. *Chicago Tribune*, 7 October 1903. Reprinted from the *Chicago Tribune*, used with permission.

building even influenced the method of construction used for the new building. During the fall of 1902 the firm had built the caisson foundations for the new building while the old one was still in operation in order to prevent any suggestion of interference with business, "of which the show windows for holiday displays were an important feature." Sullivan took pride in the fact that the method of sinking the foundations under the old building enabled work to proceed without interrupting shoppers' passage along the sidewalk, as "nothing was ever laid down in the street."[66] The importance of the windows is evident in the ground floor plan of the nine-story project drawn in 1898 (Figure III-12). Schlesinger and Mayer's corner site had enabled the store to develop a continuous base of display windows along two streets. In this early plan the show windows along both State and Madison projected forward onto the sidewalk. Conceived as bay window showrooms, the total depth of the windows varied from 6 to 8 feet to create a sufficient area for the displays, hence the size of the windows made them comparable to small showrooms along the street. In the building as built most of the windows are set flush with the structure around the perimeter of the building. When completed the show windows were lined with mirrors around their backs and sides to destroy reflections of daylight off the frontal plate glass and thus enhance the visibility of displays from the sidewalk (Figure III-13). The sense of the show window as an architecturally finished environment included provision for forced air ventilation. The air prevented condensation on the inside face of the glass within the window compartment which would otherwise have obscured the displays and ruined the goods themselves. The lighting of the displays and the popularity of moving objects powered by electric motors within the windows necessitated wiring within the raised base of the windows. The inclusion of these features in Sullivan's drawings for the original project was intended to make the base of Schlesinger and Mayer's a model of a technically up-to-date solution for the design of show windows.

Sullivan made the permanent architectural background of the windows sufficiently elegant for the display of merchandise, so that the window trimmer would not have to obscure the permanent construction with temporary decorations. A review of window displays along State Street in the summer of 1904 after Schlesinger and Mayer had sold the building noted that "No ornamental backgrounds are used in the windows of [Schlesinger and Mayer's building]. These windows are exceptionally well constructed. They are wide, deep and roomy, without columns. The permanent background is expansive mirrors, framed with highly finished dark wood, and this is all that is used to show off the goods."[67] The head trimmer, who had previously worked for Schlesin-

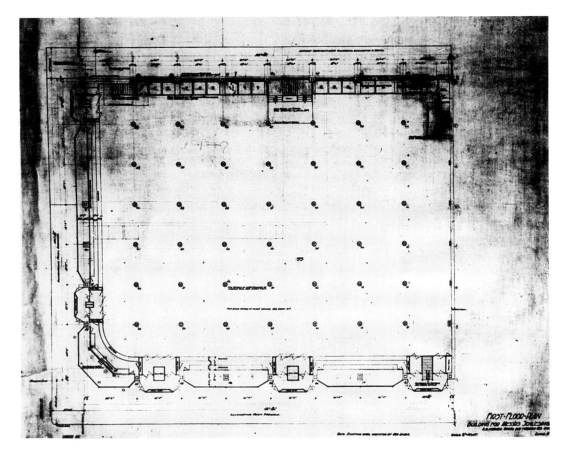

Fig. III-12. Street level floor plan of the Schlesinger and Mayer Store as projected
in 1898. Courtesy of Holabird and Root and the Art Institute of Chicago.

ger and Mayer before the business changed hands, "depends entirely
upon the draping and arrangement of goods and the harmony of colors,
for his effects which are invariably of the highest artistic order."[68]

Schlesinger and Mayer's show windows also served as important
means for introducing daylight into the interior of the lower two sales
floors. Daylight entered the store directly above the rear mirrored panels of the show windows which rose only part way from floor to ceiling.
Above the show window itself, there was a separate band of Luxfer prismatic glass flush with the plate glass of the show window below. The
Luxfer prismatic glass was a thickened glass of many plates whose ser-
rated surface performed like prisms to bend rays of sunlight from the

sky and refract them to diffuse light horizontally through the depth of a standard commercial space (Figures III-14 and III-15). Their placement above the show windows in the first and second stories of the Schlesinger and Mayer Store was designed to brighten these interiors by drawing

Fig. III-13. Detail of show windows of the Schlesinger and Mayer Store along State Street. Reprinted from *Architectural Record* 16 (July 1904), courtesy of Architectural Record.

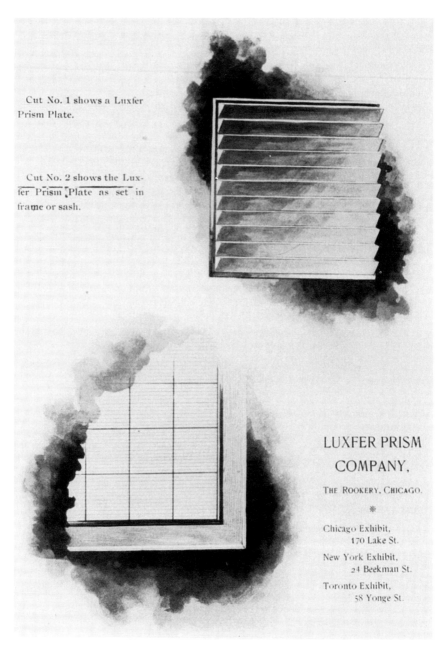

Cut No. 1 shows a Luxfer Prism Plate.

Cut No. 2 shows the Luxfer Prism Plate as set in frame or sash.

LUXFER PRISM
COMPANY,

THE ROOKERY, CHICAGO.

*

Chicago Exhibit,
    170 Lake St.

New York Exhibit,
    24 Beekman St.

Toronto Exhibit,
    58 Yonge St.

Fig. III-14. Luxfer Prism Company advertisement showing plates of prismatic glass. Reprinted from *Architectural Reviewer* (Chicago) 1 (February 1897).

Fig. III-15. Luxfer Prism Company advertisement showing interior illumination of a retail clothing store, Wabash Avenue and Madison Street. Reprinted from *Architectural Reviewer* (Chicago) 1 (February 1897).

daylight across the ceiling into areas farther back from the front to create an even ambient illumination. Elmslie recalled that in 1900 Luxfer prismatic glass was a very new building material that had been the result of scientific experiment. The material had been first developed by the Luxfer Prism Company of Chicago in the early 1890s. Owners, contractors, and real estate investors favored its use in remodeling older buildings. In the design of new structures, however, Elmslie maintained that some architects at the time did not favor its use and were not certain how to incorporate the prismatic glass into the aesthetic of a building.[69] Sullivan set this new material into the transoms of the lower windows of the Schlesinger and Mayer Store, treating it as a designed element of a wall surface conceived as a system of functional components. The transoms of prismatic glass above the second floor opened for ventilation. Iron supports for movable awnings are visible to either side of the show windows on the street. Such awnings served to shelter window shoppers along the sidewalk and to heighten the visibility of displays by inhibiting glare. The design for the show windows thus simultaneously accommodated provisions for light, ventilation, and display.

In Sullivan's view such a base was consistent with department stores as buildings in which commercial necessity implied an architecture wherein "all masonry would be reduced to a minimum, and there would be an expanse of glass for light and display."[70] The Schlesinger and Mayer Store would thus be a building conceived partly in terms of continuous glazed surfaces to extend through its whole height, but beginning at the street. The lower floors of the building were not of the traditional masonry, yet their anticipated projection beyond the lot line onto the sidewalk created a pronounced base of glass as a visual foundation for the upper floors. Sullivan's base was to be almost entirely of plate glass which, at the turn of the century, was still a relatively new material. Plate glass had not been manufactured in quantity in the United States before 1870, and widespread demand for its use in commercial buildings dated from the economic upswing of the 1880s. In many kinds of buildings in 1900, cylinder or sheet glass was still used for openings. This type of glass was blown in the form of a cylinder that was then split through its length and flattened out or stretched to form a sheet. However, in flattening out, the glass was subject to many imperfections, the most common being a wavy, watery appearance. Plate glass was manufactured with the aid of machinery to roll and form the plates directly from molten glass, helping to achieve a near uniform thickness and a near perfect evenness. From the inside, the smoothness of a plate glass surface made for clarity and brightness of daylight as illumination. On the outside, the reflectivity of plate glass could make it appear opaque, lending it an appearance of solidity rather than transparency. One proponent of plate glass wrote in 1896: "It glistens like a mirror from the outside in the sunshine, and in the shadow it reflects like one."[71] Plate glass could thus be used to complement other solid exterior materials because of its reflective sheen, an effect heightened in the renderings of the original project for the Schlesinger and Mayer Store. The glass is shown as a surface among surfaces, and, like the bronze and marble originally planned, the beauty of plate glass as a material would enhance the effect of purity in the overall design. In his specifications for the building, Sullivan stipulated that no cylinder glass was to be used and that all glass for openings in the exterior frontage from sidewalk to cornice was to be "first quality American polished plate, stiff and strong, free from blow holes, wave lines or iridescence—glass to be bright and clear, and worked to a true and even surface, giving true reflection, and must be very highly polished."[72]

The prominence of the new material is especially evident in the original scheme for the lower two floors of the Schlesinger and Mayer Store, which were to be "two-story, bay windowed showrooms, a grand display of plate glass framed in statuary bronze work."[73] In Sullivan's first design, structural supports were hardly visible around the base. The vertical columns were masked by the near complete continuity of glazing. This nearly unbroken surface of glass signified a radical change in constructive technology whereby the age-old necessity of courses or piers of masonry had now been replaced by a minimal skeleton of metal set behind the nonstructural glass. Observing new developments in Chicago's architecture in 1889, Henry Van Brunt had noted that architects in that city made "no attempt to avoid the enormous difficulty forced by the requirements of modern shop fronts, and by the priceless invention through which they can be occupied with vast single sheets of polished plate glass set under girders of iron and steel,—a condition important enough in itself to set at defiance nearly all the precepts of all the academies, and, if frankly accepted by the architect, to create, perhaps, out of this nettle, the flower of a new art."[74]

Sullivan's vision of a streetscape of show windows is more apparent in the original project than in the building as built. In his initial design the visible metal surface is almost entirely confined to the horizontal lintels above the windows on the first and second floors. Descriptions of his revised design for the Schlesinger and Mayer Store in 1902 noted that it would be "after Mr. Sullivan's style of architecture . . . , one of the distinguishing characteristics being broad windows." At this time Sullivan still intended to retain "a show window in the first story extending across uninterruptedly the space of practically 100 feet on the State Street frontage."[75] This long projecting bay window appears in one of the Fleury renderings of the project at this stage (Figure II-25), but was not included in the executed version of the base. Sullivan's colleague, architect Lyndon Smith, characterized the final form of the street level as "straightforward in its qualities of 'plate glass' architecture."[76] Sullivan incorporated the glazed base as a programmatic necessity, creating a feature expressive of the department store as an architectural type.

The ornamental enrichment of the frames around the glass signifies the importance both Sullivan, as architect, and Schlesinger and Mayer, as clients, attached to the show windows as an exhibition of decorative art. Another observer in these years wrote that "probably no architect ever designed a department store unaffected by the hobby or caprice of his client, and while this statement is likely true of every class of work, it is here fundamental, for the department store proprietor, or manager, has of necessity studied what appeals most strongly to his particular class of trade." [77] The role of the windows as part of the process of shopping made their design important for the commercial success of the store, while their extent along the sidewalk gave the architect an opportunity to exhibit the ornamental artistry acknowledged as his personal forte. By commissioning the special base of their new store and paying for its expense Schlesinger and Mayer would be displaying a unique example of the original work of Louis Sullivan as a recognized decorative artist in the service of their mercantile house. Sullivan's specifications for the original project went into great detail regarding the methods with which his design for the base was to be carried out in order to achieve the architectural effect he envisioned. The section devoted to ornamental iron in his specifications for the new building is longer than any other section of the document. Sullivan stated that the similar ornamental iron work in the Guaranty Building in Buffalo "may be taken as the basis of the elaboration of the design and the quality of materials and workmanship, with the understanding that the work called for under these plans and specifications is to be fully the equal of that of the [Guaranty] Building in its standard technical excellence, artistic finish, and delicacy of elaboration." Over the base of the building, "the use of ornamentation is to be very general. On the exterior store front work is to be exceedingly rich and delicate, and is to cover not less than, say 95% of the surface. This work will consist of geometrical and foliated designs. The scheme of ornamentation is to be very elaborate, with very fine and delicate detail." [78]

This initial conception of the lower stories was developed in a series of working drawings for the building executed in November and December 1898 (Figures III-16 and III-17). [79] Another surviving drawing for ornament around the show windows is an undated fragment of a pencil study showing motifs for the upper column and crowning lintel above the second story below the projecting metal cornice (Figure III-18). [80] In this study the motifs themselves are sketched in lightly, with touches of shadow added to indicate their degree of relief. The area rendered in the pencil study (upper column shaft, column capital, and half of lintel above second story) matches one inked in detail in the upper right of Figure III-17 drawn to the same scale, suggesting that this pencil drawing may have been a preliminary study on paper for those motifs that were later rendered in ink on linen working drawings. The fragment of the pencil study is unsigned, though as a drawing it exhibits a style of draftsmanship characteristic of George Elmslie, who later claimed to have done "all the ornamental work on the building." [81] Some later scholars have also attributed the design of the decorative cast iron along the store's base to Elmslie.[82]

The attribution to Elmslie of the surviving drawing for a section of the ornamental iron base of the Schlesinger and Mayer Store may be based on its comparison with other drawings of ornament attributed to him. One of these is a study of 1902 for a cover design for an edition of Sullivan's poem "Inspiration" (Figure III-19).[83] This sheet is composed and drawn freehand in pencil. The title page is composed with an enlarged letter *I* as the first letter of the poem's title set as a kind of graphic border along the left vertical edge of the sheet. Floral motifs are developed around the vertical stem of the letter *I* from its decorative graphic

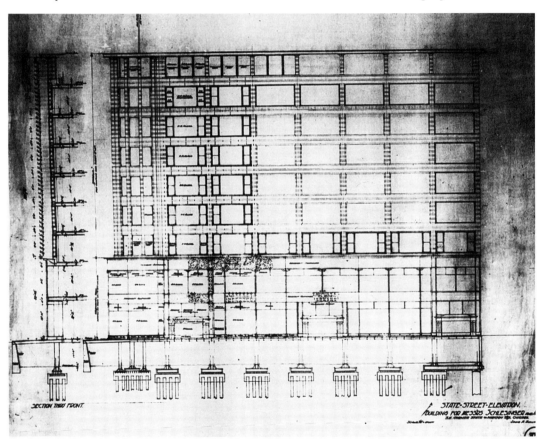

Fig. III-16. State Street elevation of the Schlesinger and Mayer Store as projected in 1898. Courtesy of Holabird and Root and the Art Institute of Chicago.

base in the bottom left, and above and below the lettering of the title word toward the upper right of the sheet. On the title page drawing the decorative motifs of tautly curved spiralling lines extending to foliate terminations closely resemble the motifs in the ornamental iron panels of the Schlesinger and Mayer drawing. The spiky profile of the leaf edges is also very similar, as is their uncertain graphic link to the tendril-like lines from which they appear to emerge. The density of shading over the area of both drawings and the technique of shading to represent surface relief, with canted strokes and biting black dots of the pencil, suggest the eye and hand of one draftsman. Finally both drawings

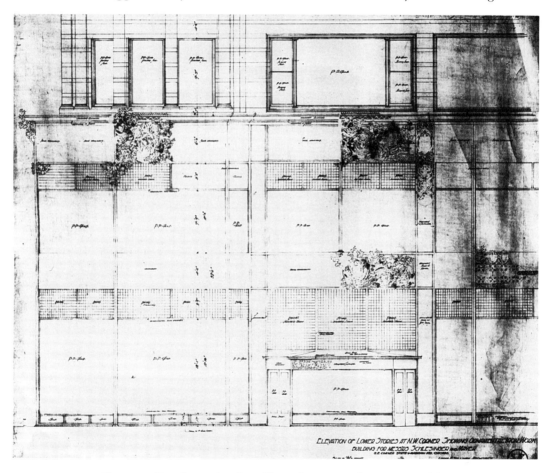

Fig. III-17. State Street elevation of lower floors at northwest corner of the Schlesinger and Mayer Store as projected in 1898. Scale of original, $\frac{1}{2}'' = 1'$. Courtesy of Holabird and Root and the Art Institute of Chicago.

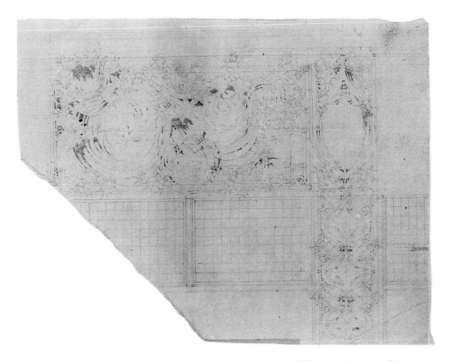

Fig. III-18. Pencil study for cast iron ornament around the second story of the
Schlesinger and Mayer Store. Scale of original, ½" = 1'. Frank Lloyd Wright Collection
of Drawings by Louis Henri Sullivan at Avery Architectural and Fine Arts Library,
Columbia University, New York. Photo courtesy of Dr. Paul Sprague.

exhibit a graphic tension between curved and straight lines. In the title
page design, the spiralling lines are composed with reference to the vertical stem of the letter *I* and the horizontal lines defining the masthead
of the rest of the title word. It is as if the straight vertical and horizontal
lines of the sheet are the graphic armature for the freer play of curvilinear foliate motifs. Similarly, in the Schlesinger and Mayer drawing, the
ruled vertical and horizontal lines of the cast iron panels serve as regular
geometric boundaries within which are set the spiralling curves and terminal leaves of the ornament. Along the vertical panel in the lower right
of the sheet, straight lines similarly form a compositional framework for
the interlacing curvilinear motifs. Writing retrospectively of his observation of Sullivan and Elmslie at work as draftsmen, William Purcell noted
that he "became fascinated with how much every little pencil press and
track had to say concerning any artist's immediate idea and the resulting
aura revealing the spirit of the man-artist."[84]

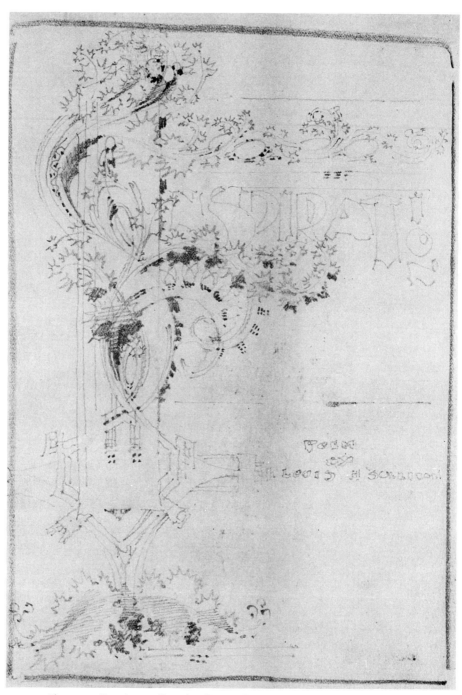

Fig. III-19. Drawing attributed to George Grant Elmslie in 1902 for a title page
for *Inspiration*, a poem by Louis Sullivan. Collection of David Gebhard,
Santa Barbara, California.

The attribution to Elmslie of the surviving drawing of architectural ornament for the Schlesinger and Mayer Store supports his assertion that he was the designer of the decorative motifs of this building. But Elmslie acknowledged that in his own development as an ornamentalist, he was a student of Sullivan's vocabulary. He wrote that Sullivan explained his theory of ornament to him and that he labored a long time to achieve facility in drawing Sullivan's forms and then to compose forms himself. Elmslie wrote that Sullivan "looked over my efforts critically and judicially and when he saw fresh interpretations and new shapes, he was greatly delighted. I never copied any of his motifs."[85] Comparison of this account with the 1898 drawings of the Schlesinger and Mayer ornament suggests that the question of attribution was not an issue for Sullivan or Elmslie, even though it has preoccupied later scholars of their work. Rather evidence of Elmslie's hand in works such as Carson Pirie Scott may be understood as the development of an apprentice under the eye of a master who had developed a novel system of expression.

If one accepts the attribution of the ornament of the Schlesinger and Mayer Store to Elmslie, then the intentions which underlay the motifs would have represented Elmslie's adaptation of Sullivan's principles of architectural ornament. Sullivan had a talent for choosing his assistants well, and Elmslie was both a capable designer and an articulate writer. In a short paper of 1935, Elmslie set down his understanding of Sullivan's ornamentation.[86] The ideas Elmslie expressed in this paper have traceable sources in nineteenth-century theories of architectural ornament which advocated that decorative forms should be derived from a fresh interpretation of nature rather than copied from history. Elmslie's essay of 1935 sets down principles articulated earlier by Sullivan in *A System of Architectural Ornament* (1924).[87] Elmslie maintained, as had Sullivan, that the source of inspiration for the ornament lay in Sullivan's "careful, accurate and deeply sympathetic studies of plant morphology."[88] Elmslie recalled that Sullivan kept a sketchbook "wherein he noted down the various elements of the origins of plant life and their final development into complete flower forms. This was a fascinating world to him as he often declared and on which he never tired talking to those who were interested. He was especially fascinated with leaf growth and the differentiations and permutations of forms within a single genus of plant, as well as the extraordinary and well nigh incredible ways in which leaves grow from the parent stems."[89]

The myriad ornamental motifs that emerged from Sullivan's studies of nature were "conventionalizations" of natural forms, meaning that the forms were not literally imitated or reproduced after their observed condition in nature.[90] Instead they became the basis of a decorative de-

sign wherein plant forms were interpreted and arranged according to a
compositional geometry. The artist subjected the natural object to his
analytical and sympathetic powers of interpretation, thereby producing
an ornamental motif which demonstrated the process of development
inherent in botanical life. As a designer of ornament Sullivan thus
heightened perception of a principle of nature because he "followed and
dramatized in poetic manner this play of organic growth in most of his
ornamental work."[91] Sullivan was fascinated by what Elmslie termed the
concept of growth and decadence as an all-pervading feature of nature.[92] Thus the theme of his motifs became "the growth from the seed
to its full exfoliation and then leaving behind, in decadence, as part of
its life, a germinal and vital substance for another springtime."[93] Sullivan
viewed his decorative art as returning to those sources in natural plant
life which had inspired the historic styles of ornament. But instead of
adopting the motifs of these styles as conventional designs, he sought to
adapt the principle of conventionalization of nature as the basis for a
modern system of architectural ornament. This system was thus to be
understood not as the imitation of historic styles of ornament but rather
an original and individually inspired equivalent of those styles. Just as
the Egyptians had studied the lotus, the Greeks the acanthus, and the
Romans the grapevine as the basis for their respective styles of ornament, so Sullivan studied the characteristic species of the American botanical environment as the basis for a renewed decorative art whose goal
was to suggest the inner vitality and not merely the outward form of
living things.[94] Thus Sullivan's view of the relation of his ornament to the
history of ornament is analogous to his view of the relation of his architecture to the history of architecture. Sullivan saw his work as an equivalent to and not an imitation of historic styles. His forms were original in
their place and time and thus corresponded in their inventive quality to
the creation of new architectures in the past.

These principles of ornamental art were those that Elmslie applied to
the design of decorative motifs for such buildings as the Schlesinger and
Mayer Store. Given that the intent of these motifs was to demonstrate
and celebrate the idea of organic vitality, the key to their visual effect was
their relation to the material surface in which they were rendered. In his
prefatory essay to *A System of Architectural Ornament*, Sullivan considered
that the substances in which the motifs were crafted were themselves
"inorganic" in that they were without vitality of their own until the designer, by virtue of his powers of expression, had breathed into these
materials the breath of life.[95] The resulting motifs rendered in materials
were thus to dramatize this process of the human mind and hand creating a living art out of inert materials. If ornamental forms were to inten-

sify perception of this idea, then they must appear to be inseparable from the surface of the materials in which and of which they are wrought. In his earlier essay entitled "Ornament in Architecture," Sullivan acknowledged that the execution of decorative designs may require the aid of different technical processes, yet the ornament "should appear, when completed, as though by the outworking of some beneficent agency it had come forth from the very substance of the material and was there by the same right that a flower appears amid the leaves of its parent plant."[96] It is this theory of expression that underlies the design and fabrication of motifs over the surface of such works as Carson Pirie Scott, as if Sullivan, in order to renew his art, were returning to its elemental principles. The sculpture of the motifs as relief signifies on one level the emergence of organic life from the realm of inorganic matter as this process occurs in nature and, on another level, the shaping of inert materials into vital forms as a demonstration of human powers of expression through the making of art.

In the design of the ornament along the base of the Schlesinger and Mayer Store, there is the suggestion of its motifs coming forth from the surface of the iron, as if an inner vitality had prompted their emergence (Figure III-13). The designs' conceptual intricacy as patterns first drawn in two dimensions and their sculptural quality when cast in relief combine to create an overall effect of an enlivened surface of metalwork. The geometric composition of the motifs along the columns is visible in the surviving pencil drawing attributable to Elmslie (Figure III-18). The drawing shows alternating oval and diamond shaped motifs drawn up the face of the column which overlap and interlace to create a suggestion of vertical movement. A larger oval appears at the top of the column as the flowering head of a natural form with leaves emerging at its base. Through such patterns the surfaces around the show windows become a field of ornamental relief wherein inert metal is transformed into a representation of the rhythms of organic growth (Figure III-20).

A similar effect is evident in the ornamental patterns along the lintel above the first floor (Figure III-21). Like the column, this design appears based on an interlaced geometric pattern in low relief. Along the upper edge of the lintel is a border composed of germinal ovals with interwoven tendrils. Like the design for the vertical column, the lintel motif's visual rhythms are suggestive of musical themes and musical structure. Elmslie asserted that there was much of the constitution of music in Sullivan's ornament. Like Sullivan, Elmslie believed in the close comparability of the arts of music and architecture, writing that "the more essential music there is in any art work, the more it approaches the natural and eternal. Since this ornament displays in its structure . . . qualities of

Fig. III-20. Detail of the northeast corner of the Carson Pirie Scott & Co. (Schlesinger and Mayer Store) on Madison Street. Reprinted from *The Idea of Louis Sullivan* by permission of John Szarkowski and the University of Minnesota Press.

rhythm, of harmony and counterpoint, and various forms of elaborate musical synthesis, just so does it approach the august throne of sound."[97] The suggestion of musicality in the ornament along columns and lintels closest to the sidewalk would certainly have been appropriate to the character of a department store, where the festive associations of window-shopping are enhanced by the lyricism of these motifs. The design for the upper border of the lintels above the first story may also be compared with a traditional egg and dart molding in classical architecture. In accounts of the history of ancient architectural ornament written at the turn of the century, motifs like the egg and dart molding were thought to have originated in antiquity as conventionalizations of the natural forms of plant life.[98] Elmslie's motif appears similarly conceived as a representation of the idea of organic vitality.

The lintels above the second story are larger than those above the first story and contain more inventive free-flowing designs of larger scale effectively seen from a slightly greater distance. The panels above the first story are 4 feet, 6 inches high while those above the second story are 6 feet high. The horizontal panels above the second story have a greater degree of relief than the lintel panels above the first story, and their sculptural depth appears heightened to enhance the visibility of motifs to be seen from below. The decorative motif of the upper lintel (Figure

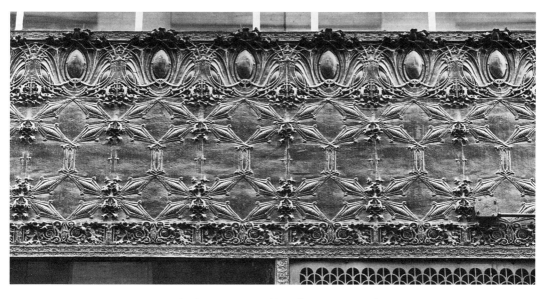

Fig. III-21. Detail of the ornamental iron lintel above the first story show windows. Richard Nickel Archive, courtesy of the Richard Nickel Committee, Chicago.

Fig. III-22. Ornamental iron lintel above second story show windows. University of
Illinois at Chicago, Arts Study Collection. Photo courtesy of Dr. Paul Sprague.

III-22) is developed as a single symmetrical composition spreading over
the full area of the iron panel, instead of a repetitive pattern in low relief
as along the lower lintel. The greater degree of relief in the upper lintels
corresponds to their greater scale and freedom of motif. The spiralling
tendrils unfold gracefully over the width of the panel across the entire
structural bay. When a series of these panels above the second floor is
viewed along State Street, their central motifs in high relief underneath
segments of the projecting cornice appear like the crowning scrolls of a
series of picture frames for the displays within the windows below. In
this way the lower floors of the building as built recall the original description of the base as a series of bay window showrooms (Figure III-
23). The effect of a row of picture frames implied by the motif of the
upper lintels recalls Elmslie's recollection that when the ornament of the
base was designed, the idea was "to frame, beautifully, the exhibits." Recalling the Schlesinger and Mayer Store, Elmslie wrote, "Is it a distrac-
tion to beautifully frame any picture whether it is in pigments or Cheney
silks?"[99]

Along State Street, in the building as first completed, there were
wreaths of ironwork set at the juncture of column and beam above the
first floor (Figure III-24). These wreaths were the most literally naturalistic motifs in the ornamental scheme for the building, their hammered
metalwork almost having the quality of a foliate decoration hung onto
the surface. These iron wreaths appear similar to natural Christmas
wreaths as a suggestion of the seasonal associations of shopping and as a
sign of welcome to passersby. The wreaths served to frame the monogram of Schlesinger and Mayer, thereby associating the name of the
house with the distinctive style of ornament which had given the store a
unique identity along the sidewalk. The wreaths above the first floor on
State Street were removed when their fastenings rusted away.[100]

Around the corner along the canopy above the Madison Street entrance there is a series of cartouches set in foliate designs which appear as another variation on the idea of the wreath (Figure III-25). The metalwork of this motif featured hammered leafwork around a central cast plaque. The position and size of the cartouches suggest that they may have been intended to mark locations for the curbing of carriages along the length of the canopy, recalling the original project's inclusion of a porte-cochere for carriages adjacent to special elevators. The cartouches above the Madison Street entrance continue the theme of the wreath around the full base of the building as an emblem signifying the invitation of greeting and suggesting the prestige of this retail store. These

Fig. III-23. View of lower stories along State Street with original cornice at right later restored at left. Richard Nickel Archive, courtesy of the Richard Nickel Committee, Chicago.

Fig. III-24. Ornamental iron wreath originally above the first floor of show windows on State Street. Richard Nickel Archive, courtesy of the Richard Nickel Committee, Chicago.

stylized insignia also may have been intended as Schlesinger and Mayer's variations on more conventional familial coats of arms displayed by some mercantile houses in Chicago in this period. The publicly accessible meaning of the wreath supports Elmslie's assertion that such architectural ornament "seemed a reasonable idiom to use and for people to enjoy, and they did enjoy it." [101] The significance of the ornament in relation to entrance is evident in an advertisement for the store's opening showing the canopied entrance on Madison Street as the focus of a crowd of well-dressed women shoppers moving toward the door (Figure

Fig. III-25. Cartouche of ornamental iron on fascia of the Madison Street canopy.
Reprinted from *The Idea of Louis Sullivan* by permission of John Szarkowski and
the University of Minnesota Press.

Fig. III-26. Advertisement for the opening of the new Schlesinger and Mayer Store. *Chicago Tribune*, 8 October 1903. Reprinted from the *Chicago Tribune*, used with permission.

III-26). The drawing emphasizes the decorative effect of the cast iron as creating a festive atmosphere that attracted visitors to the opening as if this memorable entrance was a keynote of the house. The ornament bestowed an aura of celebration which was to be re-created daily as a setting for shopping over the lifetime of the building. The advertisement is crowned with a variant of the cartouche motif framing a perspective of the building.

The most prominent adaptation of the wreath as an ornamental motif is set over the doors of the rounded corner entrance at the juncture of State and Madison streets (Figure III-27). Open wreaths are formed by tendrils of metal which appear to have germinated from the crown of the door arches below. These wreaths originally framed the monogram of Schlesinger and Mayer set on stems within the centers of the wreaths. The motif of interlacing spirals reads as a kind of allegory in metalwork depicting the process of growth and decadence universally observed in living forms (Figure III-28). The interpretation of the spiral in both the curving tendrils and curling leaves of Sullivan's design may be compared to the use of the spiral in the corner volutes and acanthus leaves of the ancient Corinthian capital. Both Sullivan's ornament and its antique counterpart may thus be understood as conventionalizations of botanical form. In this way, Sullivan's ornamental style, though highly inventive and imaginative, does nevertheless reflect considerable knowledge of historical architectural ornament and its sources of inspiration in natural phenomena.

The association between the naturalistic ornament in the building and the imagery of department stores is evident in another advertisement for the store's opening in 1903 (Figure III-29). This graphic design shows a classically garbed female figure that emerges from its train of intertwined drapery to form the right border of the sheet. The figure appears to be reaching up to place a wreath among the vinelike tendrils below the name of the store set along the top border of the page. The wreath of adornment portrayed in the advertisement corresponds to the architectural motif of the stylized wreaths over the corner doorways of the building. In the illustration the wreath resembles a crown of laurel leaves, hence the wreath surrounding the monogram of Schlesinger and Mayer in the actual building may be understood as a reinterpretation of an ancient symbol of excellence.

Sullivan set his monogram into the ornamental iron along the base of the building. The monogram, composed of the superimposed initials LHS, appears on either side of each arch above the doorways of the rounded corner entrance (Figure III-27). Sullivan's initials were also blended unobtrusively into the ornamental ironwork at the base of the

Fig. III-27. View of the corner entrance of the Schlesinger and Mayer Store.
Bob Thall Photograph.

Fig. III-28. Detail of ornamental iron over corner doors. Richard Nickel Archive, courtesy of the Richard Nickel Committee, Chicago.

In four days

Another "Largest Store."

THE new Schlesinger & Mayer building, which will be formally opened next Monday, October 12th, is the newest in Chicago. We believe it to be the most beautiful. Its location is generally regarded as the most convenient. It has been equipped from rafter to base line with the best that money could buy. We believe, too, that the many points of superior excellence in the building are more than matched by the contents.

The public is invited to see and judge for itself on the grand opening days, Monday, Tuesday and Wednesday, October 12th, 13th and 14th.

Distinctive features of the new building.

The corner circular entrance.
New combination arc and incandescent lights.
Mahogany and marble fixtures.
Largest and finest display windows in the world.
The restaurant, grill, and tea room.
Reading, writing, and rest rooms.
Telephone booths.
Emergency medical aid room.
The Paris millinery salon.
The unique French lingerie room.
The spacious art galleries.
Colonial cut glass room.
Another "largest" basement salesroom
Decorations, 10,000 crysanthemums.
The great fabric room.
The art room.
Music.
Guides, etc.

Fig. III-29. Advertisement for the opening of the new Schlesinger and Mayer Store. *Chicago Record-Herald,* 8 October 1903.

naturalistic wreaths set at the junctures of column and lintel above the first-story show windows on State Street (Figures III-24 and III-30). The architect's initials are set at the germinal base of each wreath below the initials of Schlesinger and Mayer. The exfoliations appear to have sprung from the letters LHS. Thus the ornamental motif emerges from the monogram of the architect as if to suggest that the designer's imagination was the source of the building's artistry.

The inclusion of the architect's monogram in the base of the Schlesinger and Mayer Store may be compared to a French medieval tradition of architects' and builders' seals used on documents (Figure III-31). Between the twelfth and the fifteenth century architects used these decorative emblems to ratify their deeds and contracts with building owners or patrons in lieu of a signature. The tradition of the medieval seals was brought to light in the late nineteenth century by the French scholar Adolphe Lance, who discussed their usage and reproduced many of their designs in his *Dictionnaire des architectes français*, published in Paris two years before Sullivan's arrival in 1874.[102] A seal served as the personal insignia of an architect, as a stamp of his individual methods of workmanship and expression in his art. In some seals, the initials of the owner were included with that of the architect or builder as a kind of joint signature on a document. The associated monograms of Schlesinger and Mayer and Sullivan on their department store similarly suggest the architect's claim to authorship of a distinctive building for a particular client. Sullivan's monogram in cast iron may be compared to his characteristic signature, the interwoven lines of which formed a unique linear design. As a statement of artistic identity, Sullivan's signature compares with the *signatures autographes* that French architects had used since the fifteenth century, after the use of seals had declined. Like a seal, the uniqueness of an architect's signature had helped insure the legal authenticity of the documents to which it was affixed. The autographs of the great French classical architects through the centuries were collected and reproduced in Lance's *Dictionnaire* as if to represent a succession of notable personalities through time, each of whom had left a mark on the history of his art.

The description of the original project for Schlesinger and Mayer had stated that the metalwork along its base was to be of a unique design, as if to indicate that it was the product of individual genius and could not be copied. In his specifications for the ornamental iron, Sullivan attempted to protect the uniqueness of the designs by stating that the moulds from which they were made were to be considered the property of the architect and the client, and that "in any event, they are not to be construed in any sense as being the property of the contractor for Or-

Fig. III-30. Detail of ornamental iron wreath above the State Street show windows showing monogram of Louis Sullivan below that of Schlesinger and Mayer. Richard Nickel Archive, courtesy of the Richard Nickel Committee, Chicago.

Fig. III-31. Examples of French builders' and architects' seals of Medieval and Renaissance date. Drawing by Leon V. Solon. Reprinted from *Architectural Record* 48
(August 1920), courtesy of Architectural Record.

namental Iron work, nor shall he duplicate these designs in any other
work at any time." [103] Years later, when Sullivan designed the ornamental
exterior of the Farmers' and Merchants' Union Bank in Columbus, Wisconsin, he was asked by his client, its president, J. R. Wheeler, if someone
else might not copy its design. Wheeler recalled that Sullivan replied,
"No. It won't be copied. It can't be copied." When Wheeler expressed
concern about the cost of the building, Sullivan turned to him and said,
"Just remember: you will have the only Louis Sullivan bank in the state
of Wisconsin." [104] At the turn of the century, Schlesinger and Mayer
were similarly to have the only Louis Sullivan department store in the city
of Chicago.

Sullivan's view of the process of construction informed his ideas on
the fabrication of the base of the Schlesinger and Mayer Store. In the

architectural culture of Sullivan's time the "commercial" nature of a building like a State Street department store implied not only the purpose of the finished structure, but also the predominance of the principle of expediency or least cost as a guide to decisions in design to a degree not characteristic of other building types. A department store was thus conceivable as a system of structural, mechanical, and decorative programs that corresponded to the store's system of operations as a complex enterprise. Both the store as building and the store as business were fashioned after the principle of minimal waste of time, space, and capital. The conception of such a commercial building as an economic system of elements was one aspect of its character as an architectural type. Thus one account of the Schlesinger and Mayer project emphasized that Sullivan as architect "accepts every exigency prescribed by modern commercialism. He solves every problem from the economics standpoint. . . . He conceives the building as a whole and the way in which it should be built as essential features to control his final design." [105]

Sullivan's approach to the making of a commercial building may be understood in the context of concurrent discussions in Chicago concerning the relation of mechanical production to social well-being. One focus for these discussions was the Chicago Arts and Crafts Society, organized in 1897 under the leadership of Oscar Lovell Triggs, an instructor in the English Department of the University of Chicago. The society was dedicated to the ideals of the English Arts and Crafts Movement as developed by William Morris, several of whose followers aroused the interest of Chicagoans during their tours of the United States at the turn of the century. Triggs believed that the society should consider the relation of the machine to the workingman, with the aim of reiterating "the necessity of creative workmanship in all departments of handicraft." [106] Triggs's view of this issue compares closely in spirit to the texts of Morris and Ruskin before him. In an article entitled "Arts and Crafts," published in 1897 in the society's periodical, *Brush and Pencil*, Triggs observed that in modern times "the machine methods have invaded the regions where hitherto the individual has been allowed free play." [107] He asserted that the perfection of organization and machinery had seemingly rendered the individual "powerless to undertake any great work on his own grounds and on his own initiative." [108] In the arts, this situation implied the necessity of reasserting the role of handicraft as distinct from machine methods. Triggs reasoned that, as beauty required the expression of the human soul, it could not be achieved via the agency of the machine alone. He concluded that "to have beauty in an object the human hand must touch the materials into shape, and the closer the object is to the soul the more beautiful it becomes in its ultimate form. . . . It is not possible that the things we perforce use can be beautiful until they bear the impress of hands that have taken pleasure in their formation."[109]

The ideals that Triggs presented before the turn of the century provide a context for understanding Frank Lloyd Wright's famous address of 1901 to the Chicago Arts and Crafts Society entitled "The Art and Craft of the Machine." In this address Wright expounded his vision of an architecture that would show a sympathetic utilization of mechanical processes in the creation of a new aesthetic. In Wright's view, the mechanized fabrication of building components provided a new field of opportunity for the exercise of values associated with traditional handicrafts. For Wright the array of building materials shaped and finished by machines had greatly increased the resources for architectural expression in modern times. Hence, Wright's ideal architect would be "the leader of an orchestra" whose instrumental range would include all manner of new constructive techniques.[110] Wright's advocacy of the machine as a tool for creative architecture thus stood in opposition to Triggs's romantic attachment to handiwork.

Sullivan's view of the relative value of different techniques in the making of architecture appears to embrace some ideas of both Wright and Triggs. On one hand Sullivan marvelled at the mechanical wonders of the nineteenth century, such as its great works of bridge engineering or its continental network of railroads.[111] The comparable achievement in architecture was the tall building whose steel frame and related systems of materials and services made it a constructive achievement representative of modern society. The architect when faced with such a problem "must cause a building to grow naturally, logically and poetically out of its conditions."[112] On the other hand, Sullivan was consistently passionate in his assertion of the individual artistic imagination as the unfathomable source of architecture.[113] In Sullivan's view, the quality of style in art arose from the mystery of personal inspiration apart from the material conditions of its realization. Thus he asserted that "it is within the souls of individual men that art reaches its culminations."[114] With these simultaneously held values, Sullivan apparently developed an inclusive concept of the architect's role in modern construction. He acknowledged that new materials and technical processes were conditions to be used as resources to renew architecture as an art of expression in his time.[115] Yet at the same time the resultant building as a work of architecture would bear the impress of a personal sensibility which would stamp all materials with an unmistakable individuality.[116] Such a design would be both of the times and of the man. Sullivan brought these dual values into consonance by asserting that all the means to a building's creation were merely resources for the execution of a design conceived in the mind of the architect. The architect determined those ideas he wished to express in a building's form, and his knowledge of the full range of materials and methods of construction "are part of his technical equipment whereby he has the efficiency and power to express the poetic thought—just as language and a knowledge of words are the technical equipment of the literatus." [117] If the architect was the individual who conceived the form of the building, its execution was accomplished through the labor of others, whether that labor was performed by hand, by machine, or through both of these means combined.

In an article entitled "The Machine in Art" published in *Brush and Pencil* in 1898, Louis Gibson articulated a version of these ideas in another response to Triggs's earlier statement. Citing Sullivan's method of combining modern and traditional techniques, Gibson stated that the machine "is but one class of tool" made and applied by man. [118] However, it was the capability of the mind, rather than the character of the tool, which determined the beauty or artistic value of the work which resulted from its use. Gibson asserted that the acknowledged masterpieces of detail in historic architectures, such as the egg and dart molding or the acanthus leaf of Greek architecture, were conceived by artists, yet replicated by carvers who in past times were the human counterparts of the modern machine. [119] As the architects of the Parthenon had directed the cutting of all the moldings, triglyphs, metopes, capitals, and columns, so "today the same artist would through his drawings and models, direct the machine-tool—the plane and the lathe—to carry his work just as far as was done on the Acropolis by machine men." [120] In Gibson's view Louis Sullivan was such an artist who made the drawings or models of details for his buildings which would then be interpreted, under his supervision, by the hand of a sympathetic sculptor. The final model would then be cast and replicated potentially hundreds of times by mechanical processes. Yet though both resources of craft and machine are employed as technique, "it is the artist who makes the drawing or model who makes the beauty possible." [121]

Sullivan brought an inclusive concept of the architect's role to the challenge of designing the Schlesinger and Mayer Store. He sought to utilize techniques associated with the mechanization of building and to create forms that gave evidence of the human hand in their shaping. An account of his involvement with the project as it neared completion in 1903 noted that Mr. Sullivan "accepts the modern machine, and demonstrates its capacity to assist him in evolving a work of art. He does not despise the task of designing a commercial building, but rejoices in it." At the same time, however, neither did Sullivan "neglect to use hand work, but encourages it where practicable. He is an artist himself and has a following of skilled artists whom he uses in their proper vocation."[122]

In the design of Schlesinger and Mayer's show windows, the ornamental frames of cast iron exemplified both modern techniques of metal fabrication and traditional handwork of artist and craftsman. The Winslow Brothers had executed the cast iron on the Schlesinger and Mayer Store, as they had done on other State Street buildings, including the Columbus, the Champlain, and the Reliance. The field of architectural metalwork in Chicago grew as one adjunct to development of the steel frame skyscraper. These buildings' intensity of use and their need for fireproofing had encouraged a preference for architectural metalwork in the design of storefronts, stairways, and elevator enclosures. The city's development of steel in structural skeletons by 1900 entailed "the spread of metal work to the rest of the structure, as not only appropriate but more enduring and cheaper in the end."[123] Ornamental metal's gracefulness, pliancy, and spatial economy recommended it over traditional finishes of stone and wood.[124] The proliferation of metal interior surfaces in commercial buildings was thus one of the distinguishing marks of a new architecture.

The development of the aesthetic capabilities of iron and bronze as the chief metals for architecture depended on the refinement of casting techniques. Traditional methods had limited cast metalwork to the production of cumbersome pieces whose grille work was often somewhat coarse and whose surfaces were imperfect. These limitations had prevented cast iron from achieving the refinement of detail or hand-tooled appearance of wrought iron. Even the surfaces of cast bronze in Sullivan's time also had to be chased or rubbed by hand to achieve smoothness.[125] The Winslow Brothers, however, perfected a means whereby large panels of very thin metal could be used in storefronts to surround show windows with the cast iron used as a facing for structural metal. The Winslow Brothers' sheets of iron ornamenting the renovated bays of the Mandel Brothers' building in 1897–98 were only about one half inch thick. They were so free of warping, roughness, or holes resulting from an unevenness of the molten iron's seepage into the molds that they were said to represent the state of the art in metalwork in Chicago or elsewhere.[126] Wright cited such a modern technique of casting in metal as approximating the ideal of an art and craft of the machine. The process made iron "capable of any form to which fluid will flow, to perpetuate the imagery of the most delicately poetic mind without let or hindrance—within reach of everyone."[127]

Improved techniques for casting iron challenged designers to create subtlety of pattern in ornamental surfaces. The crucial link between an architect's rendering of ornament in drawing and the manufacturer's realization of the design in casting was the hand of the modeler. The modeler was the craftsman whose clay mock-ups of architectural ornament provided the impressions from which the molds were made. Modeling ornament in clay rather than carved wood was considered essential for retaining subtleties of form in the mold and thus heightening the artistic potential of the finished metal. The expertise and sympathy of the modeler was therefore a prerequisite for the success of the new casting technologies, for only such a hand could "give the soft suggestive relief required by the nature of the sand mold into which the clay model is impressed, and the crystalline structure of the metal when cast."[128] For this purpose, Sullivan worked closely with Kristian Schneider, the Norwegian-born artist whom Sullivan commissioned to model his ornament in varied media including terra cotta and cast metal. Schneider had been a decorative plaster worker on the Auditorium Building when Sullivan discovered his facility in modeling ornament that led to their prolonged collaboration.[129] At the time of the design of the Schlesinger and Mayer Store, Schneider was employed as a modeler at the Northwestern Terra Cotta Company, which was responsible for the terra cotta on the upper exterior of the building. Sullivan employed him separately to make the clay models for the cast iron ornament surrounding the show windows along the base of the store.[130] Comparison of Schneider's clay models of this ornament with the executed metalwork shows his sympathetic understanding of Sullivan's designs and his considerable skill at rendering them in relief (Figure III-32). Purcell recalled that when he was in Sullivan's office in 1903,

> Schneider was coming in frequently to discuss the progress of the Schlesinger and Mayer work and as I had never known collaboration of that kind I was much impressed with the discussions, technical and creative, between Mr. Elmslie and Schneider concerning the models. No doubt for many years Sullivan and Wright also moved forward along with Schneider's unbelievable virtuosity, and by 1903 certainly Schneider needed nothing farther than a clear view by way of drawing or description of what was required.[131]

> Certainly the conversations which I heard between George and Schneider were plainly a section out of a long continuity in which mutual understanding and vocabulary concerned with procedure had been built up between them. Sullivan not practically active—most decisions made without consulting him.[132]

Fig. III-32. Clay model of cast iron cartouche on fascia of the Madison Street
canopy of the Schlesinger and Mayer Store. Reprinted from
Architectural Annual 2 (1901).

Schneider also modeled Elmslie's designs for terra cotta and for metal
in later buildings. In these later projects Elmslie apparently did not
make full-scale working drawings for the ornament, but rather supplied his modeler with small-scaled freehand drawings from which the
first clay models were made. The ornament then evolved into its final
form through a dialogue between Elmslie as designer and Schneider as
craftsman.[133]

Sullivan was familiar with the details of the casting process and methods of placing ornamental panels in the finished building. Elmslie recalled that on one occasion Sullivan gave an ornamental design to the
Winslow Brothers that was so intricate and delicate that they doubted
the feasibility of its fabrication. Sullivan then encouraged the Winslows
to persevere with their techniques in order to realize the design, and the
result was a grille of great virtuosity as an example of the casting art.[134]

Once the designs for the ornamental iron of the Schlesinger and Mayer Store had been developed in model form, Sullivan was careful to insure that the delicacy of detail in the clay model would be transferred to the sand mold, and thus to the molten iron. He specified that "only so much draft will be given the model as is essential to its removal from the mould, by a skillful moulder, without serious injury to the sand. The use of any further draft that may be given for facility of extrication will not be permitted." Sullivan was equally concerned that the construction of the ironwork in the building be done in such a way "as not to show any bolts or screws in any part of the work, except where absolutely necessary. Where the use of bolts and screws is unavoidable they must be symmetrically and artistically located subject to the approval of the Architect, whose attention must be called to such proposed arrangements. As far as possible work must be tapped from behind."[135] The concern of Sullivan and the Winslow Brothers for precise craftsmanship was evident to one contemporary observer of the first section of the executed base along Madison Street who noted that "the design is carried out in such rich ornamentation, the cartouches so delicate and well balanced, the lines of demarcation so carefully worked out, that it apparently expresses the climax of the capabilities of cast-iron and becomes a study for the student."[136]

The architectural potential of cast iron derived not only from its refinement of surface, but also from the exact repeatability of its forms. The technique provided an economically feasible means to create a series of identical or alternating motifs over the face of a building. The resulting rhythm of replicated ornament would endow a structure with a lyricism that would help bring it to life as architecture. Along the base of the Schlesinger and Mayer Store, Sullivan appropriated this capacity of the machine to enliven through repetition the architectural effect of ornamental designs drawn and sculpted by hand. The repeated panels of cast motifs framing the show window bays thus combine traditional craft and innovative technique to create a new system of expression in building (Figure III-23). The Winslow Brothers were highly conscious of their expertise in achieving such effects in metalwork. In the tradition of manufacturers of architectural cast iron, the firm inscribed its name in the base of the Schlesinger and Mayer Building at its northeast corner on Madison Street to proclaim its role in the realization of Sullivan's designs.

Photographs of the entrance at the time of the building's completion show a reflective sheen over the metalwork, perhaps as evidence of its painted finish (Figure III-33). The copper bronze plating that Sullivan had originally specified for the ornamental iron of the base was not used.

Fig. III-33. Corner entrance of the Schlesinger and Mayer Store as built.
Reprinted from Winslow Brothers' *Ornamental Iron and Bronze*
(Chicago, 1910).

Instead the iron was painted with a base coat of asphaltum, a thick tar-like paint, to protect the metal from moisture and weathering. Over this base coat a system of interblended colors was applied. The surface was covered with a coat of bright vermilion. Over this color was laid a translucent coat of green like the color of olive or sap. In the process of applying the paint, flecks and spots of red were allowed to show through the green overlay. According to Purcell, Sullivan likened this treatment to the fifteenth-century Italian method of applying gold leaf. In this process a base coat of Venetian red was applied, of which flecks and edges "show through and between the foil squares to give eye relief and build pointillism against the gold glints."[137] The lustrous surface of the metal visible in early photographs shows the decorative effect of this technique for painting ornamental iron.

As in Sullivan's earlier buildings, there was a close relation between the design of the ornament and the design of its polychromy. The interweaving of motifs in the decorative surface corresponded to the interblending of the painted colors over the motifs. Surviving descriptions of Sullivan's color schemes in his other works stress his consistent reliance on a single dominant tone for an entire room or surface which would then be overlaid or interlaced with accents of complementary or other contrasting colors.[138] When such a system of blended colors was applied over the iron ornament of the Schlesinger and Mayer Store, the variation of tones produced by the red seen through the green created an image of chromatic relief which corresponded to the sculptural relief of the ornamental surface itself. The effect of both the metalwork and its polychrome treatment was thus to be one of a play of delicate contrasts within an overall harmony. The individuality of particular shapes and tones is subsumed within a general impression of continuous pattern. The windows' evocation of a seasonal imagery was heightened by the painting scheme for the cast iron. The use of a softened and lustrous combination of red and green over this surface may have been intended to recall the seasonal colors of nature in passage from summer to fall. The suggestion of natural change over time would have been comparable to the suggestion of organic growth pervading the forms of the ornament. Thus, on one level, both the polychromy and the ornament would serve to convey associations of seasonal festivity appropriate as an invitation to shopping. On another level the tones of the iron relief would convey that suggestion of nature which Sullivan typically cultivated as a source of inspiration for his architecture.

The Architecture of Shopping at the
Schlesinger and Mayer Store

In its scale and ornamentation, the two-story base of the Schlesinger and Mayer Store was a special event in the eyes of passing pedestrians along State Street. The design of this most immediately visible part of the building was a means of distinguishing the identity of the house of Schlesinger and Mayer in the eyes of the shopping public. In mercantile culture at the turn of the century, the individuality of a store was perceived as an asset in achieving commercial success. John Wanamaker, founder of a leading department store in Philadelphia, wrote in 1900 that "success in some branches of mercantile life has its intense individuality, and is a matter of intense personality, much the same as in the journalistic and other learned professions. Only when personal ability and character can be translated into a franchise, can a retail business become a valuable entity."[139]

Among the merchants of Chicago, David Mayer and Marshall Field presented their retail houses as alternatives along State Street, yet in fact the two men lived close to one another in the then fashionable residential district of Prairie Avenue on Chicago's South Side.[140] Each of these merchants hoped that his store's architecture would heighten perception of its special character. In 1901 Marshall Field began construction of a twelve-story structure designed by Daniel Burnham's office (Figure III-34). The building's north section was opened in 1902 and its south section in 1907. The new Field block's steel frame was clad in a light granite from sidewalk to cornice. Show windows were set between piers within the rusticated base of the building. Though Field's window displays attracted daily crowds, the windows themselves were not as prominent an element in the architecture of new building as they were in Sullivan's Schlesinger and Mayer Store. Field's lower stories still recalled a base of stone, delineated as such by cornices above the second and third floors. Above this base the vertical lines of pilasterlike shafts of granite mark the rhythm of steel bays along the facade. These vertical piers are thicker than the horizontal lintels and project forward from them, almost as if the piers could be read as elongated and simplified classical orders. The elevation of the new Marshall Field's was crowned by a two-story attic wherein literal classical orders reappear as attached Ionic columns. Above this attic the whole facade is surmounted by a projecting bracketed cornice. The exterior design can thus be read as overlaying a steel structure with the motifs of a masonry architecture, thereby presenting the new department store as a conventionally classical edifice.

Fig. III-34. View of the new Marshall Field and Co. Store as completed in 1907.
D. H. Burnham and Co., architects. Reproduced by permission of
Marshall Field and Co.

The design for the new Marshall Field's was developed to conform to
an ideal of architectural character prescribed by Field himself. Throughout his life, Field was concerned that his buildings signify to the public
those values he considered central to his own achievement and thus to
the identity of his house. The earlier Field, Leiter & Co. building of 1868
had represented Potter Palmer's attempt to introduce to Chicago "the
free use of Vermont marbles and French designs in ornamentation" to
create a store which had been "quite original in design as compared with
other structures of that time."[141] In 1900, however, when finally given
the opportunity to create his own retail building, Marshall Field "declared himself in favor of granites, straight lines, massiveness without
bulkiness" to create not only a building that met the requirements of the
business, but also an architecture that "met the moral requirements of

Fig. III-35. Detail of the State Street entrance to the new Marshall Field and Co. Store. Reprinted from *Everybody's Magazine* 14 (March 1906).

Mr. Field himself" as "a lasting monument to his character." [142] The distinctive image of Marshall Field's was conveyed through the design of its entrance as a portico of freestanding Ionic columns over 40 feet tall, set on pedestals and supporting a projecting balustrade above the second-story cornice (Figure III-35). These columns were advertised as the largest granite monoliths erected since those of the ancient Egyptian temple at Karnak. [143]

The architecture of the new Marshall Field's not only signified the character of its founder, but also communicated an image of the store as the arbiter of Chicagoans' tastes in all facets of dress. In terms of its imported fashions, Field's maintained that "what we offer is correct," hence the house declared itself to be distinctive among Chicago's stores as "the authority of style." [144] Field's thus clothed itself with an explicitly classical architecture as an authoritative style of building from past civilizations. The use of classical orders as symbols of the stylistic authority of the house is suggested in the graphic design of an advertisement for the 1902 fall opening of the new store (Figure III-36). This advertisement shows a perspective of the Field complex at the northeast corner of State and Washington streets. The new Burnham section appears on the left, the renovated Field-Leiter (Second Singer) Building occupies the center, with the Field Annex of 1893 on the right. The view of these buildings is framed within the upper part of a show window set between two classical columns. The house's name forms a masthead for the page like a frieze. The text occupies the lower part of the show window announcing details of the opening and special features of the store's temporary decor. The text, however, reminds the public that Marshall Field's considered its reputation and policies as a retailer to be the foundation of its success. Field's was a store in which the process of retailing itself was considered the artistic act, the architecture only lending confirmation to an assumption of supremacy.

The program of advertising for the Schlesinger and Mayer Store emphasized the values of progressive innovation and popular accessibility as characteristic of both the retail business and its new building. The advertisement for the opening day of Sullivan's building in October 1903 also used the store's show window as the basis for its graphic composition (Figure III-37). The text of the advertisement is set in the lower part of the show window below the name of the store and a perspective of the building surrounded by cast iron frames of foliate lushness. Schlesinger and Mayer's advertisement presents a design of ornate metalwork as the insignia of the house in contrast to the granite columns that served as the architectural emblem for Marshall Field's.

The association between architectural character and mercantile identity in the Schlesinger and Mayer Store appeared in another advertise-

Fig. III-36. Advertisement for the opening of the north section of the new Marshall Field and Co. Store. *Chicago Tribune*, 1 October 1902.

Fig. III-37. Advertisement for the opening of the new Schlesinger and Mayer
Store. *Chicago Tribune*, 12 October 1903.

ment featuring the building's corner entrance (Figure III-3). The filigree of cast iron surrounding Sullivan's doorway was a display of festive imagery rendered in a modern material, whereas Field's portico was an assertion of stylistic authority fashioned from an ancient stone. The store through its building offered a challenge to the proverbial conclusion that "There is nothing new under the sun."[145] In his own writings, Sullivan himself invoked the phrase "something new under the sun" to characterize both the tall office building and the steel frame as unprecedented phenomena of modern times.[146] The advertisements for the new Schlesinger and Mayer Store similarly presented Sullivan's building on State Street as a statement in architecture which proclaimed to Chicago that this department store was indeed something new under the sun. By contrast Frank Lloyd Wright had characterized the architecture of Marshall Field's new building as reflecting Field's conviction that "what is most truly like the past is the safest and therefore the best."[147] Wright quoted Field as saying of his State Street retail store: "A good copy is the best we can do."[148] The ornamental iron surrounding the entrance to Schlesinger and Mayer's asserted through the language of architecture that their store was of the modern era when "each hour of the day, the world over, brings forth something new for the use and adornment of the world's children."[149]

The doorways of the Schlesinger and Mayer Store formed the link between the anticipation generated by the displays of goods along the sidewalk and direct contact with the merchandise within. Sullivan's original project of 1898 had included five doorways, three along State Street and two on Madison, their projecting glass vestibules interspersed between the show window bays (Figure III-12). In the earliest design there was to be a polygonal show window at the corner rather than an entrance. By 1903 this original plan was altered in the building to include three entrances: one projecting vestibule in the northeast corner of the store on Madison Street, one at the southwest corner on State Street, and the rounded doorway at the corner (Figure III-38). The multiple number of doorways signified the large scale of the department store as having absorbed a series of floor areas which previously would have been occupied by adjacent shops, each with its own separate entrance.

The design of the corner rotunda as built (Figure III-33) is a continuation of the architecture of show windows on either side, just as the doorways originally planned had projecting vestibules conceived as showcases set within a continuous base of plate glass. As a freestanding construction of cast iron, the corner entrance was composed of five curving sections of metal, the junctures of which were marked on the ex-

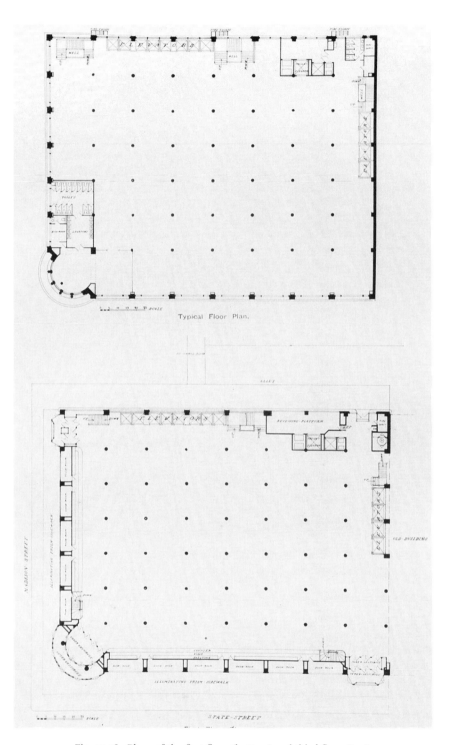

Fig. III-38. Plans of the first floor (bottom) and third floor (top).
Reprinted from *Prominent Buildings Erected by the George A. Fuller Co.*
(Chicago, 1904).

terior by slender colonnettes that acted as tubular hinges between the sections. Elmslie claimed to have worked out the details of this construction as well as the ornamental scheme of the entrance. At the sidewalk, the open filigree of ironwork around the arched doorways has a lightness and delicacy suggestive of the architecture of outdoor garden structures such as pergolas or pavilions, as if the green-tinted foliate ornament were growing over the latticework of a trellis. Inside department stores of 1900 temporary trim reminiscent of such garden architecture often served as the armature for floral decorations framing the entrance to particular departments (Figure III-39). The exterior use of similar forms in Schlesinger and Mayer's entrance re-created the effect of temporary interior imagery in a permanent architectural emblem of the

Fig. III-39. Interior decorative screen for a department store. Reprinted from
The Show Window 5 (August 1899). Photo courtesy of
the Chicago Historical Society (ICHi-20181).

abundance of delights to be discovered inside the store. The corner entrance may also have been designed for urbanistic effect. Just as the
Madison Street canopy's cartouches were sized and spaced with reference to the curbing of carriages, so the rounded profile of the main
entrance suggests the motion of streetcars whose tracks turned through
the intersection of State and Madison with a similar curvature. The semicircular sweep of the arched doors would be especially visible to pro-
spective shoppers aboard the cars as they rounded the corner (Figure
III-40).

In plan, the corner entrance was designed with a curved outer vestibule and an inner semicircular vestibule separated by a ring of doors
(Figure III-41). In warmer weather the outer doors and windows could
be set open to transform the outer vestibule into an open shelter. The
semicircular ring of doors between the outer and inner vestibules has

Fig. III-40. Intersection of State and Madison streets, looking east on Madison
showing Carson Pirie Scott's corner entrance at right and the Mandel Brothers buildings
at left, about 1908. Courtesy of the Chicago Historical Society (ICHi-04775).

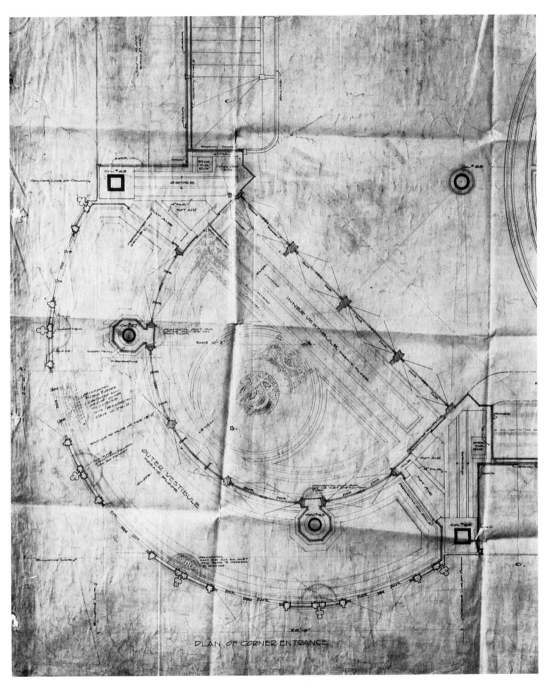

DLAN OF CORNER ENTRANCE

Fig. III-41. Floor plan of the corner entrance vestibules of the Schlesinger and
Mayer Store. Courtesy of the John Vinci Collection, Chicago.

since been removed; yet the restored vestibule still conveys an initial impression similar to that of an elegant residence (Figure III-42). The stores of State Street sought to present the image of being comparable to a downtown home or homelike club where one would be received as a welcome guest. In the vestibule of Schlesinger and Mayer's the monogram of the firm was originally set as a colorful circular mosaic in the center of the floor, as if marking the threshold to this mercantile house. Hanging directly above the monogram in the original vestibule was a bronze-plated cast iron light fixture which may have resembled a chandelier. Its illumination seen from the outside through the filigree of ornament may have been intended to recall the idea of a light glowing in

Fig. III-42. Vestibule of the corner entrance as restored in 1979. Courtesy of
the John Vinci Collection, Chicago.

the doorway of a palatial home. A suggestion of domestic warmth on the inside of the vestibule is also evident in the design of the column capitals set to either side of the central light. These capitals were made of decorative plasterwork painted orange and overlaid with an amber glaze to correspond to the sheen and chroma of the surrounding surfaces of mahogany and to respond to the source of artificial light originally hung from the ceiling between the two columns. Each element of the vestibule's architecture was thus carefully designed for harmonious effect to create a hospitable place of transition between the world of the street and the interior of the store.

The use of mahogany veneer for the ceiling and panelling of the corner vestibule helped to distinguish this entrance to a department store from the lobbies of office buildings which typically featured marble wainscoting. The San Domingo or Mexican mahogany used throughout the Schlesinger and Mayer Store was known for its fine grain and rich tone. The treatment of this material exemplified Sullivan's tendency to seek effective combinations of both new mechanized techniques and traditional crafted detail in his work. The broad areas of carefully chosen and matched veneer in the vestibule were made possible by improvements in veneer machines during the late nineteenth century. Frank Lloyd Wright cited the veneer machines of his time as facilitating a new aesthetic of simplicity in wood whereby elegant planes of veneer would reveal the natural grain, color, and texture of the material.[150] Wright noted that the machine in a generic sense, "by its wonderful cutting, shaping, smoothing, and repetitive capacity, has made it possible to so use it without waste that the poor as well as the rich may enjoy to-day beautiful surface treatments of clean strong forms that the branch veneers of Sheraton and Chippendale only hinted at, with dire extravagance."[151] In Sullivan's entrance for Schlesinger and Mayer the room's mahogany surfaces are made up of several laminated planes of wood. The visible expanses of veneer are edged in moldings of rich yet delicate profile that testify to the personality of their designer in creating subtle variations on traditional classical motifs. The curvilinear sweep of the moldings around the ceiling suggests a sense of plasticity in architecture whereby spatial forms are delineated through continuity of materials. At the same time the surfaces of veneer edged in molded relief helped to convey associations of domestic refinement characteristic of a department store conceived as a mercantile house.

Inside its doors, the main floor of the Schlesinger and Mayer Store was intended to give an impression of spaciousness (Figure III-43). The open plan made possible by steel construction was of particular value to department stores that sought to maximize usable sales area and enjoy near complete flexibility in its arrangement. In 1900 the lack of interior structural walls was representative of a building's modernity. In older assemblages of annexed properties, masonry partitions survived as remnants of party walls between adjacent buildings formerly used as separate stores. The structural necessity of such walls prevented their complete removal even when adjoining buildings came under single ownership as part of one store. By 1898 the consensus along State Street was that "partitions make a store seem crowded, cut off the light, and make the arrangement of counters and departments like so many stalls, giving no opportunity for deviation from this." [152] In place of the patch-work salesrooms resulting from partitions, the model interior arrange-ment for new stores was thought to be one large space on each floor. The ideal building for retailing had an interior without barriers to the movement of people over its floors to facilitate inspection of goods, as shown in an advertisement for the "opening" of one retailer of men's

Fig. III-43. Interior of the main floor looking northwest, about 1919. Courtesy of the John Vinci Collection, Chicago.

Fig. III-44. Advertisement for the opening of Willoughby, Hill and Co.
Chicago Tribune, 9 October 1881.

furnishings located two blocks west of Schlesinger and Mayer (Figure
III-44). Thus Sullivan's plans for the new Schlesinger and Mayer Building showed an open area of 26,000 square feet on every floor, with all
special elements such as stairways and elevators, set along the south and
east walls at the edges of the sales areas. What appears today as a simple
rectangular grid of columns in Sullivan's plans represented a remarkable
clarification of space and structure when compared with the earlier
building which had an arrangement of irregular partitions and columns
with "no definite alignment" due to many interior modifications over
the years.[153]

The open plan permitted stores like Schlesinger and Mayer to maximize return on their rental investment in the most highly valued properties in Chicago. The unmatched cost of land on State and Madison
streets determined that every available cubic inch of Sullivan's building
be revenue-generating sales space. Probably for this reason the plans of
the Schlesinger and Mayer Store included no interior skylit court com-

parable to those of Marshall Field's and The Fair. Such a generous spatial gesture had been a convention of Parisian department stores, where
the need for interior daylight became the opportunity for the creation
of skylit atria with elegant stairways. Such a central space had been a
memorable feature of the second A. T. Stewart Store on Broadway and
the earlier buildings for Field, Leiter & Co. As a rule, however, the gen-
eration of large department stores along State Street built between 1890
and 1910 did not include the amenity of an interior court. Sullivan's floor
plans reflected the need for spatial economy in their smallest detail. Elevators were thought to be advantageous because they permitted the
number of space-consuming stairways to be reduced to the minimum
needed to satisfy municipal regulations for fire egress. The compact arrangement of the entrance vestibules and interior staircases, the consoli-
dation of ventilating shafts and pipe chases, even the use of cast iron
panels and mahogany veneer as the thinnest of finish materials all implied the need to minimize space-occupying features throughout the volume of the building.

  The floors of the department store nearest the sidewalk were considered to be the most valuable sales space because of their proximity to the
entrances. These floors were greater in height and in their degree of
architectural embellishment to create a first impression of spaciousness
and elegance in the minds of shoppers. Except for the top story the
height of the floors decreased with their distance above the street level.
The variation in floor heights from the basement up is shown in Figure
III-45, a sectional drawing looking east through the first (1899) and the
third (1903) sections of the Schlesinger and Mayer Store. In terms of
height, the ground floor was 20 feet floor to floor, the second 16 feet 3
inches, the third 14 feet 8 inches, those from the fourth through the
ninth 13 feet 9 inches, the tenth and eleventh floors 11 feet 2 inches,
and the twelfth story 12 feet 11 inches from its floor to the upper edge
of the roof. Schlesinger and Mayer's total annual rent of $112,000 on the
corner property was accordingly assessed in terms of unequal sums for
each floor above the street. The largest proportion of the annual rent
was paid for the street level, the next largest for the second floor, and so
on, with each story farther from the sidewalk contributing proportion-
ally less to the total rental value of the building. In 1904 the street level
was valued at $32,380 in annual rent, the second floor at $11,870, and
so on to the topmost floors which were valued at $2,158 per year.[154] The
second or mezzanine floor, like the basement and ground floor, was considered accessible from the street without the use of elevators. Thus the
inclusion of the second floor within the lower zone of the exterior elevation does correspond to its heightened value as a sales floor associated
with the traffic of shoppers who came in off the sidewalk.

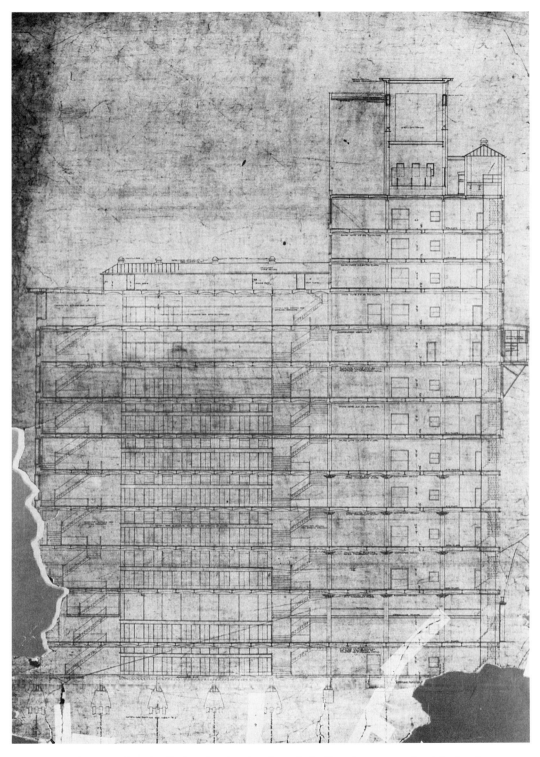

Fig. III-45. Longitudinal section drawing through the first nine-story section (1899) and the third twelve-story section (1903) of the Schlesinger and Mayer Store, looking east. Courtesy of the Architectural Collections, Chicago Historical Society.

The uses of the different floors in the Schlesinger and Mayer Store derived from both the desire to induce trade and the need to ease handling of inventory. All merchandise arrived at the building from the east service alley for initial transfer to stockrooms on the topmost floors. Heavier wares were arranged in departments on upper floors nearest the stockrooms to minimize the effort in their handling. The fashionable articles on the floors nearest the sidewalk were those most likely to be sold to the casual shopper on impulse through the attractiveness of their display. Ideally the inducement of small eye-catching items at the entrance would lead customers to more substantial goods on the upper floors. Hence the arrangement of merchandise by floor in the Schlesinger and Mayer Store at its opening was first floor: gloves, handkerchiefs, hosiery, jewelry, laces, and ribbons; second floor: silks, fabrics, and material for dressmaking; third floor: millinery, lingerie, shirtwaists, women's dressing gowns, and infants' wear; fourth floor: women's costumes including suits, formal and evening gowns, wraps, and furs; fifth floor: an art exhibition of imported pottery, bronzes, and displays of cut glass; sixth floor: tapestries, draperies and curtains, and beds and bedding; seventh floor: rugs and carpets, with the store's administrative offices located in the southwest corner. The eighth floor was devoted to the restaurant, grill, and tearoom with their kitchen facilities on the south side of the floor. The ninth floor housed a dressmaking department, and the tenth through twelfth stories housed stockrooms and workers' locker and rest rooms.[155]

One spatial feature characteristic of the sales floors in new retail buildings along State Street in the 1890s was the width of their aisles. In the revised Chicago building code of 1905, the floor space of a department store was defined as "the actual amount of space which is available for employees and patrons, exclusive of the space occupied by counters, showcases, shelving, and other fixtures."[156] The code's regulations included dimensions for minimum widths of aisles and number of exits per floor area. These specifications for department stores resembled regulations for theaters. Provisions for both building types were designed to insure safe egress for crowds in case of fire.[157] The width of the aisles determined the novel sense of spaciousness that distinguished the experience of shopping in department stores from that of older smaller stores. The aisle width of the State Street stores was advertised in published views of their interiors, where the perspective of photographs typically emphasized the linear sweep of open space between the counters (Figure III-46). Interiors from Field's to The Fair's were designed around the admonition that "customers do not like to walk through a store where there is a squeeze and a crush every few steps."[158]

Schlesinger and Mayer stressed that in their new building "avenue-like aisles lead from section to section," thus denoting a generously wide and elegantly lined thoroughfare as the urbanistic model for passage between the counters.[159] On opening day, the main aisle on the ground floor was described as the widest store aisle in the city, having a width of 16 feet.

Shoppers' freedom of movement was considered a higher priority than generous arrangements for storage of stock or elbow room for workers, "for where it means crowded aisles a limited space behind counters will suffice as plenty."[160] The spatial prerogative of the clientele in the Schlesinger and Mayer Store is evident in the minimal dimension between counters and shelving shown along the interior perimeter of the first-floor plan. The issue of the relative allotment of space for shoppers and workers is only one illustration of the pervasive distinction in department stores at that time between the women who shopped and the women who served them. The working conditions of the shop girls on State Street were a focus for sociological concern in Chicago

Fig. III-46. Interior view of the main floor of The Fair Store. Reprinted from *Chicago Dry Goods Reporter* 28 (1 January 1898).

at the turn of the century. In a study entitled "Two Weeks in a Department Store," a social worker described her experience of these conditions from the perspective of the average worker.[161] Taking employment in one of the large popular department stores, the investigator detailed a daily routine of long hours, minimal wages, and fatiguing stress. One of the problems she noted in these stores was the lack of lounge space provided for employees to eat their meals or to take short breaks. Their only place of respite might be a table in a darkened stockroom out of view of the sales departments. It was reported that "there were comforts in the customers' waiting-rooms, but discharge was the fate of the employé who dared go in there."[162] The new Schlesinger and Mayer Store included lockers and washrooms for men and women employees on the topmost floors not devoted to sales. In the design of shoppers' rest rooms on different sales floors below, considerable attention was given to lighting, ventilation, and privacy. The ornamentation of surfaces in these rooms indicated the degree to which architectural amenities throughout the store were reserved for its patrons.

The spacious sales floors in department stores needed adequate lighting to make them usable for the display of goods. The old Schlesinger and Mayer Building had not had electricity until a generating plant and electric lights were added in the remodeling of 1890. Sullivan's new Schlesinger and Mayer Store, however, was planned from the beginning to be wired for electricity supplied by the building's own new power plant. The system of artificial lighting in the new store, like that in the old building, was a combination of arc lamps and incandescent lamps.[163] The principal sources of illumination were the arc lamps, which used a strong electric current bridging carbon poles to create a luminous arc through a chamber of air enclosed in glass. The arc lamp had originally been developed for use in street lights as an improvement over gaslights. Inside the sales floors of the department store they were intended to provide more powerful areal illumination than incandescent fixtures. The disadvantages of arc lamps were the strength and expense of the electric current they used, the harsh local intensity of their light, which required a panoply of diffusers to even and spread its brightness, and their tendency to produce a blue violet glow that discolored the surrounding interior. Incandescent lights were used as supplementary sources to balance the quality and chroma of the light provided by the arc lamps. Their warmer, softer illumination was used to highlight displays or objects in showcases, offsetting the arc lights overhead with a complementary red yellow glow. The outlets for the arc lamps were located in the ceiling in the center of the structural bays on each floor (Figure III-47). Sullivan enhanced these utilitarian devices with his distinctive style of

metalwork, housing the mechanism of the lamps in ornamental bronze-
plated cast iron fixtures (Figure III-48). The ornamentation of the fixtures gave them an architectural presence as designed objects hung
throughout the sales spaces. The embellishment of these visually prevalent elements helped establish the dual impression of technical up-to-
dateness and decorative completeness cultivated by Schlesinger and
Mayer's as a leading mercantile house.

The dimness, discoloration, and unevenness of illumination from
even the most improved sources of artificial lighting of 1900 made them
at best a poor substitute for adequate daylight as essential to a setting for
merchandising. The usefulness of floor area for the display of goods
depended on natural light sufficient to permit shoppers to inspect the
subtleties of merchandise, which could be difficult to see under artificial
illumination. In 1903 one account of Chicago retailing noted that "in
some stores one could observe a procession of women going to the doorway to match colors and fabrics."[164] The consensus among State Street
retailers was that "money can buy plenty of gas or electricity, but nothing
is so conducive to satisfactory shopping as the light of day."[165] Given the
limited powers of artificial sources, introduction of a maximum of daylight into the depth of sales floors was considered the only means of
preventing both customers and workers from being seriously handi-

Fig. III-47. Interior view of the seventh floor of the Carson Pirie Scott Store
(formerly Schlesinger and Mayer) in 1906. Courtesy of
the John Vinci Collection, Chicago.

Fig. III-48. Ornamental fixture for a
typical arc lamp. Reprinted from
Architectural Record 16 (July 1904), courtesy
of Architectural Record.

capped in the daily operations of buying and selling. The need to com-
pensate for inadequacies of artificial light provoked what one account
termed an epidemic of remodeling of older building fronts along State
Street in 1900 to open up the walls of department stores to the outside.[166] One firm named its remodeled facility the Daylight Clothing
House while another of Schlesinger and Mayer's neighbors was advertised as the "daylight" store because its refitting with prismatic glass identified its interiors as progressive in design, "in contradistinction to those
stores which still depend upon artificial light to dispel darkness during
the day."[167]

The need for a maximum amount of daylight underlay the design of
the upper elevations of the Schlesinger and Mayer Store. Echoing a contemporary preoccupation of State Street merchants, Sullivan cited this
requirement as a basic programmatic criterion for the design of a department store, emphasizing that in a building of this type, "all masonry
would be reduced to a minimum, and there would be an expanse of glass
for light and display."[168] His design for the upper exterior of the Schlesinger and Mayer Store accentuates the windows as the characteristic motif of the elevations, as if the wall proclaims the need for introducing
natural light to the interiors of the sales floors (Figure III-49). The upper windows of Sullivan's building have traditionally been identified as
"Chicago windows," meaning that they contain a large central fixed sheet
of plate glass flanked by two smaller double hung windows for ventilation. The three sections of the window together fill the rectangular area
defined by the columns and beams of a typical bay of the structural
frame. This type of window appeared on other commercial buildings of
steel in Chicago's Loop during the 1890s as a solution to the problem of
bringing light and air to the interior floors of tall buildings.[169] The windows of the upper stories have terra cotta frames whose edges project
forward from the plane of the wall, so that the light-giving opening is
outlined as a rectangular figure against the neutral ground of the surrounding surface (Figure III-50). In the original project of 1898, these
windows had similarly been framed by projecting moldings of marble to
convey an impression of the upper exterior as an array of picture windows set in a wall of glistening stone. In the elevations as built, the ornamental frames of terra cotta call attention to the units of fenestration
as repeated motifs that celebrate the accessibility of light.

Sullivan's design of the upper elevations may be understood as the
accentuation of a practical requirement, thus exemplifying the polemic
ideal of a new architecture developed from the expression of function.
The upper elevations of the Schlesinger and Mayer Store emerged at a
time when there was extensive debate between those who advocated the

Fig. III-49. Interior view of an upper floor. Richard Nickel Archive, courtesy of
the Richard Nickel Committee, Chicago.

use of historic styles and those who embraced new conditions of society
as a basis for architecture. The Architectural League of America,
formed in 1899, flourished briefly as an advocate of the latter view. Inspired partly by the example of Sullivan's work, the league's constitution
stated that it sought "to encourage an indigenous and inventive architecture, and to lead architectural thought to modern sources of inspiration."[170] In the literature of the league, commercial architecture was
cited as a field for design wherein adherence to function would prove a
fruitful method of developing appropriate new forms. In 1901 William
Furber wrote that large retail stores were among those types of buildings
which exemplified the ideal of style in architecture fitting to purpose, as
distinct from the adaptation of historic styles derived from past civilizations. Furber advocated that the need for display windows in such buildings "should be the dominant note of the design. The piers and super-
structure should not be treated as to convey the impression that the large

windows were begrudgingly put in by the architect, only on the imperative order of the owner. If the style proposed to be used does not lend itself readily to an 'open' treatment, it is evident that the style selected is not a fitting one." [171]

If the show windows were to be the keynote for the architecture appropriate to department stores, then their upper stories could be conceived as extensions of the same idea of a building's fabric opened up for light and display. Hence the base of the Schlesinger and Mayer Store may have been a partial inspiration for the formal treatment of the elevation above, as if the conceptual development of the design had proceeded from the bottom up. In the original project of 1898 the upper

Fig. iii-50. Detail of the upper elevation on State Street. Richard Nickel Archive, courtesy of the Richard Nickel Committee, Chicago.

windows are described as plate glass framed in bronze, just like the show
windows below. In the building as built, the upper windows have mullions of cast iron between the central and flanking panes with diminutive
capitals like the colonnettes that divide the areas of glass in the lower
stories. Though the openings above the base were for interior lighting
rather than sidewalk display, their accentuated frames suggest the exhibition of goods inside the store on its upper floors. It is as if the upper
windows were a metaphor for the experience of the sales space within
the building, after shoppers had been given a literal presentation of its
merchandise in the show windows along the street. A comparable relation between show windows along the sidewalk and windows lighting
upper stories appears in Parisian department stores of the later nineteenth century. The base of the Bon Marché featured tripartite display
windows of plate glass divided by slender colonnettes, echoed in tripartite openings with columnar mullions set into the marble facade above.
In Le Printemps the three upper stories above the street level were sales
floors and thus featured bays of windows that similarly followed the design of the iron and glass *vitrines* along the base. The treatment of these
stores' upper elevations as extensions of the design for their mezzanine
and ground floors may have derived from the use of the upper windows
as showcases for merchandise that could be seen from the street like the
show windows closer to the sidewalk.

The need for ventilation was closely related to the ideals of spaciousness and daylight as criteria for a modern retailing environment. Conventional older systems of heating department stores used low pressure
steam trapped and circulated as a by-product of the steam engines used
to provide an in-house source of power for the building's mechanical
equipment, primarily the elevators.[172] When steam from the engines was
inadequate for heating the building, steam generated by a supplementary furnace was forced into pipes to augment that drawn from the engines. The heat was introduced through radiator coils set in the floors
and encased in the walls of the lower stories to save sales room, and
through freestanding steam radiators on the upper floors. Common
complaints about such systems were their unevenness of distribution of
heat through the buildings and their inadequacy in winter weather. Beyond this arrangement there were often no provisions for ventilating or
circulating air through the buildings. In summer with the heat off and
the doors and windows closed to keep out the dust and noise of State
Street, the sales force sweltered and the stores offered complimentary
palm fans and glasses of ice or mineral water to their clientele.[173]

The mechanical system for moving air through the new Schlesinger and Mayer Store was considered one of the building's most outstanding features at the time of its opening. The store's mechanical plant had three main parts: first, a coal-burning power plant for generating electricity designed by Adler and located within Schlesinger and Mayer's Wabash Avenue properties; second, a heating and ventilating plant located in the subbasement of the new building 40 feet below the sidewalk; and, third, a machinery house on the roof, which contained the large electric motors that powered the elevators and freight and package conveyors.[174] The mechanical system from subbasement to rooftop was a focus of the guided tour of the building arranged by Schlesinger and Mayer for visitors to its opening days.[175] The tour, which began underground, culminated in the roofscape where visitors viewed the large tanks that supplied water for the store's sprinkler system of fire protection and the pumps that kept the tanks full. The array of machinery was promoted as a crowning feature of the store's design, the equipment gathered at the top of the building "thus taking far from the knowledge of the shoppers the heat, dirt, and noise incident to the mechanical equipment of such a structure."[176] Palpable evidence of the efficacy of this system was the enveloping sense of moving air throughout the store. Accounts of the opening cited mechanical ventilation as an innovation of decisive importance to the design, with the system supposedly providing a complete change of air through the volume of the building every five minutes.[177] Warm air plenums set adjacent to the structural columns around the periphery of the interiors were claimed to have provided an evenness of distribution over the floors "so well arranged that the atmosphere in the lowest basement forty feet below the street is as pure as in any part of the building."[178]

The sense of the vitality of mechanical systems as central to the nature of a modern building made them objects of wonder worthy of architectural expression. Their description in accounts of Schlesinger and Mayer's opening resembled Sullivan's comments on the physiological nature of mechanical systems in the tall office building. He wrote of the topmost attic story as that space in which "the circulatory system completes itself and makes its grand turn, ascending and descending. The space is filled with tanks, pipes, valves, sheaves, and mechanical etcetera that supplement and complement the force-originating plant hidden below ground in the cellar."[179] Sullivan's fascination with such systems as novel phenomena that could be overlaid with an appropriate aesthetic appears in the design of the decorative metalwork inside the entrance vestibule (Figures III-51 and III-52). Semicylindrical inlets were set just inside the

Fig. III-51. Ornamental hot air inlet in the corner entrance vestibule. Richard Nickel Archive, courtesy of the Richard Nickel Committee, Chicago.

Fig. III-52. Ornamental hot air grille in the corner entrance vestibule. Richard Nickel Archive, courtesy of the Richard Nickel Committee, Chicago.

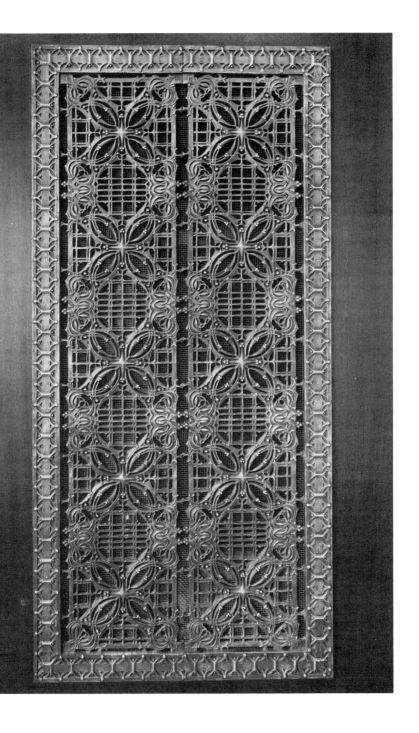

outer doors while rectangular grilles were set in the walls on either side of both vestibules. These ornate designs call attention to the passage of air through their delicate metal tracery.

A fundamental requirement for the design of department stores was the creation of a completely fireproof covering for the steel structure with a smooth envelope of baked clay. Adler emphasized that the weakness of terra cotta fireproofing lay in the joints between individual pieces that surrounded columns, girders, and floor beams. He advised that the ideal system of fireproofing for steel assemblies would be attainable if "porous terra cotta could be applied to pillars and beams in continuous jointless masses."[180] This principle underlay Sullivan's specifications for the interior finish of ceilings and columns of the Schlesinger and Mayer Store. He noted that the thoroughness of protection depended on a continuous terra cotta soffit for the flooring of each level in the building "so as to make flat ceilings throughout without disclosing the girders." Sullivan also intended to "finish all columns . . . to a round section, and to avoid sharp angles wherever possible."[181] The rationale for cylindrical columns and other smooth surfaces was that angular edges represented weak joints between encasing pieces of terra cotta which would be most likely to sustain damage from the heat and flame or in firefighting when water would tend to knock loose sections of fireproofing. Sullivan's desire for continuity of surface as approaching an ideal of fireproof construction is evident in the smooth ceiling and rounded columns of the main floor (Figure III-43). The original finish for both columns and ceiling was a lime based white wash known as calcimine. This finish was more resistant to fire than ordinary paint. Additional precaution against fire is evident in the sprinkler system whose piping was left visible beneath the ceiling.

Neighboring department stores such as Marshall Field's had encased steel structural columns on their sales floors to look like conventional classical orders sometimes supporting beamed ceilings with architraves rendered as moldings in plaster. In Field's new store, completed in 1907, the street level featured fluted Corinthian orders with Ionic columns above apparently supporting the upper floors around the interior light court (Figure III-53). The architectural effect of Schlesinger and Mayer's main floor was created in part by the design of the columns and their ornamental capitals, which were executed in decorative plasterwork finished with calcimine (Figure III-54). The capitals of the columns are convex in profile on the first and second floors, while those on the third and fourth floors are concave in their line of transition from shaft to ceiling. Above the fourth floor the columns without capitals meet ceilings where arches of terra cotta fireproofing were left exposed (Figure III-

47). The ornamental capitals through the fourth floor reflect the art of the modeler in plaster rather than the carver in stone, just as the surfaces of the cylindrical columns below and the ceiling above reflect the use of clay fireproofing. The columns are thus, in one sense, true to their materials and to their role in the construction, and they have an originality of form that distinguishes them from conventional re-creations of ancient orders.

Schlesinger and Mayer's showcases helped to shape the spatial impression of their shopping floors. Showcases of glass were a novel commercial furnishing characteristic of the department store of 1900. State Street stores of the turn of the century featured long display cases set on marble bases with all surfaces glazed except for the minimal mahogany

Fig. III-53. Main aisle of the new Marshall Field and Co. Store about 1907. Photo courtesy of the Chicago Historical Society (ICHi-20290). From *Marshall Field and Company: The World's Greatest Merchandisers* (Chicago, 1907).

Fig. III-54. Interior column capitals on the first and second floors (bottom) and third and fourth floors (top) of the Schlesinger and Mayer Store. Richard Nickel Archive, courtesy of the Richard Nickel Committee, Chicago.

framing that formed the edge of their top and sides. Such showcases had evolved from heavier cruder tables and closed cabinets into continuous counters of polished plate glass lining the aisles of the sales floors. The reduced height of the department store's showcases was considered a mark of urbane modernity relative to the high shelves and vertical piling of goods familiar in older rural dry goods stores.[182] As a means of display the interior showcases were analogous to the exterior show windows, presenting attractive arrangements of merchandise to customers as they moved through the store, just as the show windows initiated shoppers' involvement with articles exhibited along the street.

The distribution of merchandise over the upper floors of a modern store building required Schlesinger and Mayer and their competitors to convince shoppers of the ease and safety of vertical movement by elevator. The use of the elevator was an unfamiliar experience for a considerable part of the clientele.[183] Thus the tours of the store building on its opening days helped cultivate familiarity with the passenger lifts by taking visitors vertically through each shopping level from the basement to the roof. The floor-by-floor progression of the tour as a gentle tool for shaping behavior was accompanied by advertisements for Schlesinger and Mayer which noted that "roomy elevators run from floor to floor with the regularity of rail road trains."[184] The main banks of elevators were set along the interior of the glazed east wall as indicated in the floor plans of the completed building (Figure III-38). The moving elevator cars and their enclosing metalwork on each floor would be seen from the interior as silhouetted against the background of a luminous wall of windows. Stairways set between the elevators were designed not to be spatially intrusive. They were ornate in detail with cast iron grilles set as balusters between the railings above and the steel beams supporting the stair below (Figure III-55). The repetition of the grilles up the stairway creates a stepped cadence of ornament whose intricate metalwork continued the theme of decorative screens set against a rear wall of glass on one side, with the stairs open to the sales floors on the other. Ornament along the face of the risers and on the underside of the stairs also greeted the eyes of shoppers as they ascended or descended. Today the original stairways have been closed off from the floor areas for fire safety and the rear east wall has been filled with masonry.

Ladies' waiting and writing rooms adjacent to rest rooms were set in the round northwest corner bay of the third and ninth floors (Figure III-38). These rooms were not included in the original project of 1898 but were added as part of the revised design of 1902, when Schlesinger and Mayer sought to enhance the cachet of their house. At the turn of the century ladies' waiting and writing rooms in a department store were like the parlor or reception hall in an elegant residence or club.[185] The

Fig. III-55. Northeast stairway of the Schlesinger and Mayer Store. Richard Nickel Archive, courtesy of the Richard Nickel Committee, Chicago.

Fig. III-56. Rest room in the northwest corner of the third floor, about 1906.
Courtesy of the John Vinci Collection, Chicago.

store's writing room included desks, chairs, and stationery to facilitate correspondence just as telegraph offices did in the lobbies of office buildings. In the case of the department store, the letterhead of the stationery atop a handwritten note was comparable to the printed designs crowning the writing paper of a businessmen's club or hotel. Schlesinger and Mayer's main waiting and rest rooms were located in the rounded corner of the third floor to enhance their proximity to the light and thus create the effect of an outdoor veranda or pavilion. At Schlesinger and Mayer's, "rest rooms, as soothing as shady nooks in a summer garden, await use by the weary. There one may repose in quiet, read, write letters, call friends by telephone and command every convenience and luxury." [186] The sense of these spaces as a cross between a club lounge and the parlor of a spacious residence appears in an early photograph (Figure III-56) which shows a homelike melange of furnishings with decorative plants and oriental carpets overlaying the sheen of the mosaic floor.

The design of the woodwork in the ladies' waiting and writing rooms reveals how Sullivan sought to achieve decorative art through machine production. Sullivan had long shown interest in the woodworker's craft as a means of realizing his ornamental art in architecture through carving, moldings, and the choice of veneers.[187] In the third-floor writing room, the partitions of mahogany included large lower horizontal panels of wainscoting above which were set ornamental screens made up of layers of the same wood (Figure III-57). Surviving working drawings for the design of these decorative wood screens are in Elmslie's hand, and

Purcell testifies to having watched Elmslie draft the designs for the screens in both the ladies' rest rooms and the restaurant of the store.[188] The screens were to be fabricated using fret saws that could cut intricate ornamental patterns in very thin planes of wood. The use of the fret saw

Fig. III-57. Ornamental fret-sawed mahogany screen for the third floor writing room. Reprinted from *Architectural Record* 16 (July 1904), courtesy of Architectural Record.

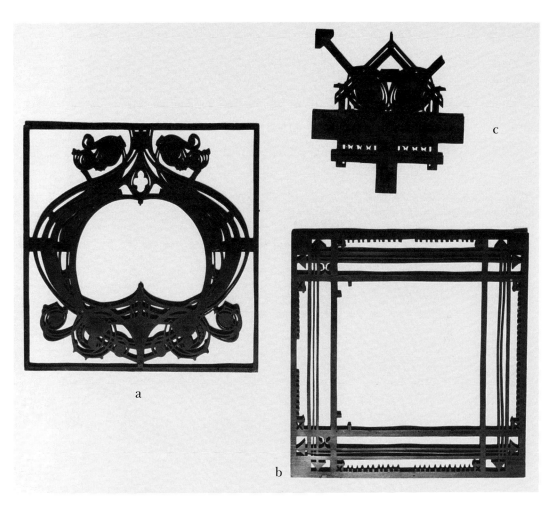

Fig. III-58. Individual motifs that form different layers of the fret-sawed mahogany screen for the third floor writing room. Richard Nickel Archive, courtesy of the Richard Nickel Committee, Chicago.

to create the filigree of the screens was a technique adapted to the nature of the mahogany as a relatively soft and porous wood effectively cut and shaped with sharp tools. To create each panel of the decorative screen in the writing room, layers of finely sawed mahogany in three different patterns were used (Figure III-58). These planes of wood were glued together in such a way that their grains were rotated, thereby helping to strengthen the screen. The outer layers on the front and back of each panel of the screen had an oval design (a), the next inner two were formed from straight lines (b), and the innermost panels had a design combining curved and straight lines (c). The layering of complementary patterns was likened to the overlaying of counterpoint or harmonic variation over a melody in music (Figure III-59).[189] The finely sawed planes of wood were "all placed in sequence to produce a fine orchestration of ornamental form."[190]

The most celebrated of the special rooms was the eighth-floor dining facility that served as a composite grille, tearoom, and restaurant (Figure

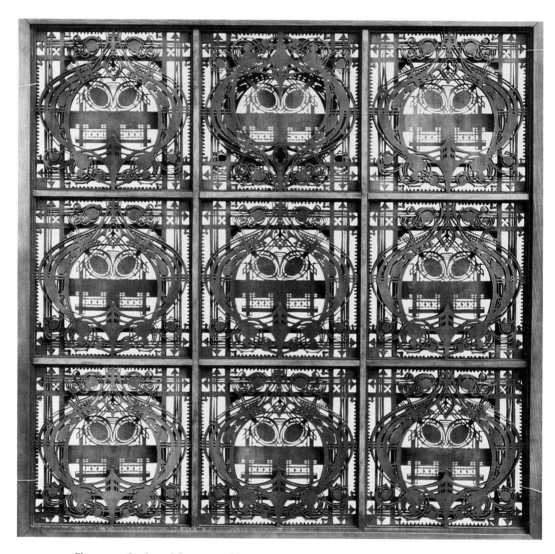

Fig. III-59. Section of the reassembled mahogany screen for the third floor writing room. Richard Nickel Archive, courtesy of the Richard Nickel Committee, Chicago.

Fig. III-60. Eighth floor restaurant about 1906. Courtesy of
the John Vinci Collection, Chicago.

III-60). Such a facility was a means of drawing visitors to the store who
might not enter with the thought of shopping but who, once involved
with the experience of being in the building, were likely to buy something. Benjamin Schlesinger of Carson Pirie Scott noted that "the store
cafes are a great trade bringer. If it were not for them there would be
vastly less patronage than now, for hundreds of women come to this
store at the lunch hour only to eat—and stay to make purchases."[191]
When Berlage visited Chicago in 1911, William Purcell, Sullivan's former
draftsman, took him to lunch in the eighth-floor restaurant of Schlesinger and Mayer's to show him the details of this room.[192] One precedent
for the new restaurant was the French cafe that Sullivan had designed
for an upper floor added to Schlesinger and Mayer's expanded Bowen
Building in 1897. The ornamental designs of this earlier room were said
to be most beautiful, with no expense spared in its appointments.[193] Siegel's partnership in Schlesinger and Mayer's predates the drawings for
their dining room, suggesting that the inclusion of this space may have
reflected Siegel's and Mayer's desire to heighten the elegance of their
house. One of Siegel's Manhattan stores, Simpson, Crawford, and Simpson, among the most elegant and established in the city, had created a
dining facility intended to compare with exclusive metropolitan restaurants.[194] Sullivan's restaurant for Schlesinger and Mayer was highly unconventional in its ornamental design. The room was advertised as "the
most sumptuous of its kind to be found in any mercantile house in Amer-

ica," with a seating capacity of 1,000 operating through the shopping
day.[195] The floors were marble mosaic and the columns were polished
red African onyx with gilded plaster capitals. Jewel-studded holophotes
or lenses surrounded the electric lamps to create polychrome sources of

Fig. III-61. Ornamental fret-sawed mahogany screen separating the elevator area
from the restaurant on the eighth floor. Reprinted from *Architectural Record* 16
(July 1904), courtesy of Architectural Record.

illumination within the decorative plasterwork of the beamed ceiling. The profusion of materials from remote sources may have signified the idea of the department store as an importer of goods from all over the world.[196] In the center of the room an octagonal bandstand was planned for daily violin recitals and other musical events.[197] The dining room itself was set apart from the elevator area by mahogany screens designed as an arcade (Figure III-61). These arches were composed of an intricate tracery of multiple layers of fret-sawed wood. Their ornamental pattern and the rich moldings framing the screen were designed by George Elmslie.[198] In this screen the architects had accentuated the possibility of treating materials in new ways by combining the resources of a formal imagination with the techniques of machines. Throughout the Schlesinger and Mayer Building Sullivan and Elmslie sought to explore this approach toward creation of a new architecture.

Sullivan's Design for the Exterior of Carson Pirie Scott

When one stands today across State Street opposite Carson Pirie Scott, it is evident the degree to which Sullivan developed the upper exterior of his building to give the store an architectural presence in the heart of the city (Figure III-62). Surveying the height and extent of the State Street front, an observer is presented with the great scale of its repeated rectangular bays and their expanse of inset glass. When the Schlesinger and Mayer Store was first opened in 1903, the steel frame was still a dramatically innovative way to build buildings. The resulting structures were new phenomena in the history of architecture. As is evident from the development of State Street department stores, the use of steel was the logical consequence of the need to create a maximum of spatial volume in a minimum amount of time. Only steel could then permit the necessary large and open sales floors and accommodate the need to increase the size of the buildings over time. The frame was thus a response to conditions of use, and the resulting skeleton of steel became the constructive fact out of which Sullivan sought to make a work of architecture.

Sullivan himself implied that in the design for the Schlesinger and Mayer Store, he had been centrally concerned with the development of "a logical and poetic expression of the metallic frame construction."[199] From the time it was introduced in commercial architecture in Chicago, the steel frame had posed an unprecedented challenge to designers. The width of typical steel bays and the total height of typical steel buildings did not easily lend themselves to artistic treatment according to formal conventions of historic architecture. Perhaps for this reason, Sullivan

Fig. III-62. View of the State Street front. Reprinted from *The Idea of Louis Sullivan* by permission of John Szarkowski and the University of Minnesota Press.

and his colleagues sought an architectural solution for steel logically developed from requirements of its structural engineering. In 1891, William Le Baron Jenney, Sullivan's first employer in Chicago, stated the basic criteria for structural design in steel with reference to the building for The Fair then under construction. Jenney asserted that in a modern steel building "the design must be such that the material is used in the most economical manner, every piece must be calculated. There must be sufficient material and no more, for it is essential, not only for economy but also to reduce the weights on the foundations, that the construction should be as light as possible consistent with stability."[200]

Sullivan developed the design of the Schlesinger and Mayer exterior in part according to this criterion of the minimum amount of material to be supported by its structure. In the case of a department store, the need for a wall opened to daylight converged with the idea of minimal cladding for the skeletal frame. Sullivan alluded to this issue in his discussion of an anonymous department store in *Kindergarten Chats*. He praised the design for its windows, which were as large as possible to admit light to the interior. The architect had eschewed the use of irrelevant historical motifs and had instead proceeded "by a process of elimination" to create a structure that was "a logical, though somewhat bald, statement of its purpose, an unmistakable . . . index of the business conducted within its walls."[201] Sullivan wrote of the building as if the paring away of historical motifs were comparable to the elimination of excess material. The principle of rigorous economy of materials in structural design was thus comparable to the principle of rigorous adherence to function in architectural design. In Carson Pirie Scott the intention of paring away the wall to its skeletal minimum can thus be read as evidence of an attitude toward expression of type as well as a constructive ideal. The impression of a light, open building in the upper elevation was heightened in the rounded corner as originally built. There each window between the vertical colonnettes was at first a single sheet of curved glass which filled the entire opening between the head, sill, and jambs. These windows opened by swinging horizontally with the glass pivoted at the center of the head and sill. This elegant detail of glazing at the rounded corner accentuated the impression of lightness and purity of expression visible in early photographs. In a later renovation, these pivoting sheets of glass were replaced with conventional double hung windows between the colonnettes on each story (Figure II-28).

The architectural effect of the upper elevations on State and Madison streets depended on the size and shape of the window openings relative to the surrounding wall surface of columns and lintels (Figure III-63). Elmslie recalled that Sullivan himself "formed the window shapes in the

upper stories, which were the characteristic element of the design." [202]
The width and height of the window openings relative to the wall surface of the columns and lintels between them produces ratios of void to
solid that create the visual rhythms of the elevation. On State Street the
width of a steel bay between column centers on a typical upper floor
(fourth through ninth) is 21 feet, 11 inches (263 inches), while the floor
to floor height is 13 feet, 9 inches (165 inches). [203] Within each steel bay,
if the window area is understood to exclude the dimensions of its projecting frame of terra cotta, the void of the opening between its reveals
is about 18 feet, 9 inches (225 inches). The width of the column face
between adjacent windows on the same story is about 3 feet, 2 inches (38

Fig. III-63. View of the upper elevation on State Street. Richard Nickel Archive,
courtesy of the Richard Nickel Committee, Chicago.

inches). Given these dimensions the resulting ratio of void to solid (225 inches/38 inches) produces a horizontal visual rhythm across the length of any given story of about 6:1:6:1:6:1. In the vertical dimension, the void of the window opening between its head and sill is about 9 feet, 3 inches (111 inches), while the height of the terra cotta lintel between windows on successive stories is about 4 feet, 6 inches (54 inches). The ratio of window void to solid lintel (111 inches/54 inches) produces a vertical visual rhythm through the height of the building on these stories of about 2:1:2:1:2:1. These visual rhythms produce the architectural effect of the upper wall, whose elegance of proportion has often been noted in discussions of the design. Elmslie wrote that Sullivan conceived of "rhythm as the over all element of significance in architecture."[204] In Carson Pirie Scott the rhythms of void to solid in the upper wall dramatically present the span of the steel beams between their columnar supports through the height of the building, as if Sullivan had created a distinctive cadence of structural elements that made vivid the architectural potential of a new means of construction.

Another significant proportion of the upper elevation is the degree of recession of the glass of the windows from the outer surface of terra cotta. The recession of the windows creates a depth of reveal around the openings that gives the elevation the image of a cage of piers and lintels as the elemental expression of the metal frame. The recession of the windows contributes significantly to the perception of visual rhythms in the upper elevation when viewed from the street. The upper exterior thus reads as a wall of windows set within a tectonic outline, rather than a window wall of glass as a continuous surface set forward of, or flush with, the plane of the structure. The conception of the upper elevation as a series of windows set in a wall is accentuated in older photographs which show awnings mounted within the reveals of individual windows to keep sunlight off their large expanses of glass. The 18-inch depth of the sills also fulfilled the functional purpose of providing a platform within each window bay for the work of window washers necessary to keep the glass clean. In his accounts of the history of architecture through the ages, Sullivan identified the pier and lintel as the essential beginning of architecture; these first constructive forms were "the basic origins of our art—elements and origins independent of time, of period, epoch, style, or styles."[205] The sudden prevalence of a new form of trabeated construction in steel as a condition of modern building thus provoked Sullivan to rethink the potential for expression in the seemingly timeless elements of column and beam, or pier and lintel. The perennial challenge to the designer, ancient or modern, was "to breathe into the simplest elements, lintel and pier, the breath of life," in order that the resulting architecture may become once again a living art, the source of whose vitality was the soul of the individual artist-architect.[206]

The potential for personality or individuality of expression in the new architecture of the steel frame lay in the design of the cladding materials necessary for fireproofing the metal. The frame had not been simply a novel mode of assembling structure; it had also redefined the relation between structure and expression in architecture. In the masonry buildings of the past, the art of architecture had its focus in the details that marked the points of juncture of structural parts. Wright characterized the historic styles of architecture as art fashioned after the handicraft ideal, wherein "structural parts were laboriously joined in such a way as to beautifully emphasize the manner of joining."[207] This process had produced traditional stylistic vocabularies of motifs which were in essence different means of beautifully fashioning and assembling elements of construction. The steel frame, however, as a product of the modern machine, could be assembled as a self-supporting structure, "complete in itself without the craftsman's touch."[208] In Wright's view, the advent of the frame had separated the human hand from its traditional task of embellishing structure through the process of its assembly. Given this new condition of building, a prime resource for renewing the potential for human expression in architecture was the system of terra cotta fireproofing which provided a continuous envelope for steel members throughout the frame. The completed building of 1900 was a composite construction of metal encased in clay. Thus, Jenney characterized the modern era of architecture as "an age of steel and clay" succeeding the earlier ages of wood, masonry, and iron building.[209] Jenney and others believed that continued development of the steel frame and its terra cotta sheathing would become the basis for a new architecture characteristic of their time wherein the design of the frame's covering would produce works of expressive power that would rival those of earlier ages. Dankmar Adler wrote that in the new architecture of steel, the fireproofing materials provided the "media for artistic treatment which may be handled solely with reference to the desire to adapt 'form' to 'function.'"[210] Adler felt that the influence of these new materials would "tend toward a more free and less trammeled treatment of architectural design, and that the striving for creation of ideally perfect form will be less hampered by limitations incident to the use of refractory materials of construction."[211]

In Chicago certain kinds of terra cotta were developed as internal fireproofing packed around the structural members of the metal frame, while others were developed as exterior cladding materials to provide a continuous finished surface for the street fronts of steel buildings.[212]

The distinguishing properties of terra cotta when developed as an exterior finish material were its glazed or enamelled finish, which could be produced in a variety of colors, its lightness relative to stone, the possibility of manufacturing it in large quantities so that individual pieces could be fitted precisely together in the shop, and, most important, its plasticity, which meant that it could be fashioned into any ornamental or architectural form. The possibilities of architectural terra cotta endeared it to Sullivan and his contemporaries who believed that this material would "at last permit steel construction to have an architectural expression of its own," equivalent to, yet not imitative of, historic architectures.[213] Just as the essential criterion for steel construction was rigorous economy of materials, so the logic of fireproofing dictated that the clay surfaces used for fireproofing the frame be completely continuous without breaks or disjunctures that would mark weak points of fire resistance. The requisite continuity of terra cotta had been likened by Wright to the flesh that covers the bones of the human skeleton.[214] In Sullivan's usage, the literal plasticity of terra cotta as clay was a tangible metaphor for a conceptual ideal of plasticity in architectural design. In theoretical terms a plastic architecture would be one in which, according to Sullivan, the forms under the hand of the architect "would grow naturally out of the needs and express them frankly, and freshly."[215]

The concept of plasticity in Sullivan's thought was closely related to the larger idea of an organic architecture. Sullivan wrote to Russell Sturgis in 1897: "I presume you are aware how deeply I am committed to the reality of a creative, plastic, responsive architectural art, an art productive of *organisms*, not 'compositions'; an art coming from the man, not from his books; an art deep and natural, not thin and artificial."[216] In Sullivan's view, a building was organic to the degree that its outward form was responsive to, and expressive of, the logic of its internal life. His observations of materials like terra cotta had suggested this principle of a work of architecture as an object permeated by a single idea of functional essence transformed into visible character. In this way a building might be like a work of nature. Sullivan developed this theme in a short essay of 1910 entitled "Suggestions in Artistic Brickwork," in which he recalled that the development of new types of brick and terra cotta had prompted his awareness of the ideal of a building as a completely enveloped whole. Sullivan wrote that with these new materials at his disposal, the architect "began to feel more sensible of the true nature of the building as an organism or whole. . . . And with this sensibility began to come the vision that the building is, in essence, the expression, the full expression of the plan."[217] In another context he asserted that any building which is truly a work of art "must have, almost literally, a life."[218] If a building could be conceived as analogous to a living thing, then its form would possess a literal wholeness or continuity of surface like that of a form in nature.[219] The ideal of organic wholeness appears to have informed the design of Carson Pirie Scott.

Sullivan's conception of the upper elevation as a continuous surface of plastic terra cotta accentuated the nature of the State Street department store as a building of broad expanses of interior space extending along the block through multiple floors (Figure III-64). The horizontal emphasis of the exterior treatment is heightened through both proportional rhythm and ornamental detail. In the vertical dimension at the corner, the slender colonnettes rise through the full height of the elevation from the base to the cornice. The colonnettes as part of the corner tower are particularly prominent in a watercolor rendering of the project by Albert Fleury (Figure III-65). The viewpoint of the rendering heightens the apparent scale of the building in its urban context as well as the picturesque character of the corner's verticality contrasted with the horizontal sweep of the major elevation down State Street.

The allusion to vitality in Fleury's rendering is heightened by the color of the lower stories depicted as a deep and lush verdure, as if the metalwork were overgrown with springtime foliage. The suggestion of natural greenery along the building's base may have been intended by Sullivan as a representation of the fertile landscape surrounding his city.[220] In his text entitled *Democracy*, written in 1907–8, Sullivan consistently contrasted man-made Chicago with the beauty of surrounding nature, emphasizing the power of the land as a source of renewal for urban society. He wrote, "As we walk together in the heart of the Great City, is there aught greeting our eyes to suggest or even hint the nearby presence of a noble Lake, the teeming prairies, green and radiant, half-encircling the Great and gloomy City?"[221] The introduction of such a suggestion within the base of a department store would have been particularly meaningful given the link between mercantile life of the city and agricultural life of the region. The white color of the upper terra cotta and the reflections of the windows in Fleury's depiction may hint at an affinity between the building's surfaces and the blue and white of the clouded sky against which its profile is sharply drawn as if the architecture was responsive to a perception of surrounding nature. The watercolor gives the scene an atmospheric quality, as if the building were animated by the light and air of the passing hour, and the movement of the crowds along its base.

In the upper elevation of the Schlesinger and Mayer Store, the design of the terra cotta covering conveys the architect's attitude toward the properties of the material. The terra cotta lends delicacy of scale to a structure of steel. The individual pieces in each course are about one-tenth the width of a typical steel bay. The blocks of clay, which are a little over two feet long, can thus be read as rectangles one order of magnitude smaller than the rectangular windows they surround. Hence the terra cotta carries upward a suggestion of the intricate detail established by the ornamental relief along the base. In this way the upper surface of the wall helps unify the appearance of the building. The alternation of thick and thin courses of terra cotta in the upper wall of Carson Pirie

Fig. III-64. View of the Carson Pirie Scott Store showing the 1906 addition by D. H. Burnham and Co. Courtesy of the Chicago Historical Society (ICHi-01571).

Scott is a visual refinement that may be read as a vestige of the original design for the surface in marble. The thin courses read from a distance as lines that add a degree of horizontal emphasis and visual tautness to the elevation.

The overall effect of the terra cotta as an unbroken skin for the building is heightened by the precision with which its pieces were fitted together. This effect was achieved through methods of craftsmanship developed by the Northwestern Terra Cotta Company, the manufacturer of exterior architectural terra cotta used on the Schlesinger and Mayer Store and on a number of other State Street buildings in this era. Each section of the wall was actually tested for fit in the manufacturer's shop where adjacent pieces were smoothed by machine to create a tight fit between blocks along the same course and between successive courses. When the prefitted blocks were then set in the building, the result was a surface of clay remarkable in its time for the precision of its joints, a technical refinement that made the terra cotta into a material with an exactness of tolerance like that associated with the construction of the steel frame itself. The joints between courses of terra cotta were rounded to one-sixteenth of an inch, a narrower dimension than that which Sullivan had specified for joints between courses of marble envisioned in the original design.[222]

The realization of the Schlesinger and Mayer Store in terra cotta enabled Sullivan to explore the decorative potential of the material as he had done in earlier works. The plasticity of clay made it an ideal medium for Sullivan's style of architectural ornament. He viewed the ornamentation of architectural terra cotta in works such as his Bayard Building in New York as a treatment befitting the nature of the material. A description of this design proclaims the virtues of the clay as a substance that suffered itself "to be shaped, with marvelous readiness, into every conceivable delicacy and variety of form and movement."[223] Sullivan viewed architectural terra cotta as permitting the reassertion of human sensibility in the design and modeling of its surfaces. He was quoted in 1894 as asserting that "this material, which will record the impress of a thumb, has still further capabilities of refinement in this direction looking forward to the time when even the plain terra cotta blocks shall be hand modelled."[224] Terra cotta was thus one medium in which the values of individual imagination and handwork could be reasserted in the new architecture of steel.

Sullivan chose to apply a light raiment of ornament over the upper elevation of his building which helps to unify the design throughout its height. The progression of decorative surfaces begins with the metal-

Fig. III-65. Watercolor rendering of the Carson Pirie Scott Store (formerly Schlesinger and Mayer) by Albert Fleury. Gift of John Dern, Jr. (1979.223). Reproduced by permission of the Architectural Collections, Chicago Historical Society. Photo courtesy of the John Vinci Collection, Chicago.

work around the show windows along the sidewalk. In the wall of terra cotta above the base, ornamental patterns were introduced within the reveals of the windows along their jambs and heads but were omitted from their sills, which would not be visible from the sidewalk. A detail of the terra cotta motifs within the reveals of the upper windows shows a pattern of alternating foliate and geometric shapes (Figure III-66). From a distance this pattern reads as a floral border strung like festoons around the windows. The decorative outline of the reveals of the upper windows heightened their image as festive picture frames when viewed from the street below, inviting shoppers as they look up to visit the floors of merchandise above (Figure III-67). The reveals echo the more lavish ornament at the base of the building, as if to carry through the theme of framed display established below. Their architectural effect as part of Sullivan's design is apparent by contrast to the upper wall of the adjacent Burnham addition, where ornamental terra cotta was omitted from the window reveals.

The incised horizontal motif running along the lintels on the face of the building plays a role similar to the string courses of the preexisting building, visually dividing the structure by floors, just as the experience of the interior space was arranged by levels. The decorative courses heighten the perception of the breadth of the building, an effect echoed by the thinner courses of plain terra cotta that lead the eye across the face of the wall. The horizontal bands of ornament bear a resemblance to taut garlands perhaps to convey the festive character of a department store. In these bands, interlaced sinusoidal motifs run across the blocks of terra cotta (Figure III-68). This detail may suggest Sullivan's attitude toward ornament in architecture as a means to accentuate formal themes legible in the major lines of a building. As the eye sweeps over the upper elevation the filigree of ornamental motifs creates a flickering pattern of light and shadow along the decorative courses of clay. Such lyricism of detail helps to intensify perception of rhythmic movement evident at a larger scale in the proportions of the steel bays (Figure III-63). Sullivan wrote that when an ornamental design is part of the surface or substance that receives it, "there exists a peculiar sympathy between the ornament and the structure. Both structure and ornament obviously benefit by this sympathy—each enhancing the value of the other. And this, I take it, is the preparatory basis of what may be called an organic system of orna-mentation."[225] Sullivan believed that if the building could be conceived as a lifelike whole, then "it follows from this living principle that an or-namented structure should be characterized by this quality, namely, that the same emotional impulse shall flow throughout harmoniously into its varied forms of expression—of which, while the mass composition is the

Fig. III-66. Detail of the ornamental patterns along the reveal of an upper story window. Richard Nickel Archive, courtesy of the Richard Nickel Committee, Chicago.

more profound, the decorative ornamentation is the more intense. Yet
both must spring from the same source of feeling."[226]

Looking up from the sidewalk in 1904, one would have seen the culmination of the exterior ornamental scheme in the top story, which

Fig. III-67. View of the ornamental reveals around the upper story windows.
Photo by Juan Pablo Bonta.

Fig. III-68. Sample block of ornamental terra cotta from courses running along the face of the upper wall between stories. Richard Nickel Archive, courtesy of the Richard Nickel Committee, Chicago.

featured an open colonnade supporting a flat overhanging cornice of minimal thickness. The plane of the wall was thus discontinued at the top of the building, with only the essential elements of column and soffit remaining to complete the construction. Behind the colonnade a continuous band of glass ran along the entire length of the topmost story, as if to recall the continuous glazing first planned along the building's base. Sullivan's original termination for the Schlesinger and Mayer Store was described as "a cornice based on the projecting roof beams and rationally functional."[227] From the exterior, the top story appeared as a distinctive silhouette with decorative bands of terra cotta around the shafts of the columns capped by large decorative capitals. The ornamental face of the overhanging soffit above the columns completed the progression of ornamental surfaces up the face of the building when viewed from the street. The visible prominence of the crowning elements was suggested in one account of Sullivan's design which stated that "the terminal foliations of the stem-like columns and the cornice detail [were] correspondingly enlarged for their additional distance from normal viewing."[228] Such an effect is evident in an advertisement for the store's opening in 1903 (Figure III-69). Here the graphic design accentuates the ornamental surfaces through the whole height of the building from sidewalk to cornice.

The Schlesinger and Mayer Store as first built may be read as a unified design which adapts a traditional tripartite scheme for the whole mass of the building. The first two stories of dark ornamental iron form the base, marked as such by the line of the slender cornice of metal projecting above the second story. The upper floors are treated as a shaft or midsection of the elevation, a reading accentuated by the rising colon-

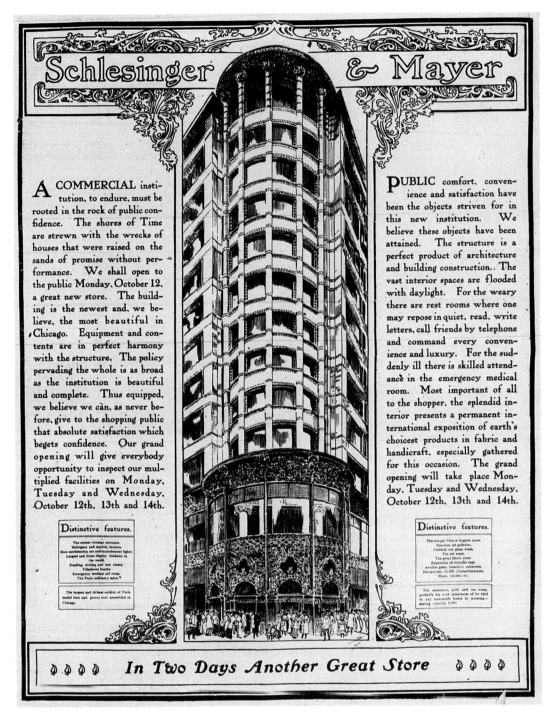

Fig. III-69. Advertisement for the opening of the new Schlesinger and Mayer Store. *Chicago Tribune*, 10 October 1903.

nettes at the rounded corner running through the height of the building from base to cornice. These upper floors are in turn crowned by the colonnade at the top story, whose projecting cornice creates a depth of shadow as a terminating visual effect across the upper edge of the building. Read as a tripartite form, the design of Carson Pirie Scott exhibits a formal convention of classical architecture. In presenting a schematic design for a prototypical office building in his essay "The Tall Office Building Artistically Considered," Sullivan acknowledged that thoughtful critics of his day had proposed that "the true prototype of the tall office building is the classical column, consisting of base, shaft and capital—the molded base of the column typical of the lower stories of our building, the plain or fluted shaft suggesting the monotonous, uninterrupted series of office-tiers, and the capital the completing power and luxuriance of the attic."[229] Although Sullivan noted critics' perceptions of his works as observing the traditional tripartite form of the classical orders, he regarded their interest in this formal resemblance as "secondary only, non-essential, and as touching not at all upon . . . the true, the immovable philosophy of the architectural art."[230] Sullivan's goal as a designer and a polemicist was to foster an architecture whose inspiration was derived from a principle of expression found in nature rather than from stylistic traditions of history. As he sought to create "organisms, not compositions," Sullivan developed the concept of organic form as an alternative to dependence on historical precedent. For Sullivan the former ideal represented a future for his art pursued in accord with the timeless laws of natural creation, while the latter approach signified architecture's decline through imitation of forms that had lived only in earlier eras of humanity's past. Sullivan wanted his art to live again in the present. He thus invoked as its first principle what he believed to be the animating idea that underlay the form of all living things: "that the life is recognizable in its expression, that form ever follows function. This is the law."[231]

Sullivan acknowledged that one source of this principle of expression in his architecture had been his exposure to the theoretical tradition of the Ecole des Beaux-Arts. In 1904 Sullivan wrote to Claude Bragdon in response to an article Bragdon had written on the influence of the Ecole on recent American architecture. Reflecting on his education in Paris as compared to that of other architects who studied at the Ecole, Sullivan wrote:

> On the whole, and personally, my view is favorable to the school. On the whole, and as regards others, my view is unfavorable.
>
> I believe I *absorbed* the real principles that the school *envelops*, so to speak—my work has consistently shown this. I can scarcely believe that the others did. Their work certainly gives no evidence of it. It was certainly at the school, and because of the teachings of the school, that there entered

my mind, or fructified in my mind, the germ of that law which later, after much observation of nature's processes, I formulated in the phrase, "Form follows Function." It was at the school also, that I first grasped the concrete value of logical thinking; and it is doubtless due to this first impulse that I later developed a scientific system of thought and expression of my own.[232]

Though Sullivan distanced his position from the practice of directly imitating classical forms, he traced the origin of his ideas in part to his period of contact with the school that he termed "the fountain head of theory."[233] Throughout the later eighteenth and nineteenth centuries one emphasis of French architectural theory had been on a systematic distinction between different types of buildings according to their uses and associations. In the earlier history of the classical tradition the concept of type had been developed as a rationale for varied expressive treatment of buildings for different purposes.[234] This idea may be understood as an antecedent of Sullivan's principle that form follows function. A call for a clear ordering of architectural expression according to type serves as a principal theme in early numbers of his *Kindergarten Chats*. Sullivan discusses certain buildings as exemplifying a class of structures that did not clearly convey their purpose through the language of their forms. In this view such works may be artfully clothed in motifs of classical architecture, yet they do not fulfill the theoretical ideal of coherent expression of type.[235] In his praise for an unnamed department store, Sullivan proclaims its chief virtue to be its direct statement of purpose. In this building "the form follows the function in a simple straightforward way."[236] The structure's use and associations are clarified through its form, hence "no one can mistake it for a hotel, an office building, a railway station, or a bank—and yet it is not rigged out in the guise of a Roman temple."[237]

The idea of type conceived as the expression of functional identity underlies Sullivan's approach to design as presented in the essay "The Tall Office Building Artistically Considered." In describing a sequence of conceptual steps toward the creation of such a structure, Sullivan emphasizes that as "I am seeking not for an individual or special solution, but for a true normal type, the attention must be confined to those conditions that, in the main, are constant in all tall office buildings, and every mere incidental and accidental variation eliminated from the consideration, as harmful to the clearness of the main inquiry."[238] Sullivan appears to have brought this same logic to the problem of the Schlesinger and Mayer Store. This department store was to be "a type of what the modern mercantile structure should be."[239] Hence Sullivan's design can be read as an attempt to give definitive expression to a new kind of building with a distinctive function. If Sullivan's statement that form follows function is interpreted in part to mean that expression follows type, then the Schlesinger and Mayer Store emerges as the application of a principle of classical architecture to modern conditions.

Sullivan believed that he had "*absorbed* the real principles that the [Ecole] *envelops*," as if to say that rather than being enamored with outward forms of the classical tradition, he had grasped an idea known to that tradition whose range of application made it transferable to the novel architectural tasks of his own place and time. Thus, on one level, Sullivan's department store on State Street may be interpreted as the work of a radical classicist who was seeking to renew his art through return to a basic principle of design. During his first trip to Paris in 1900, N. Max Dunning, a friend and follower of Sullivan, visited the atelier of Louis Pascal at the Ecole des Beaux-Arts. As Dunning was a visitor from Chicago, the conversation turned toward the Columbian Exposition and to the work of Sullivan. Pascal, a distinguished architect and teacher at the Ecole, had apparently kept in close touch with Sullivan's architecture in general and expressed admiration for it. Dunning wrote that M. Pascal stated: "I consider that Louis H. Sullivan in his work, has exemplified better the real essence of Beaux-Arts teaching than any other American."[240] In paying Sullivan this tribute, Pascal may have been alluding to the same essential theory that Sullivan cultivated as a source of his art.

Pascal was the teacher of Paul Philippe Cret, the French architect who became a prominent educator in the United States. Cret studied in Pascal's atelier at the Ecole for seven years, from 1896 to 1903, when he came to Philadelphia to teach at the University of Pennsylvania. In Cret's view, what the Ecole had offered American students through the late nineteenth century was not so much a stylistic vocabulary of classical forms but rather what he termed a method of work or science of design adaptable to the full range of modern building types. He believed that the Paris school had aided the development of American architecture through its teaching of those general principles which he himself had assimilated during his years with Pascal. In 1908, Cret wrote that "the Ecole develops in an admirable way the study of design, respect for the program and the research of a special character proper for each kind of building. It is as a result of this that in merely looking at a building designed under such principles, one knows immediately its purpose, simply because its plan and elevation correspond to its needs, and it is executed throughout with a respect for artistic truth."[241]

Louis H. Sullivan. Reprinted from *Architectural Annual* 2 (1901).

CONCLUSION

Few places on earth at the juncture of the nineteenth and twentieth centuries presented a more insistent statement of modern conditions than the world of State Street in Chicago. The degree to which Louis Sullivan gave vivid architectural definition to new realities is one source of Carson Pirie Scott's vitality as a work of art. Seen in this context, the modernity of his building is rooted in the larger historical process of social transformation through the world's first industrial century which had produced the department store as a characteristic institution. Sullivan was an acute observer of his era, and his attempt to express its identity through the medium of building was not unlike Zola's search for literary characterization of the Parisian department store in which he saw "the poetry of modern activity."[1] Sullivan similarly viewed a building like the Schlesinger and Mayer Store as a "poem of the modern," whose memorable image may be understood as an architectural interpretation of the life of its place and time.[2] In such a building, Sullivan sought to realize his conception of the architect as an observer of that life who had the capacity to characterize it in built form. From this perspective Sullivan asked "whether a final analysis does not reveal the great artist, not as creator, but rather as interpreter and prophet."[3] Sullivan presented such an idea in a statement entitled "The Modern Phase of Architecture," addressed to the inaugural convention of the Architectural League of America in 1899. He wrote that in a new era of human history the architect would be a poet of the national life of his time. Sullivan assured his colleagues that

> If you take the pains truly to understand your country, your people, your day, your generation; the time; the place in which you live; if you seek to understand, absorb, and sympathize with the life around you, you will be understood and sympathetically received in return. . . .
>
> The greatest poet will be he who shall grasp and define the commonplaces of our life—those simple, normal feelings which the people of his day will be helpless, otherwise, to express—and here you have the key with which, individually, you may unlock, in time, the portal of your art.[4]

Carson Pirie Scott's identity as a work of modern architecture thus does not derive solely from its expression of the steel frame, but also from its architect's inclusive and profound sense of the emerging society for which he was building. Sullivan undoubtedly prized the opportunity to design the Schlesinger and Mayer Store. The project's location, scale, and prominence made it one of the most challenging architectural problems of its day. Since the building type was representative of its time, the commission permitted its architect to demonstrate his vision of a new architecture appropriate to that time. Sullivan viewed the superficial application of historic styles to modern buildings as a misrepresentation of the character of contemporary civilization, and a misuse of forms whose cultural significance derived from the life of past societies. He is quoted as saying that "architecture is an expression rather than a style and is the outcome of certain conditions in a certain civilization. . . . For instance, if instead of speaking of a Louis Quatorze style you speak of putting a Louis XIV civilization in State Street it is easy to see how fearful [is] the anachronism."[5] Sullivan believed that the realities of modern life could be given visible definition through an architecture responsive to its rhythms and institutions. Such buildings would mark the renewal of the architectural art in the modern period. When given the opportunity to design the new house of Schlesinger and Mayer, Sullivan sought to create a building that, rather than representing a misappropriation of past styles, would instead demonstrate architecture's capacity to reassert its vitality as an art symbolic of a living present.

As an alternative to the adaptation of historic styles in architecture, Sullivan developed the concept of organic form as an approach to his art. In his view a building like an organism would have an outward form as the visible characterization of its internal life. Sullivan sought to realize the concept of wholeness or continuity of form implicit in this organic ideal, as if each of his buildings were to exhibit a unity of expression like that found in living things. In articulating this thesis, Sullivan allied his position with a seemingly universal law of nature. He ostensibly conceived of a work like Carson Pirie Scott as a consistent demonstration of this principle at all levels. As Elmslie wrote, "the ornament, as I looked at it, was as the exfoliation of a germinal idea—just as the plan is the exfoliation of a need."[6]

As a department store Carson Pirie Scott's design responded to functional criteria and symbolic associations of this building type. The ornamental enrichment of the base was closely linked to techniques of display of goods in the show windows, where decorative detail would be appreciated in this particular context. A gradation of ornament continued over its upper stories, whose fenestration proclaimed the spatial logic and the need for daylight characteristic of the sales floors inside. Sullivan had reinterpreted conventions of design for department stores to make a work of architecture that stood as a logical and poetic expression of its purpose. He presented Carson Pirie Scott as a definitive solution for a mercantile structure, much as he had earlier sought a prototypical solution for the problem of the tall office building.

Sullivan's department store on State Street was rationally conceived in so far as its design responded to a well-defined program. It was distinct from similar buildings around it in part because of the way in which characteristics of the type were given accentuated formal expression. Yet Carson Pirie Scott was also a work animated by the spirit of its designer. The building's identity as architecture derives in part from a certain persona of style found in Sullivan's other works. In this way its form is a statement of his belief that vitality of expression in his art emerged not only from clear presentation of a building's purpose, but also had its origins in the depths of an artist's imagination. Carson Pirie Scott is thus testimony to Sullivan's faith in the romantic ideal that an individual's creative sensibility is what makes a building come alive as a work of art.

Sullivan's concern for clarity of expression according to purpose and his belief in the architect as an interpretive form-giver can be seen as part of his broader aspiration for the cultural significance of his work. In this sense he evidently understood the concept of type in architecture to mean not only a building that gave formal identity to a set of programmatic conditions, but also a structure that typified or symbolized the society of its place and period. Hence his designs for both the tall office building and the department store were intended to be works of architecture that gave expression to the life of their time. In seeking to fulfill such an enhanced concept of type, Sullivan found models in great monuments of the past like the Parthenon. This structure had set a standard for works that aspired to be records of their civilization. Such architectural types were of decisive importance for the history of the art. For

Sullivan the Parthenon was a work created "in the Greek subjectivity." It stood for its own and for later generations as the "sign and image of Greek civilization."[7] In his view such a building's power to interpret and signify the ideals and aspirations of a society touched some element of the essential in architecture as a mode of human expression. It was this breadth of historical perspective that underlay the design of Carson Pirie Scott as a work in which one could read certain facets of a culture. The design not only represented the development of the building art in Chicago to 1900, but also exemplified the idea of an architectural monument in the original sense of a building that calls to mind the life and rituals of a people.

Sullivan and his contemporaries in Chicago were conscious of the paradox that a work of architecture which achieved a universal stature in the history of the art was nevertheless the product of a specific moment in the life of a particular society. In a discussion of 1887 entitled "Style," Sullivan's colleague in Chicago, John Wellborn Root, wrote that "A great type in architecture, like that of the Parthenon, became great not only because of its perfection as a solution of a given problem, but because in a hundred small respects it expresses the immediate influence of essentially local conditions."[8]

In Chicago's architectural culture through this period, emphasis on the interpretation of historic monuments as emerging from a specific social or even geological situation may have been prompted by what might be termed a regional self-awareness. An observer of the city's built environment in 1879 concluded that "before Chicago attain[s] a complete success in its architectures, it must have a school of its own. . . . What this city needs are architects who have been reared in what may be termed a Chicago atmosphere. An architect of this school should be permeated by the peculiar surroundings of our locality. He must be in sympathy with the soil, so to speak, for the reason that Chicago is sui generis, and must have a construction such as would suit no other city."[9] By 1900 Sullivan's followers in Chicago thought of their work as that of an independent regional school centered in the West which would serve to promote a future for an American architecture authentic to their country's way of life. They thus understood themselves to be the true conservators of their art as the expression of societal identity. The Chicago of 1900 was perceived as the center of a region whose architecture had begun to achieve such an indigenous character. Claude Bragdon compared Chicago's commercial buildings to a "plant, which, having its roots deep in the native soil, may grow and put forth, some day, some rare blossom."[10] The example of Sullivan's work was decisive for his younger colleagues. He was the architect who had forcefully articulated these ideals and whose buildings had provided the model of works that were, as George Maher wrote, "expressive of a living truth."[11]

Sullivan's work by the turn of the century was not only seen as proof of the vitality of a regional school, but was also compared to European Art Nouveau as a kindred effort to free architecture from dependence on historic styles. Hence Chicago developments, though springing from local origins, were interpreted as part of the international creation of a new architecture. Claude Bragdon wrote that the ideal of Art Nouveau was to attempt "to be truthful and to show, ugly or beautiful, the living face of the Seit-geist [sic]."[12] Though Bragdon in 1903 believed that America had not imported this new style to any appreciable degree, he asserted that the country had, in the work of Louis Sullivan, "L'Art Nouveau architecture which is all our own; not less radical and original than its foreign prototype."[13] This characterization of Sullivan's achievement corresponded to Henry Desmond's account of Carson Pirie Scott, which he labeled as the work of "our only Modernist," implying that Sullivan, like the European avant garde, was seeking a new architectural language not imitative of past styles.[14]

Later historians have also compared buildings like Carson Pirie Scott to the simultaneous appearance of Art Nouveau architecture in European capitals.[15] There, urbane commercial cultures had produced an unconventional mode of ornamental art not unlike Sullivan's own. But, instead of searching for European influence on the ornamental art of Sullivan and his circle or vice versa, it might be more accurate to assume that there were parallel developments in different centers of artistic innovation. What may have linked Sullivan's work in Chicago with simultaneous experiments in Paris and even Vienna was a search for symbols consonant with modern urban society, variations of which were characteristic of these Western cultures by the turn of the century. At this time A. W. Barker wrote of Sullivan's work as prophetic of a new architecture of the twentieth century which would reflect just such a universal condition as the common predicament of both Europe and the United States. He concluded in 1901 that

> a fact that must not be overlooked is this: that with the spread of the modern means of communication of thought and matter, in all essentials sectional distinctions are being wiped out, except those arising from climate and other natural conditions, even the influence of national temperament having been reduced to a minimum by the railroad and the telegraph.
>
> The result of this will be that all art of the future must tend toward the expression of the modern cosmopolitan spirit, rather than a distinctively national idea, and that the architectural renaissance so much desired will sweep without much variation about the whole world.[16]

Sullivan's contemporaries could thus see his works as both the assertion of a regional identity in American architecture and, at the same
time, the prophetic equivalent of the emergence of a new architecture
abroad. In the case of Carson Pirie Scott, the design exhibited the architect's faithfulness in addressing the specific character of a Chicago department store of 1900. At the same time, however, Sullivan saw the
building as having the general character of a work of art that gave voice
to its age. Since the time of Carson Pirie Scott's completion, the design
of its upper wall has received acclaim as a canonical image of a universal
modernity of architecture. Thus Sullivan's last major building fulfills the
ideal of a memorable architectural type as developing from distinctive
local conditions, yet eventually finding a position within the broad history of architecture as a symbolic form whose meaning transcends the
particularities of its origin.

Carson Pirie Scott has traditionally been seen as an important point
of departure for the new architecture of this century because of its forth-
right expression of a new structural technique. While Sullivan's design
does vividly clarify the constructive fact of its steel frame, it also represents his creation of a unified work of architecture out of the many facets
of a building's use and context. Its form is sympathetically inclusive of
those features that gave the design life and meaning for those who were
to experience it on the State Street of 1900. In this way, Carson Pirie
Scott exemplifies what might be achieved when individual critical imagination is brought to the making of the built environment. As a symbol
of its city and its era, the building is still a resource for those who wish
to learn about the making of significant works of art. Louis Sullivan's
landmark stands as an affirmation of architecture's power to renew itself
in modern times.

NOTES

Introduction

1. Henry W. Desmond, "The Schlesinger and Mayer Building, Another View—What Mr. Louis Sullivan Stands For," *Architectural Record* 16 (July 1904):67.

2. Claude Bragdon, "An American Architect: Being an Appreciation of Louis Henry Sullivan," *House and Garden* 7 (January 1905):53.

3. F. W. Fitzpatrick, "Chicago," *Inland Architect and News Record* 45 (June 1905):46.

4. H. A. Caparn, "The Riddle of the Tall Building: Has the Skyscraper a Place in American Architecture?" *Craftsman* 10 (April 1906):488.

5. A. W. Barker, "Louis H. Sullivan, Thinker and Architect," *Architectural Annual* (Philadelphia), 2(1901):52. The Danish reviewer to whom Barker refers was Alfred Ravad, "American Architecture and Louis H. Sullivan," *Tidsskrift for Kunstindustri* (Copenhagen), 4 (1898):189–200.

6. William Purcell, quoted in Leonard K. Eaton, *American Architecture Comes of Age: European Reactions to H. H. Richardson and Louis Sullivan* (Cambridge, Mass.: M.I.T. Press, 1972), 214.

7. Hendrik Berlage, "The New American Architecture" (1912), reprinted in Don Gifford, ed., *The Literature of Architecture* (New York: E. P. Dutton & Co., 1966), 609.

8. Louis H. Sullivan, *The Autobiography of an Idea* (1924; New York: Dover Publications, 1956), 257–59, 298–99, 310–14.

9. Obituaries of Sullivan include Fiske Kimball, "Louis Sullivan—An Old Master," *Architectural Record* 57 (April 1925):289–304; Frank Lloyd Wright,

"Louis H. Sullivan—His Work," *Architectural Record* 56 (July 1924):28–32; Andrew N. Rebori, "Louis H. Sullivan (1856–1924)," *Architectural Record* 55 (June 1924):587; Claude Bragdon, "Louis H. Sullivan," *A.I.A. Journal* 12 (May 1924): 241; William L. Steele, "Tribute to Louis Henri Sullivan," *A.I.A. Journal* 12 (June 1924):275–76; C. Howard Walker, "Five Architects and One Truth," *A.I.A. Journal* 12 (September 1924):401–5. Discussions of Sullivan and the Chicago school appear in Fiske Kimball, *American Architecture* (Indianapolis and New York: Bobbs-Merrill Co., 1928), 153–60, 191–99; Thomas E. Tallmadge, *The Story of Architecture in America* (New York: W. W. Norton & Co., 1927), 214–33; George C. Edgell, *The American Architecture of Today* (New York: C. Scribner's Sons, 1928), 69–84.

10. Edgell, *American Architecture*, 76.

11. Fiske Kimball, "Louis Sullivan—An Old Master," 299.

12. Ludwig Hilbersheimer, *Groszstadt Architektur* (Stuttgart: Julius Hoffmann, 1927), 55–57. Similar reference to Sullivan's work as a forerunner of the new architecture is found in Bruno Taut, *Modern Architecture* (London: The Studio Limited, 1929), 66–68.

13. Lewis Mumford, *The Brown Decades: A Study of the Arts in America* (1931; reprint, New York: Dover Publications, 1955), 113–14.

14. Ibid., 156.

15. Quoted in John McAndrew, "Who Was Louis Sullivan?" *Arts Magazine* 31 (November 1956):23.

16. Siegfried Giedion, *Space, Time and Architecture*, 5th ed., revised and enlarged (Cambridge, Mass.: Harvard University Press, 1982), 10.

17. Ibid., 382.

18. Ibid., 389.

19. Carl Condit, "The Chicago School and the Modern Movement in Architecture," *Art in America* 36 (January 1948):19–36. This article anticipated Condit's later works on the same subject, *The Rise of the Skyscraper* (Chicago: University of Chicago Press, 1952) and *The Chicago School of Architecture: Commercial and Public Building in the Chicago Area, 1875–1925* (Chicago: University of Chicago Press, 1964).

20. Condit, "The Chicago School and the Modern Movement," 21.

21. Condit, *The Chicago School of Architecture*, 164–65.

22. The range of critical opinion on the Carson Pirie Scott building is partially documented in Juan Pablo Bonta, *Architecture and Its Interpretation: A Study of Expressive Systems in Architecture* (New York: Rizzoli International Publications, 1979), 91–129, and in Rochelle Berger Elstein, "Enigma of Modern Architecture: An Introduction to the Critics," in Wim de Wit, ed., *Louis Sullivan: The Function of Ornament* (New York: W. W. Norton & Co., 1986), 199–211. Exemplary analyses of Carson Pirie Scott are in William Jordy, *American Buildings and Their Architects: Progressive and Academic Ideals at the Turn of the Twentieth Century* (1972; reprint, New York: Oxford University Press, 1986), 135–64, and the same author's essay, "The Tall Buildings," in Wim de Wit, ed., *Louis Sullivan*, 128–37.

Chapter I: The Development of Chicago's State Street and Its Department Stores to 1898

1. On the early development of the wholesale trade in Chicago in the 1850s, see Harold I. Cleveland, "Fifty-Five Years in Business: The Life of Marshall Field—Chapter II," *System: The Magazine of Business* 9 (June 1906):561–63, and William J. Cronin, "To Be the Central City: Chicago, 1848–1857," *Chicago History* 10 (Fall 1981):130–37.

2. On the character of Lake Street to the 1860s, see Edgar Lee Masters, *Levy Mayer and the New Industrial Era* (New Haven, 1927), 14–15; Homer Hoyt, *One Hundred Years of Land Values in Chicago* (Chicago: University of Chicago Press, 1933), 65; Harold M. Mayer and Richard C. Wade, *Chicago: Growth of a Metropolis* (Chicago: University of Chicago Press, 1969), 36.

3. On the early career of Potter Palmer in the 1850s, see Robert W. Twyman, "Potter Palmer: Merchandising Innovator of the West," *Explorations in Entrepreneurial History* 4 (December 1951):58–64. Cf. Twyman, *History of Marshall Field & Co., 1852–1906* (Philadelphia: University of Pennsylvania Press, 1954), 1–9.

4. Potter Palmer, "Memoirs," quoted in Cleveland, "Life of Marshall Field—Chapter III," *System* 10 (July 1906):24.

5. On the development of the A. T. Stewart Store, see Harry E. Resseguie, "A. T. Stewart's Marble Palace—The Cradle of the Department Store," *New-York Historical Society Quarterly* 48 (April 1964): 131–62, and Mary Ann Clegg Smith, "John Snook and the Design for A. T. Stewart's Store," ibid., 58 (January 1974):18–33.

6. *Chicago Tribune*, 30 September 1858, cited in Twyman, *History of Marshall Field*, 5.

7. Potter Palmer, "Memoirs," quoted in Cleveland, "Life of Marshall Field—Chapter III," 22.

8. Perry R. Duis and Glen E. Holt, "The Many Faces of State Street," *Chicago* 27 (June 1978):100.

9. Accounts of Potter Palmer's development of State Street are in Hoyt, *Land Values in Chicago*, 89–90; Bessie Louise Pierce, *A History of Chicago*, 3 vols. (Chicago: University of Chicago Press, 1937) 2:138–39. See also "The Making of State Street," Chicago Bureau of Statistics and Municipal Library, *Chicago City Manual* 5 (1912), 56–59.

10. On the origins of Chicago's horse-car railway, see Ronald J. Weber, "Rationalizers and Reformers: Chicago Local Transportation in the Nineteenth Century" (Ph.D. diss., University of Wisconsin, 1976), 10–15, 76; "Our First Street Cars," *Chicago Tribune* (30 August 1896):44.

11. Palmer, "Memoirs," quoted in Cleveland, "Life of Marshall Field—Chapter III," 24; Twyman, *History of Marshall Field*, 22–24; James W. Sheahan and George P. Upton, *History of the Great Conflagration* (Chicago: Union Publishing Co., 1871), 51, quoted in Hoyt, *Land Values in Chicago*, 90.

12. On Palmer's trip to Europe, see Twyman, *History of Marshall Field*, 22. Contemporary assessment of his activity on State Street is quoted in Mayer and Wade, *Chicago*, 54.

13. *The Land Owner* 3 (April 1871):103.

14. *The 1866 Guide to New York City* (1866; reprint, New York: Schocken Books, 1975), 22. On the development of New York's shopping district in the late nineteenth century, see M. Christine Boyer, *Manhattan Manners: Architecture and Style, 1850–1900* (New York: Rizzoli, 1985), 87–101.

15. *Chicago Tribune* (13 October 1868):4.

16. Ibid. On the first and second A. T. Stewart stores, see Winston Weisman, "Commercial Palaces of New York, 1845–1875," *Art Bulletin* 34 (December 1954):288, 295.

17. On the financial aftermath of the Great Fire, see Pierce, *History of Chicago*, 3:10–16.

18. Merchant John Farwell's account of this meeting is quoted in Cleveland, "The Life of Marshall Field—Chapter IV," *System* 10 (August 1906):137–38.

19. *Two Years after the Fire* (Chicago: Land Owner Publishing Co., 1873), Preface.

20. Illustrations and descriptions of the Palmer House after the Fire are in *The Land Owner* 4 (January 1872):1, and in Everett R. Chamberlain, *Chicago and Its Suburbs* (Chicago, 1874; reprint, New York: Arno Press, 1974), 231–34. See also Randall, *Development of Building Construction in Chicago*, 54.

21. Apartment blocks along Parisian boulevards contained boutiques with glazed fronts on both the street and mezzanine levels as early as the 1830s. Examples of such designs are illustrated in Louis-Marie Normand, *Paris moderne: ou, choix de maisons construites dans les nouveaux quartiers de la capitale et dans ces environs* (Paris: Normand fils, 1857). Hugh Morrison, *Louis Sullivan, Prophet of Modern Architecture* (New York: W. W. Norton & Co., 1935), 53, cites Cesar Daly, *Architecture privée au XIXième siècle sous Napoleon III*, 1st ser. (Paris: A. Morel, 1864) as Van Osdel's principal source for the design of the exterior.

22. On the rounded domed corner as a convention of Parisian apartment houses in the late nineteenth century, see P. Frantz Marcou, "Corner Houses in Paris," *Architectural Record* 6 (January–March 1897):318–22. This motif was also adapted from Parisian residential buildings to become an architectural convention of Parisian department stores like the Bon Marché and Le Printemps.

23. *The Land Owner* 4 (December 1872):206.

24. On Boyington's career, see Peter B. Wight, "Memorial to the Late W. W. Boyington," *Inland Architect and News Record* 32 (November 1898):32.

25. *The Land Owner* 4 (November 1872):187.

26. The subtle nonalignment of State and Madison streets at their intersection is not a unique condition in the street grid of Chicago. The intersection occurs at the juncture of four separate early subdivisions of the town surveyed at different times. The area northwest of the site was the first to be laid out, in 1830; the area to the southwest was part of an expansion of the original town plan in 1833; the area to the southeast was laid out in 1836; and that to the northeast of the intersection in 1839. See Hoyt, *Land Values in Chicago*, 32.

27. Accounts of the widening of State Street until 1870 are found in the references cited in note 9, above.

28. Anonymous editorial entitled, "Architectural," *Chicago Times* (2 November 1879):9.

29. *The Land Owner* 4 (November 1872):187.

30. On the effects of the Panic of 1873 and its aftermath in Chicago, see Pierce, *History of Chicago*, 3:194–96; Hoyt, *Land Values in Chicago*, 117–25.

31. Pierce, *History of Chicago*, 3:181, "The World's Largest Store," *Chicago Dry Goods Reporter* 28 (1 January 1898):53.

32. "The Department Store in the West," *Arena* 22 (September 1899):321. The Fair's account of its history is Forrest Crissey, *Since Forty Years Ago: An Account of the Origin and Growth of Chicago and Its First Department Store* (Chicago: The Fair, 1915).

33. Samuel Adams, "The Department Store," *Scribner's Magazine* 21 (January 1897):4–6.

34. "The World's Largest Store," 53.

35. Crissey, *Since Forty Years Ago*, 17.

36. On the buying and retailing policies of Field, Leiter & Co., see Twyman, *History of Marshall Field*, 24–29.

37. Crissey, *Since Forty Years Ago*, 24–25. For a contemporary view of the role of fairs in the history of trade, see H. Gordon Selfridge, *The Romance of Commerce* (New York: John Lane Co., 1918), 121–38.

38. Pierce, *History of Chicago*, 3:181.

39. "The Fair," *Chicago Tribune* (9 October 1881):20.

40. Twyman, *History of Marshall Field*, 108–9.

41. Cleveland, "Life of Marshall Field—Chapter XI," *System* 11 (May 1907): 463.

42. Crissey, *Since Forty Years Ago*, 23.

43. Ibid., 17.

44. Twyman, *History of Marshall Field*, 175–76.

45. *Rand McNally Bird's-Eye Views and Guide to Chicago* (Chicago: Rand McNally & Co., 1898), 47, in Frank A. Randall, *History of the Development of Building Construction in Chicago* (Urbana: University of Illinois Press, 1949), 165.

46. Chicago's population compared to other cities of the western world in 1850 and 1890 is documented in Adna F. Weber, *The Growth of Cities*, Columbia University Studies in History, Economics and Public Law, vol. 11 (New York, 1899), 450. The eight largest cities in Europe and the United States in 1890 were, in order of size: London, New York, Paris, Berlin, Vienna, Chicago, Philadelphia, and St. Petersburg, Russia. On Chicago's population from 1870 to 1890, see Pierce, *History of Chicago*, 3:20–21.

47. Illustration and description of the first Singer Building are in *The Land Owner* 4 (June 1872):92–94.

48. "The World's Largest Store," 53.

49. "A Huge Operation," *Economist* 3 (10 May 1890):575; Pierce, *History of Chicago*, 3:181.

50. *Chicago Tribune* (7 June 1885):2.

51. Twyman, *History of Marshall Field*, 84–85. Other major stores on State

Street included that of Charles A. Stevens located on the east side of the street between Madison and Washington streets just north of Mandel Brothers. The Stevens store had a mercantile character patterned after that of Marshall Field's, and Stevens' building, like Field's present structure, was designed by Daniel Burnham & Co. in 1912. Toward the south end of the shopping corridor, architects Holabird and Roche also designed the store of Maurice L. Rothschild, the first part of which was completed in 1906 at the southwest corner of State and Jackson streets.

52. Duis and Holt, "The Many Faces of State Street," 102.

53. On the technology, financing, and politics of the introduction of cable cars to Chicago in the 1880s, see Weber, "Rationalizers and Reformers," 92–101.

54. Brian J. Cudahy, *Destination: Loop; The Story of Rapid Transit Railroading in and around Chicago* (Brattleboro, Vt.: Stephen Greene Press, 1982), 9, cites this account of the origin of the term *Loop* as the consensus of the Chicago Historical Society. A confirming account of this original meaning of the term *Loop* appears in Milo R. Maltbie, ed., *The Street Railways of Chicago: Report of the Civic Federation of Chicago*, reprinted from *Municipal Affairs* (New York: 1901), 55 (note). Maltbie quotes the president of the South Side's Chicago Railway Co., who in an 1883 meeting with the company stockholders stated that cable cars commenced running in January 1882 along State Street south to 39th Street "and also around the eight blocks north of Madison St., commonly known as the loop." Since 1897, the "Loop" has referred to that portion of Chicago's business center that falls within the Union Loop of the elevated electric railroad completed in that year. The circuit of elevated tracks which define the Loop runs above Lake, Wabash, Van Buren, and Wells streets to turn trains through the downtown coming from the city's north, south, and west sides.

55. *Chicago Tribune* (7 June 1885):2.

56. On the concept of elevated sidewalks for Chicago, see *Economist* 11 (20 January 1894):68–70; 11 (27 January 1894):95; 12 (15 December 1894):659; 13 (19 January 1895):73.

57. "The Renovation of State Street," *Economist* 4 (16 August 1890):258.

58. "As to Street Congestion," *Economist* 6 (17 October 1891):650; Hoyt, *Land Values in Chicago*, 172.

59. *Chicago Inter Ocean* (9 February 1890):10. Local characterization of State and Madison streets as "The World's Busiest Corner" is quoted in Mayer and Wade, *Chicago*, 132.

60. "The Renovation of State Street," 258.

61. The Bee Hive was founded by the two pairs of brothers, Maximilian and Gustav L. Morgenthau and Joseph H. and Jacob H. Bauland. On their operation and Adler and Sullivan's renovation of their buildings, see Pierce, *History of Chicago*, 3 : 183 and note 102; *Chicago Inter Ocean* (11 February 1884):6; *Chicago Tribune* (8 March 1885):3; *Economist* 5 (21 February 1891):294.

In 1887–88 Adler and Sullivan also renovated the Springer Block, a four-story commercial building at the southwest corner of State and Randolph streets built in 1872 by the architects Carter, Drake, and Wight. The Springer Block as renovated by Adler and Sullivan was subsequently known as the Bay State and

Kranz Buildings. See Sarah Bradford Landau, *P. B. Wight: Architect, Contractor, and Critic, 1838−1925* (Chicago: Art Institute of Chicago, 1981), 30−32; Morrison, *Louis Sullivan*, 299−300; Randall, *Development of Building Construction in Chicago*, 62, 66−67; and Historic American Buildings Survey, HABS No. IU-1008, "Springer Block (Bay State Building and Kranz Building)."

    62. "The Attractions of Central Property," *Chicago Tribune* (4 March 1888):6.

    63. Hoyt, *Land Values in Chicago*, 149−53.

    64. "The Needs of the Retail Quarter," *Economist* 3 (22 February 1890):200.

    65. On aspirations for Chicago's development in anticipation of the World's Columbian Exposition, see Hoyt, *Land Values in Chicago*, 171−78. The Masonic Temple and the Reliance Building are discussed in Donald Hoffmann, *The Architecture of John Wellborn Root* (Baltimore: Johns Hopkins University Press, 1973), 196−204, 177−91. On the Venetian and Champlain Buildings, see Randall, *Development of Building Construction in Chicago*, 126, 138, and on the Champlain, Condit, *Chicago School of Architecture*, 124. The first large steel frame department store in New York was that of Siegel, Cooper & Co. (1896) at Sixth Avenue between 18th and 19th streets. This was followed by a new generation of department stores including R. H. Macy & Co. at 34th Street and Broadway (1902). See "All Kinds of a Store," *Architectural Record* 12 (August 1902):287−303, and Robert A. M. Stern, Gregory Gilmartin, and John Massengale, *New York 1900: Metropolitan Architecture and Urbanism 1890−1915*. (New York: Rizzoli, 1983), 190−94.

    66. On the Second Leiter Building see the *Economist* 2 (1 June 1889):452−53, and (22 June 1889):524. See also *Inland Architect and News Record* 14 (August 1889):10−11. The First Leiter Building (1879) was also designed by William Le Baron Jenney for Levi Leiter at the northwest corner of Monroe and Wells streets. Previous accounts of the Second Leiter Building appear in Giedion, *Space, Time, and Architecture*, 5th ed., revised and enlarged, 382−85; Condit, *Chicago School of Architecture*, 89−90; Jordy, *American Buildings and Their Architects: Progressive and Academic Ideals at the Turn of the Twentieth Century*, 38−41; and Theodore Turak, *William Le Baron Jenney; A Pioneer of Modern Architecture* (Ann Arbor, Mich.: UMI Research Press, 1986), 269−76.

    67. An example of Jenney's early commercial architecture in the era of the Gothic Revival would be the Portland Block (1872), at the southeast corner of Dearborn and Washington streets. On this building and Jenney's early interest in Gothic architecture see "Messrs. Jenney and Mundie," *Architectural Reviewer* (Chicago) 1 (February 1897):2−9, and Jordy, *American Buildings and Their Architects: Progressive and Academic Ideals at the Turn of the Twentieth Century*, 38−41. On Jenney's attitude toward light construction see his account, "The Chicago Construction, or Tall Buildings on a Compressible Soil," *Inland Architect and News Record* 18 (November 1891):41. On daylight and minimal walls see his discussion of the Home Insurance Building's design in *Inland Architect and News Record* 4 (September 1884):24.

    68. "The Leiter Building on State Street," *Economist* 2 (22 June 1889):524. The Second Leiter may exemplify Jenney's views on rational subordination of ornament to construction in architecture as presented in his lecture before the

Chicago Architectural Sketch Club, entitled "A Few Practical Hints," *Inland Architect and News Record* 13 (February 1889):7-9. Jenney's rationalism may also have been informed by his education in French academic and technical traditions. See Theodore Turak "The Ecole Centrale and Modern Architecture: The Education of William Le Baron Jenney," *Society of Architectural Historians Journal* 29 (March 1970):40-47. The slender colonnettes within the major bays of the Second Leiter front may also derive from a cast iron aesthetic of commercial architecture dating back to the 1870s. The use of slender cast iron colonnettes to maximize daylight in storefronts appears in the work of Richard Morris Hunt in New York of this period. Jenney was an admirer of Hunt and included cast iron members set in large windows in his designs for storefronts of the 1870s. On Hunt's commercial work, see Winston Weisman "Commercial Palaces of New York, 1845-1875," 301, and Sarah Bradford Landau, "Richard Morris Hunt: Architectural Innovator and Father of a 'Distinctive' American School," in Susan R. Stein, ed., *The Architecture of Richard Morris Hunt* (Chicago: University of Chicago Press, 1986), 54-60.

69. William Le Baron Jenney, "Building Stone," paper read before the Chicago Academy of Sciences, *Inland Architect and Builder* 3 (February 1884):7.

70. *Industrial Chicago*, 6 vols. (Chicago: The Goodspeed Publishing Co., 1891-96), 2:205. The author(s) of *Industrial Chicago* wrote of the Second Leiter Building as one example of what was perceived as a new commercial style characteristic of the city's office and mercantile buildings whose principal attributes were light, space, air, and strength combined with massiveness. Emphasis on a utilitarian aesthetic as a theme of Chicago's architectural criticism around 1890 is discussed in Jordy, *American Buildings and Their Architects*, 4:22-23, and the same author's "The Tall Buildings," in Wim de Wit, ed., *Louis Sullivan*, 79. See also Wichit Charnernbhak, *Chicago School Architects and Their Critics* (Ann Arbor, Mich.: UMI Research Press, 1981), 61-86.

71. Louis Sullivan, Kindergarten Chat VI: "An Oasis," *Kindergarten Chats and Other Writings*, ed. Isabella Athey (New York: George Wittenborn, 1947), 30.

72. Charles D. Warner, "Studies of the Great West, Part III: Chicago," *Harper's New Monthly Magazine* 76 (May 1888):872-73.

73. "The Siegel-Cooper Fire," *Economist* 6 (8 August 1891):247; "The Leiter Building," *Economist* 6 (26 September 1891):533; *Rand McNally Bird's-Eye Views of Chicago* (1898), 39, 47, reprinted in Randall, *Development of Building Construction in Chicago*, 165, 174; "The Department Store in the West," 324; and Pierce, *History of Chicago*, 3:181.

74. "A Huge Operation," *Economist* 3 (10 May 1890): 575. Cf. "New Fair Store is Open," *Chicago Tribune* (12 September 1897):33. On the new Fair building, see also Theodore Turak, *William Le Baron Jenney*, 286-95.

75. Theodore Turak, *William Le Baron Jenney*, 289.

76. John J. Flinn, *Chicago, The Marvelous City of the West* (Chicago: The Standard Guide Co., 1892), 582-89.

77. The relation of the Field Annex to the World's Fair is noted in "Marshall Field's New Store," *Economist* 7 (26 March 1892):461. The construction of the Annex is discussed in George M. R. Twose, "Steel and Terra Cotta Buildings in

Chicago and Some Deductions," *Brickbuilder* 3 (January 1894):2. See Ann Lorenz Van Zanten, "The Marshall Field Annex and the New Urban Order of Daniel Burnham's Chicago," *Chicago History* 11 (Fall and Winter 1982):130–41.

78. Montgomery Schuyler, "D. H. Burnham and Company," *Great American Architect Series for the Architectural Record* (1899; reprint, New York: Da Capo, 1977), 59–61.

79. Louis Sullivan, Kindergarten Chat V: "An Hotel," *Kindergarten Chats and Other Writings*, 27.

80. "A Long Frontage on State Street," *Economist* 11 (16 June 1894):676.

81. "A State Street Building," *Economist* 11 (14 April 1894):400.

82. On the painting of the State Safety Building, see P. B. Wight, "Soap and Water in Relation to Architecture," *Inland Architect and News Record* 25 (May 1895): 38–39.

83. "The State Street Deal," *Economist* 11 (30 June 1894):736; "A Great Department Store," *Economist* 12 (13 October 1894):898. The State Safety Building and neighboring structures were replaced by a new Rothschild Store also designed by Holabird and Roche and completed in 1912. See Randall, *Development of Building Construction in Chicago*, 245.

84. "Mandel Brothers' New Front," *Chicago Tribune* (19 September 1897):21.

85. "Modernizing Commercial Buildings," *Inland Architect and News Record* 32 (September 1898):19; "Extend and Remodel," *Chicago Dry Goods Reporter* 28 (12 March 1898):25.

86. "Extend and Remodel," 25.

87. "State and Madison," *Economist* 15 (9 May 1896): 573–74.

88. "Extend and Remodel," 25.

89. "Modernizing Commercial Buildings," *Inland Architect and News Record* 32 (September 1898):18. A comparable conception of the tall building as a contemporary example of the historic principle of the rational development of style appears in C. H. Blackall, "Legitimate Design of the Casing of Steel Structures," *Construction News* 9 (22 November 1899):635–36. The renovated Mandel Brothers Store of 1897–98 was replaced by a new structure for this same house on the same site designed by architects Holabird and Roche and built 1912–15. See Randall, *Development of Building Construction in Chicago*, 150.

Chapter II: A Chronology of the Schlesinger and Mayer Store

1. "Schlesinger and Mayer," in Alfred Theodore Andreas, *History of Chicago*, 3 vols. (1886; reprint, New York: Arno Press, 1975), 3:718. Obituaries of Leopold Schlesinger in the *Chicago Tribune* (16 March 1914):4 and David Mayer, *Chicago Tribune* (16 March 1920):17. Existing accounts of the chronology of the Schlesinger and Mayer (Carson Pirie Scott) Building include those found in Narciso Menocal, *Architecture as Nature: The Transcendentalist Idea of Louis Sullivan* (Madison: University of Wisconsin Press, 1980), Appendix B, 168–79, and in Robert Twombly, *Louis Sullivan, His Life and Work* (New York: Viking, 1986), 335–38, 344–48, 358, 378–82.

2. Andreas, *History of Chicago*, 3:718.

3. *Chicago Inter Ocean* (9 February 1890):10.

4. "Schlesinger and Mayer's Leases," *Chicago Tribune* (26 July 1891):10.

5. Andreas, *History of Chicago*, 3:718.

6. Theodore Dreiser, *Sister Carrie*, Pennsylvania Edition (Philadelphia: University of Pennsylvania Press, 1981), 42.

7. Ibid.

8. Ibid., 68.

9. Ibid., 70.

10. Obituary of Leopold Schlesinger, *Chicago Tribune* (16 March 1914):4. On the founding of the Jewish Training School, see Hyman L. Meites, ed., *History of the Jews of Chicago* (Chicago: Jewish Historical Society of Illinois, 1924), 160–62.

11. Early description of Sullivan's ornamentation for the interior of Sinai Congregation's synagogue appears in the *Chicago Times* (21 May 1876), quoted in Willard Connely, *Louis Sullivan: The Shaping of American Architecture* (New York: Horizon Press, 1960), 84. See also Twombly, *Louis Sullivan*, 87–92.

12. A detailed description of the renovated interior of Sinai's sanctuary appears in the *Reform Advocate* (Chicago) 4 (30 September 1892):135–36. See Spertus Museum of Judaica, *Faith and Form: Synagogue Architecture in Illinois* (Chicago: Spertus College Press, 1976), 40, 76.

13. Notice of Adler and Sullivan's commission for the Schlesinger residence in *Inland Architect and Builder* 4 (December 1884):70.

14. Obituary of Leopold Schlesinger, *Chicago Tribune* (16 March 1914):4.

15. On the 1885 remodeling of the Bowen Building for the Schlesinger and Mayer Store, see the *Chicago Tribune* (21 June 1885):8. Their acquisition of 133–35 State Street is noted in the *Chicago Tribune* (4 June 1885):3.

16. Announcements of Schlesinger and Mayer's renovation plans in 1890 appeared in the *Economist* 3 (8 February 1890):139; *Chicago Inter Ocean* (9 February 1890):10; *Chicago Tribune* (9 March 1890):28; *Economist* 3 (22 March 1890):348; *Building Budget* (Chicago) 6 (May 1890):7; *Economist* 4 (16 August 1890):258; *Economist* 5 (2 February 1891):293–94.

17. Schlesinger and Mayer's control of properties at 141–43 State Street south of the Bowen Building is documented in *Chicago Tribune* (26 July 1891):10; *Chicago Inter Ocean* (26 July 1891):10; (9 August 1891):10.

18. *Industrial Chicago*, 6 vols. (Chicago: Goodspeed Publishing Co., 1891), 1:230.

19. Addition of upper fifth and sixth floors to the Schlesinger and Mayer properties at 137–43 State Street was noted in the *Economist* 17 (13 March 1897):274; *Chicago Inter Ocean* (5 September 1897):21; *Economist* 18 (18 September 1897):320; *Chicago Tribune* (19 September 1897):34.

20. *Chicago Inter Ocean* (9 August 1891):10.

21. *Chicago Inter Ocean* (31 May 1896):20.

22. *Economist* 15 (27 June 1896):789.

23. *Economist* 15 (30 May 1896):666–67. Sullivan's new entrance at 141–13 Wabash Avenue of 1896 closely resembled that designed by Adler and Sullivan at 141–43 State Street as part of their earlier renovation of Schlesinger and Mayer's ground floor in 1892. See *Chicago Tribune* (3 July 1892):22.

24. *Economist* 17 (27 February 1897):224.

25. *Chicago Tribune* (28 June 1896):39; *Chicago Inter Ocean* (5 July 1896):38.

26. *Chicago Tribune*, Golden Jubilee Edition (10 June 1897):7.

27. Menocal, *Architecture as Nature*, 169. Sullivan's bridge is compared to the passerelle connecting the Gare St. Lazare and the Hôtel Terminus, designed by Juste Lisch and completed by 1889. See Paul Chemetov and Bernard Marrey, *Architectures à Paris 1848–1914* (Paris: Dunod, 1984), 71.

28. Andrew McLeish to Samuel C. Pirie, 2 April 1898, Carson Pirie Scott & Co. Archives, Chicago. Leiter's acquisition of the property on the southeast corner of State and Madison streets is recorded in Deed No. 180037, 10 May 1878, Book 828, page 116, Recorder's Office, Cook County, Illinois.

29. Lease of 2 May 1898, between Levi Z. Leiter and Leopold Schlesinger and David Mayer, recorded 14 July 1898 as Document 2710116, Recorder's Office, Cook County, Illinois. Archives, Field Museum of Natural History, Chicago.

30. Frank Lloyd Wright, *Genius and the Mobocracy*, 2nd ed. (New York: Horizon Press, 1971), 85.

31. *Economist* 31 (18 June 1904):860.

32. Andreas, *History of Chicago*, 3:718.

33. Ibid. See obituary of Leopold Schlesinger, *Chicago Tribune* (16 March 1914):4.

34. Biographical file on Florence Blum Mayer (1872–1934), Printed Books Collection, Chicago Historical Society.

35. "David Mayer, Mary Garden's Sponsor, Dies," *Chicago Tribune* (16 March 1920):17.

36. Leonard K. Eaton, *Two Chicago Architects and Their Clients: Frank Lloyd Wright and Howard Van Doren Shaw* (Cambridge, Mass.: M.I.T. Press, 1969), 41, 46–49.

37. On Mayer's association with the amusement park project, see *Construction News* 20 (30 September 1905):254, which notes Frank Lloyd Wright as architect. An earlier notice in *Construction News* 20 (29 July 1905):82, states that D. H. Burnham & Co. had been commissioned to prepare plans for this project.

38. Notice of the formation of David Mayer & Co. as a firm devoted to the development of commercial real estate appears in the *Economist* 33 (1 April 1905):461. David Mayer's major holdings in downtown real estate and his building projects after 1905 are listed in the *Economist* 48 (28 December 1912):1078. Mayer commissioned Burnham's office to build the Chicago Business College (1910) of eight stories at the southeast corner of Adams Street and Wabash Avenue, the Goddard Building (1913) of thirteen stories at the southwest corner of Monroe Street and Wabash Avenue, and the Wells-Quincy Building (1914) of eleven stories on the southeast corner of Quincy Street and Fifth Avenue (Wells Street).

39. Frank Lloyd Wright, *Genius and the Mobocracy*, 2nd ed., 85.

40. *Chicago Tribune* (28 May 1898):1.

41. "Million Dollar Marble Building," *Economist* 19 (28 May 1898):613.

42. *Chicago Tribune* (28 May 1898):1.

43. "Million Dollar Marble Building," *Economist* 19 (28 May 1898):613.

44. On the commission for the Gage facade, see Morrison, *Louis Sullivan*, 194–97, and Twombly, *Louis Sullivan*, 350–53. Renderings of the Gage facade and the Schlesinger and Mayer Store appeared on facing pages of the *Architectural Record* 8 (April 1899):424–25. On McCormick's project, see "To Concentrate Millinery Trade," *Chicago Dry Goods Reporter* 28 (16 July 1898):13.

45. "Chicago Millinery Houses," *Chicago Dry Goods Reporter* 28 (13 February 1898):45. On the original design for the three buildings, see "McCormick Improvement to Begin," *Chicago Tribune* (16 October 1898):34.

46. Hugh Morrison, *Louis Sullivan*, 194–95.

47. "Brick and Terra Cotta in American and Foreign Cities," *Brickbuilder* 8 (December 1899):253–54.

48. First announcements of Sullivan's project for the new Schlesinger and Mayer Store appear in the *Chicago Tribune* (28 May 1898):1; *Economist* 19 (28 May 1898):612–13; *Chicago Inter Ocean* (29 May 1898):20.

49. "Sketch of Schlesinger and Mayer's Proposed $1,000,000 Building," *Chicago Tribune* (29 May 1898):30; *Chicago Inter Ocean* (29 May 1898):20.

50. *Economist* 19 (28 May 1898):612.

51. *Chicago Tribune* (19 September 1897):34.

52. *Economist* 19 (28 May 1898):612.

53. *Construction News* 7 (20 July 1898):51.

54. The terms of Schlesinger and Mayer's agreement with Marshall Field appeared in the *Chicago Tribune* (14 July 1898):10; *Economist* 20 (16 July 1898):77; *Chicago Inter Ocean* (17 July 1898):21; *Economist* 20 (23 July 1898):105. Leiter's sale of the property back to Field is discussed in Lloyd Wendt and Herman Kogan, *Give the Lady What She Wants!: The Story of Marshall Field & Company* (Chicago: Rand McNally & Company, 1952), 233–34.

55. Record of Elmslie's account of the corner of the Schlesinger and Mayer Store in Burnham Library/University of Illinois Architectural Microfilming Project, Daily Progress Records and Notes, 2 vols., I: Entry for 29 March 1951, Burnham Library, Art Institute of Chicago.

56. Real Estate, 50–56 Madison Street; Construction Account, Carson Pirie Scott & Co. Archives, Chicago.

57. Municipal Ordinance of 5 December 1898 regarding construction of Schlesinger and Mayer on city property is recorded in the *Journal of the Proceedings of the Chicago City Council 1898–1899*, Municipal Reference Library, Chicago, 1067. Reference to this ordinance recurs in correspondence between Carson Pirie Scott & Co. and the City of Chicago through the years 1905–9, Carson Pirie Scott & Co. Archives, Chicago. On the issue of department stores' encroachments onto public property, see Perry R. Duis, "Whose City? Part Two," *Chicago History* 12 (Summer 1983):11–12.

58. Set of Specifications for the Schlesinger and Mayer Store Building, Louis H. Sullivan, Architect, 10 December 1898, Section F, page 4. Architectural Collections, Chicago Historical Society.

59. The use of bronze ornamentation on the Magasins du Printemps is noted in "Grands Magasins du Printemps à Paris," *Encyclopédie d'Architecture*, 3rd ser., 4(1885):4–5. On the distinctive properties of bronze as an architectural metal,

see Charles DeKay, "Decorative Work in Iron and Bronze," *Architectural Record* 15 (June 1904):529.

60. Set of Specifications for the Schlesinger and Mayer Store Building, Louis H. Sullivan, Architect, 10 December 1898, Section D, pp. 1–2. Architectural Collections, Chicago Historical Society.

61. Henry-Russell Hitchcock and William Seale, *Temples of Democracy: State Capitols of the USA* (New York: Harcourt Brace Jovanovich, 1976), 213.

62. Rhode Island Capitol Commission, Minutes of 15 February to 27 June 1896, Rhode Island Department of State, Providence, R.I., quoted in Hitchcock and Seale, *Temples of Democracy*, 219.

63. Henry W. Desmond, "The Works of Ernest Flagg," *Architectural Record* 11 (April 1902):5–9. On the Corcoran Gallery of Art see Mardges Bacon, *Ernest Flagg: Beaux-Arts Architect and Urban Reformer* (New York: Architectural History Foundation, and Cambridge, Mass.: M.I.T. Press, 1986), 65–69, 77–89.

64. Louis Sullivan to Marshall Field, 19 May 1899. Archives, Field Museum of Natural History, Chicago.

65. On the imposition of the 1893 height limit, see the Chicago Real Estate Board, *Studies on Building Height Limitations in Large Cities* (Chicago: Chicago Real Estate Board Library, 1923), 14. The reduction in the height of the Schlesinger and Mayer design was noted in the *Economist* 20 (5 November 1898):538. The cost of the revised building was noted in *Construction News* 8 (11 January 1899).

66. *Economist* 21 (6 May 1899):552.

67. Rapid progress of construction was noted in the *Economist* 22 (7 October 1899):419. Announcements of the opening of the first section of the new Schlesinger and Mayer Store on Madison Street appeared in the *Chicago Tribune* (3 December 1899):16, and (5 December 1899):7. The earlier delay in rebuilding State Street properties was noted in the *Economist* 2 (1 July 1889):451.

68. *Economist* 20 (16 July 1898):78. Sullivan and Adler are mentioned as associated architects of the Schlesinger and Mayer Store at the time of the granting of the building permit in November 1898; *Economist* 20 (5 November 1898):538 and *Economist* 21 (8 April 1899):423. Notice of Sullivan's responsibility for the store building and Adler's responsibility for its power plant in *Economist* 19 (4 June 1898):644 and in *Chicago Inter Ocean* (5 June 1898):20.

69. Payments to Adler and Sullivan for the first section of the building are listed in Real Estate, 50–56 Madison Street; Construction Account, Carson Pirie Scott & Co. Archives, Chicago.

70. Set of Specifications for the Schlesinger and Mayer Store Building, Louis H. Sullivan, Architect, 10 December 1898, Section A, page 8. Architectural Collections, Chicago Historical Society.

71. *Economist* 22 (7 October 1899):419.

72. "Architecture in the Shopping District," *Inland Architect and News Record* 34 (January 1900):46–47.

73. Mention of the stonecutters' strike in Chicago and its relation to the terra cotta industry appears in the *Brickbuilder* 7 (June 1898):129; 7 (July 1898):148. On the relation of the stonecutters' labor actions to the use of machinery for stonecutting in Chicago, see [United States Industrial Commission], *Report of the*

Industrial Commission on the Chicago Labor Disputes of 1900, with Especial Reference to the Disputes in the Building and Machinery Trades (Washington: Government Printing Office, 1901), lxxv–lxxvi, 132–33, 211–19, 355–61, 389–93.

74. *Economist* 22 (7 October 1899):419.

75. Specifications for the Schlesinger and Mayer Store Building, Section D, page 2.

76. Real Estate, 50–56 Madison Street; Construction Account, Carson Pirie Scott & Co. Archives, Chicago.

77. Notice of Siegel's activities and his agreement with Schlesinger and Mayer appear in the *Economist* 27 (14 June 1902):763; *New York Times* (14 June 1902):1; *Chicago Tribune* (14 June 1902):1; (6 August 1902):13; *New York Times* (6 August 1902):2.

78. *Chicago Tribune* (14 June 1902):1.

79. *Chicago Tribune* (6 August 1902):13.

80. *Economist* 27 (1 March 1902):264; *Economist* 27 (5 April 1902):435. Change in the city's height limit noted in Chicago Real Estate Board, *Studies on Building Height Limitations*, 14. The new retail store for Marshall Field & Co. of 1902–7 is discussed in Twyman, *History of Marshall Field*, 154–59, and in Randall, *Development of Building Construction in Chicago*, 133. On the Boston Store and the Mandel Brothers Store, ibid., 226, 150. The Mandel Brothers Annex is described in P. B. Wight, "Fireproofing: The Central Trading Company's New Building at Chicago," *Brickbuilder* 10 (May 1901):103.

81. *Economist* 28 (23 August 1902):249. In his account of construction in 1902–3 Sullivan wrote that the first nine-story section of the store built on Madison Street in 1899 was to "be raised to a height of twelve stories to correspond" to the new corner building; yet the first section of nine stories had steel columns and foundations "designed accurately for their loads." Thus the nine-story section might not have been raised to match the adjacent twelve-story sections because of inadequate structural capacity. See Sullivan, "Sub-Structure at the New Schlesinger and Mayer Store Building," *Engineering Record* 47 (21 February 1903):194, 196. See also Menocal, *Architecture as Nature*, 169, and Jordy, "The Tall Buildings," in Wim de Wit, ed., 155, note 87.

82. Louis Sullivan to Joel Hurt, Atlanta, Ga., 30 August 1904. Copybook of Business Letters of Louis H. Sullivan, April 1, 1903 to January 9, 1905; Burnham Library, Art Institute of Chicago.

83. Comparison of the corner of the Schlesinger and Mayer Store with that of Le Printemps is suggested in Menocal, *Architecture as Nature*, 69. On Le Printemps, see "Grands Magasins du Printemps à Paris," *Encyclopédie d'Architecture*, 3rd ser., 4 (1885):1–35, and Bernard Marrey, *Les grands magasins: des origines à 1939* (Paris: Picard, 1979), 97–110. On the influence of Le Printemps see Claude Mignot, *Architecture of the Nineteenth Century in Europe* (New York: Rizzoli, 1984), 247, and André Saint-Martin, *Les grands magasins* (Paris: Rousseau, 1900), 58

84. The new Schlesinger and Mayer Store is documented with plans and views in *Fireproof Building Construction: Prominent Buildings Erected by the George A. Fuller Co.* (New York and Chicago, 1904), 140–45. A. E. Wells was the general

contractor for the first section of the Schlesinger and Mayer Building on Madison Street built in 1899.

85. "Builders Work under Shoppers," *Chicago Tribune* (4 January 1903):6.

86. Louis H. Sullivan, "Sub-Structure at the New Schlesinger and Mayer Store Building," *Engineering Record* 47 (21 February 1903):194–96.

87. Andrew McLeish to John T. Pirie, 31 March 1903. Carson Pirie Scott & Co. Archives, Chicago.

88. "The New Schlesinger and Mayer Building, Chicago," *Brickbuilder* 12 (May 1903):103–4.

89. Ibid., 104.

90. Louis H. Sullivan to J. M. Henderson of Carson Pirie Scott & Co., 23 May 1903. Copybook of Business Letters of Louis H. Sullivan, April 1, 1903 to January 9, 1905. Burnham Library, Art Institute of Chicago.

91. Accounts of the grand opening of the new Schlesinger and Mayer Store appeared in the *Chicago Journal* (12 October 1903):2; *Chicago Record Herald* (13 October 1903):13; *Chicago Inter Ocean* (14 October 1903):7.

92. Fleury was the artist who painted the murals of spring and autumn as part of Sullivan's decorative program for the interior of the Chicago Auditorium. One exhibition of his oil paintings, watercolors, and drawings was entitled "Picturesque Chicago," held at the Art Institute of Chicago in October 1900.

93. Andrew McLeish to John T. Pirie, 22 October 1903, Carson Pirie Scott & Co. Archives, Chicago.

94. Schlesinger and Mayer's losses in sales during construction in 1902–3 are noted in Andrew McLeish to John T. Pirie, 31 March 1903, Carson Pirie Scott & Co. Archives, Chicago. The store's initiation of a wholesale department is recorded in *Economist* 13 (4 May 1895):524.

95. Andrew McLeish to John T. Pirie, 31 March 1903, Carson Pirie Scott & Co. Archives, Chicago.

96. Andrew McLeish to John T. Pirie, 7 April 1903, Carson Pirie Scott & Co. Archives, Chicago.

97. Notices of Schlesinger and Mayer's acquisition of the leases to 155 State Street and 45–49 Monroe Street appear in *Economist* 30 (15 August 1903):210–11 and *Economist* 30 (22 August 1903):242.

98. *Chicago Tribune* (19 June 1904):22.

99. Accounts of Selfridge's acquisition of Schlesinger and Mayer in *Economist* 31, Special News Bulletin, 14 May 1904; *Chicago Tribune* (15 May 1904):57; *Chicago Inter Ocean* (15 May 1904):5; *Chicago Dry Goods Reporter* 34 (21 May 1904):37; *Merchants Record and Show Window* 14 (June 1904):234–35. See also Twyman, *History of Marshall Field*, 162–64.

100. *Chicago Tribune* (15 May 1904):57.

101. Selfridge's sale of building and leaseholds to Young in *Chicago Tribune* (15 June 1904):11 and (19 June 1904):22. The transfer of the Carson Pirie Scott property to the Field Museum is recorded in the will of Marshall Field, pages 36–38, a certified copy of which is found in the Archives, Field Museum of Natural History, Chicago.

102. Reginald Pound, *Selfridge: A Biography* (London: William Heinemann,

1960), 25. See also Harry Gordon Selfridge, "Selling Selfridge, Some Random Reflections of an American Merchant in London," *Saturday Evening Post* 208 (27 July 1935):18−19, 51, 53.

103. "Selfridge Sells Out," *Economist* 32 (13 August 1904):212−13; *Chicago Dry Goods Reporter* 34 (13 August 1904). See also Memorandum of John G. Shedd on Carson Pirie Scott & Co.'s purchase of H. G. Selfridge & Co., 1904, Carson Pirie Scott & Co. Archives, Chicago.

104. *Economist* 32 (31 December 1904):871.

105. Carson Pirie Scott & Co., Letter of Recommendation for Mr. Louis H. Sullivan, 7 May 1906, Sullivan Centennial Exhibition File, Museum Archives, Art Institute of Chicago.

106. *Chicago Tribune* (1 October 1907):20.

107. Randall, *Development of Building Construction in Chicago*, 148. Illustration of the 1927 addition to Carson Pirie Scott at the northwest corner of Monroe Street and Wabash Avenue in Condit, *The Chicago School of Architecture*, Figure 184.

108. Randall, *Development of Building Construction in Chicago*, 290. Illustration of Monroe Street section of Carson Pirie Scott in Condit, *The Chicago School of Architecture*, Figure 185.

109. Sale of the building from the estate of Otto Young to Carson Pirie Scott is recorded in a document of 3 October 1955, Book 52585, page 477, Recorder's Office, Cook County, Illinois. On the Holabird and Root addition to Carson Pirie Scott of 1960−61, see Condit, *The Chicago School of Architecture*, 165−6. Carson Pirie Scott was added to the National Register of Historic Places on 17 April 1970, Federal Register No. 70000231. The bulding was given the status of a National Historic Landmark on 15 May 1975.

110. John Vinci, "Carson Pirie Scott: 125 Years in Business," *Chicago History* 8 (Summer 1979):92−97.

Chapter III: Sullivan's Department Store on State Street

1. "The World's Largest Store," *Chicago Dry Goods Reporter* 28 (1 January 1898):43.

2. Samuel K. Adams, "The Conduct of Great Businesses, Part I: The Department Store," *Scribner's Magazine* 21 (January 1897):3−4.

3. Louis Sullivan, Kindergarten Chat III: "A Terminal Station," *Kindergarten Chats and Other Writings*, 24.

4. Louis Sullivan, "The Tall Office Building Artistically Considered" (1896), *Kindergarten Chats and Other Writings*, 202.

5. Louis Sullivan, Kindergarten Chat XXXIX: "On the Historic Styles" (1901), original version reprinted in *Roots of Contemporary American Architecture*, ed. Lewis Mumford (1952; reprint, New York: Dover, 1972), 78. One probable source of Sullivan's views on the relation of art and society was the work of the French art historian and philosopher, Hippolyte Taine (1828−93). Sullivan wrote of the impact of Taine's writings on his own thought in *The Autobiography of an Idea* (New York: Dover, 1956), 233−34. On Sullivan's relationship to Taine,

see Sherman Paul, *Louis Sullivan: An Architect in American Thought* (Englewood Cliffs, N.J.: Prentice-Hall, 1962), 20−21, and Menocal, *Architecture as Nature*, 11−12. An example of Taine's views on the relation of art and society is found in his *Philosophy of Art*, trans. John Durand (New York: Holt & Williams, 1873), 19−30.

6. Ibid., 77. Sullivan's ideal of a work of architecture developed logically and poetically out of all its conditions also recalls Gottfried Semper's definition of style in architecture as a "harmony of a building with the conditions primary to its coming into existence." On the influence of Semperian theory in Chicago, see Roula Mouroudellis Geraniotis, "German Architectural Theory and Practice in Chicago, 1850−1900," *Winterthur Portfolio* 21 (Winter 1986):304−6.

7. Louis Sullivan, "The Tall Office Building Artistically Considered" (1896), *Kindergarten Chats and Other Writings*, 208. This statement may be compared with Sullivan's unpublished manuscript, "May Not Architecture Again Become a Living Art?" n.d., Burnham Library, Art Institute of Chicago. See also Frederick Baumann, "Two Questions Considered: First: Is Architecture a Living Art? Second: Can Architecture Again Become a Living Art? Preceded by a Historical Review of Art," *Inland Architect and News Record* 29 (February 1897):23−26.

8. On the relation between State Street department stores and the Columbian Exposition, see Russell Lewis, "Everything under One Roof: World's Fairs and Department Stores in Paris and Chicago," *Chicago History* 12 (Fall 1983):41−43.

9. On the Manufactures and Liberal Arts Building at the Columbian Exposition, see Joseph K. Freitag, "The Greatest of All Fair Buildings," *Engineering Magazine* 3 (July 1892):503−11, and Donald Hoffmann, "Clear Span Rivalry: The World's Fairs of 1889−1893," *Society of Architectural Historians Journal* 29 (March 1970):48−50.

10. Advertisement for Schlesinger and Mayer, *Chicago Record-Herald* (7 October 1903):8.

11. Advertisements for Schlesinger and Mayer, *Chicago Inter Ocean* (8 October 1903):12, and (15 October 1903):12.

12. "Autumn Festival," *Chicago Dry Goods Reporter* 29 (7 October 1899):25.

13. H. Gordon Selfridge, *The Romance of Commerce* (London and New York: John Lane, 1918), 363.

14. Lyndon Smith, "The Schlesinger and Mayer Building," *Architectural Record* 16 (July 1904):59.

15. Adams, "The Conduct of Great Businesses, Part I: The Department Store," *Scribner's Magazine* 21 (January 1897):4−6, 9−10, 12−14.

16. Advertisement for Schlesinger and Mayer, *Chicago Inter Ocean* (9 October 1903):12.

17. Advertisement for Marshall Field & Co., quoted in *Merchants Record and Show Window* 13 (September 1903):122.

18. H. Walter Scott, "One American Principle: Some Comparisons of the Manner in Which American and European Merchants Treat Their Customers," *Merchants Record and Show Window* 15 (October 1904):17−18. See also J. H. Phillips, "London Shopkeeping Methods," *Merchants Record and Show Window* 12 (January 1903):3.

19. "Practical Store Service: Present Day Retailing," *Chicago Dry Goods Reporter* 33 (15 August 1903):41.

20. "Modern Store Making," *Chicago Dry Goods Reporter* 33 (15 October 1903):12.

21. Daniel J. Boorstin, *The Americans: The Democratic Experience* (New York: Random House, 1973), 99.

22. Ibid., 91–92.

23. Quoted in Boorstin, *The Americans*, 100.

24. Advertisement for Schlesinger and Mayer Store opening, *Chicago Inter Ocean* (8 October 1903):12.

25. John Dennis, Jr., "Marshall Field: A Great Mercantile Genius," *Everybody's Magazine* 14 (March 1906):297.

26. *Rand McNally & Co. Bird's-Eye Views and Guide to Chicago*, reprinted in Randall, *Development of Building Construction in Chicago*, 165.

27. Ibid., 166. See also "The Expansion of Retail Houses," *Economist* 5 (21 February 1891):293–94.

28. "New State Street Firm: H. G. Selfridge & Co. Buys Out Schlesinger and Mayer," *Chicago Dry Goods Reporter* 34 (21 May 1904):37.

29. On the range of special rooms and activities within buildings like Schlesinger and Mayer's, see "The Modern Department Store and the Features Which Most Tend to Make It So," *Dry Goods Economist* (New York) 57 (24 October 1903):51–53.

30. Benjamin F. Schlesinger, "How to Bring Visitors into the Store," *System* 9 (March 1906):202.

31. Advertisement for Marshall Field & Co. quoted in "Hints to Retailers and State Street Observations," *Chicago Dry Goods Reporter* 28 (22 October 1898):45.

32. "The Needs of the Retail Quarter," *Economist* 3 (22 February 1890):200.

33. Crissey, *Since Forty Years Ago*, 23.

34. "Modern Store Making," *Chicago Dry Goods Reporter* 28 (19 November 1898):12.

35. Lyndon Smith, "The Schlesinger and Mayer Building," *Architectural Record* 16 (July 1904):59.

36. Ibid.

37. On the design of show windows in the early nineteenth century, see David Dean, *English Shop Fronts from Contemporary Source Books 1792–1840* (New York: Transatlantic, 1970), and Hector Lefuel, *Boutiques parisiennes du Premier Empire* (Paris: Morancé, 1925).

38. On A. T. Stewart's show windows, see Harry E. Resseguie, "A. T. Stewart's Marble Palace—The Cradle of the Department Store," *New-York Historical Society Quarterly* 48 (April 1964):140–41. On Potter Palmer's early adaptation of the show window, see Twyman, *History of Marshall Field & Co.*, 5.

39. On Macy's development of window displays at the Christmas season, see Ralph M. Hower, *History of Macy's of New York, 1858–1919* (Cambridge, Mass.: Harvard University Press, 1943), 118, 169, 275, and Leonard S. Marcus, *The American Store Window* (New York: Watson-Guptill, 1978), 13.

40. Sullivan, *The Autobiography of an Idea*, 226–27. The architecture of Pari-

sian shop windows through the era of the Second Empire is selectively documented in Cesar Daly, *L'Architecture privée au XIXième siècle*, 2nd ser., 3 vols. (Paris: Ducher, 1872), vol. I, sec. 1.

41. John Crawford Brown, "Early Days of the Department Stores," *Valentine's Manual of Old New York*, n.s., 5 (New York, 1921), edited by Henry Collins Brown, 118–19.

42. Contemporary discussions of the relation between the show window and newspaper advertising include: A. Mershon, "Window Dressing an Art," *Merchants Record and Show Window* 13 (July 1903):26; W. Sawyer, "Advertising That Pays," ibid. 14 (June 1904):227–28; E. Oldham, "The Kinship between the Show Window and the Newspaper Ad," ibid. 15 (July 1904):33–34.

43. Mershon, "Window Dressing an Art," 26.

44. Ibid.

45. "Hints to Retailers and State Street Observations," *Chicago Dry Goods Reporter* 28 (15 October 1898):71.

46. "Window Dressing and Interior Store Decoration," *Chicago Dry Goods Reporter* 29 (4 November 1899):51.

47. Remark of Professor Edmund Buckley, University of Chicago, cited in "Art through Windows," *Merchants Record and Show Window* 15 (December 1904):29.

48. Ibid.

49. Mershon, "Window Dressing an Art," 26.

50. Lillie H. French, "Shopping in New York," *Century* 41 (March 1901):651.

51. Advertisement for Schlesinger and Mayer Store opening, *Chicago Daily News* (14 October 1903):3.

52. "The World's Largest Store," *Chicago Dry Goods Reporter* 28 (1 January 1898):45–47.

53. Leonard S. Marcus, *The American Store Window*, 12, 16. The trimmers' publication appeared as *The Show Window* (1897–1902), changing its editor and ownership to become *The Merchants Record and Show Window* (1903–38).

54. Report on the Third Annual Convention of the National Association of Window Trimmers of America, *The Show Window* 5 (August 1899):61.

55. "Window Gazers Earn Money," *The Show Window* 5 (August 1899):107.

56. The principles of display design are elucidated in handbooks such as Charles A. Tracy, *The Art of Decorating Show Windows and Interiors: A Complete Manual of Window Trimming* (Chicago: Merchants Record Co., 1903). See also L. Frank Baum, *The Art of Decorating Dry Goods Windows and Interiors* (Chicago: Show Window Publishing Co., 1900).

57. "Art through Windows," *Merchants Record and Show Window* 15 (December 1904):29.

58. Reginald Pound, *Selfridge*, 28. See also H. Allen Brooks, "Chicago Architecture: Its Debt to the Arts and Crafts," *Society of Architectural Historians Journal* 30 (December 1971):312. On the analogy between department stores and museums, see Neil Harris, "Museums, Merchandising and Popular Taste: The Struggle for Influence," in Ian Quimby, ed., *Material Culture and the Study of American Life* (New York: W. W. Norton & Co., 1978), 149–54.

59. Representative of the trade in artificial foliage for display design were the advertisements of Carl Netschert in Chicago, *Merchants Record and Show Window* 15 (August 1904):xxvi–xxvii.

60. "Window Trimming," *Chicago Dry Goods Reporter* 33 (26 September 1903):83.

61. On the use of natural imagery in store decoration, see "A Great Exposition," *Merchants Record and Show Window* 15 (November 1904):19–21. On the associations of spring in mercantile culture, see "The Coming of the Flower," *Chicago Dry Goods Reporter* 29 (25 March 1899):11.

62. Tracy, "Interior Decorations," in *The Art of Decorating Show Windows and Interiors*, 4th ed. (Chicago: Merchants Record Co., 1909), 171.

63. "Large Crowds at Big New Store," *Chicago Journal* (12 October 1903):2. The floral imagery prevalent in the temporary decor of State Street's department stores may have been linked to a broader societal preoccupation with the cultivation and display of flowers, as suggested in articles such as Candace Wheeler, "The Decorative Use of Wild Flowers," *Atlantic Monthly* 95 (May 1905):630–34, and periodicals such as *Garden and Forest* (New York, 1888–97) and *Gardening* (Chicago, 1892–1925). Living flowers in gardens and landscapes were also the focus of a genre of American painting at the turn of the century. See William H. Gerdts, *Down Garden Paths: The Floral Environment in American Art* (Cranbury, N.J.: Associated University Presses, 1983). Sullivan's abiding interest in floral gardens is described in Lyndon P. Smith, "The Home of an Artist-Architect: Louis H. Sullivan's Place at Ocean Springs, Mississippi," *Architectural Record* 17 (June 1905):471–90.

64. On the relation between agricultural prosperity and the dry goods trade, see editorials entitled "Another Big Wheat Crop," *Chicago Dry Goods Reporter* 28 (4 June 1898):9, and "The Horn of Plenty," ibid. 28 (23 July 1898):23.

65. "State Street Observations Valuable," *Chicago Dry Goods Reporter* 28 (23 July 1898):87.

66. "The New Schlesinger and Mayer Building, Chicago," *Brickbuilder* 12 (May 1903):103, 102.

67. "Along State Street," *Merchants Record and Show Window* 15 (August 1904):104.

68. Ibid.

69. George Grant Elmslie, Notes on Hugh Morrison's Account of the Gage Brothers Building, undated typescript in the Purcell and Elmslie Collection, Northwest Architectural Archives, University of Minnesota, St. Paul, Minn.

70. Louis Sullivan, Kindergarten Chat V: "An Hotel," *Kindergarten Chats and Other Writings*, 27.

71. "Plate versus Cylinder Glass," *Inland Architect and News Record* 28 (January 1897):42. See also Warren C. Scoville, *Revolution in Glass Making: Entrepreneurship and Technological Change in the American Industry, 1880–1920* (Cambridge, Mass.: Harvard University Press, 1948), 19–21, 46, 52, 78.

72. Set of Specifications for the Schlesinger and Mayer Store Building, 10 December 1898, Louis H. Sullivan, Architect, Section N, page 2. Architectural Collections, Chicago Historical Society.

73. "Marble Building at State and Madison Streets," *Chicago Inter Ocean* (29 May 1898):20.

74. Henry Van Brunt, "Architecture in the West," *Atlantic Monthly* 64 (December 1889):782, reprinted in William A. Coles, ed., *Architecture and Society: Selected Essays of Henry Van Brunt* (Cambridge, Mass.: The Belknap Press of Harvard University Press, 1969), 192.

75. *Economist* 28 (23 August 1902):249.

76. Lyndon Smith, "The Schlesinger and Mayer Building," *Architectural Record* 16 (July 1904):59.

77. John L. Mauran, "The Department Store Plan," *Brickbuilder* 17 (November 1908):252.

78. Specifications for the Schlesinger and Mayer Store Building, Section F, pages 1−2.

79. Blueprints of an early set of working drawings for the Schlesinger and Mayer Store Building, Louis H. Sullivan, Architect, dated from 18 November to 23 December 1898, are in the Architectural Collections, Chicago Historical Society. These drawings document the design when the upper exterior was still envisioned in marble. Almost all of this set is also recorded in the Burnham Library/University of Illinois Architectural Microfilming Project, Art Institute of Chicago, Microfilm Roll #4: Adler and Sullivan; Louis H. Sullivan, Frames 345−94. Blueprints of later drawings from the period of construction 1902−3 also survive in the Architectural Collections, Chicago Historical Society.

80. The pencil drawing, titled "Ornamental Iron Spandrel, Schlesinger and Mayer Building, Chicago, Ill.," is 6 1/16 inches × 7 3/4 inches on heavy weight drawing paper, unsigned and undated. The drawing is No. 100 in the Frank Lloyd Wright Collection, Avery Architectural Library, Columbia University. See Paul Sprague, *The Drawings of Louis Henry Sullivan* (Princeton, N.J.: Princeton University Press, 1978), Catalogue No. 114, p. 61.

81. George Grant Elmslie to Frank Lloyd Wright, 12 June 1936, reprinted in *Society of Architectural Historians Journal* 20 (October 1961):140.

82. Attribution to Elmslie of the ornamentation of the Schlesinger and Mayer Store is found in Morrison, *Louis Sullivan*, 200−201, and David Gebhard, "Louis Sullivan and George Grant Elmslie," *Society of Architectural Historians Journal* 19 (May 1960):64. On Elmslie's role in the design of ornamentation for Sullivan's buildings, see Paul Sprague, "The Architectural Ornament of Louis Sullivan and His Chief Draftsmen" (Ph.D. diss., Princeton University, 1968), 119−54.

83. The pencil drawing of a title page for Sullivan's poem "Inspiration" (5 1/4 inches × 8 inches, unsigned and undated) was included as Plate No. 1 in the exhibition catalogue by David Gebhard entitled *Drawings for Architectural Ornament by George Grant Elmslie, 1902−1936* (Santa Barbara, Calif.: Art Gallery, University of California, Santa Barbara, 1968).

84. William Gray Purcell, Memorandum for Louis Sullivan Exhibit, 8 June 1956, Sullivan Centennial Exhibition File, Museum Archives, Art Institute of Chicago.

85. George Grant Elmslie to Frank Lloyd Wright, 12 June 1936, reprinted in *Society of Architectural Historians Journal* 20 (October 1961):140.

86. George Grant Elmslie, "Sullivan Ornamentation," *Illinois Society of Architects Monthly Bulletin* 19–20 (June–July 1935):6, reprinted with modifications in *American Institute of Architects Journal* 6 (July 1946):155–58.

87. Louis Sullivan, "The Organic and the Inorganic," *A System of Architectural Ornament* (1924; reprint, New York: Eakins Press, 1967).

88. Elmslie, "Sullivan Ornamentation," 156. On Sullivan's study of botanical forms, see Paul Sprague, "The Architectural Ornament of Louis Sullivan and His Chief Draftsmen," 61–70.

89. Ibid., 156–57.

90. The theory of architectural ornament as the conventionalization of natural botanical forms extends back into the nineteenth century in both English and French variations. See, for example, Christopher Dresser, *The Art of Decorative Design* (1862; reprint, New York: Garland Press, 1977), 36–37, cited in Landau, *P. B. Wight*, 25. See also Theodore Turak, "French and English Sources of Sullivan's Ornament and Doctrine," *Prairie School Review* 11 (Fourth Quarter 1974):5–30, and Sprague, "The Architectural Ornament of Louis Sullivan and his Chief Draftsmen," 47–60. Architectural ornamentation is described as the conventionalization of natural forms in William Le Baron Jenney, "A Few Practical Hints," *Inland Architect and News Record* 13 (February 1889):7, and in Frank Lloyd Wright, "On Ornamentation," *Oak Leaves* [Oak Park, Ill.] (16 January 1909), reprinted as "Ethics of Ornament," in *Prairie School Review* 4 (First Quarter 1967):16–17.

91. Elmslie, "Sullivan Ornamentation," 157.

92. Ibid., 157. Sullivan developed the themes of growth and decadence as a poetic perception of nature in his "Essay on Inspiration" of 1886, reprinted in Menocal, *Architecture as Nature*, Appendix A, 155–67. On possible sources for Sullivan's theories of ornament, see Menocal, pp. 10–31. An alternative view of the sources of Sullivan's position is developed in Lauren S. Weingarden, "Louis H. Sullivan's Metaphysics of Architecture (1885–1901): Sources and Correspondences with Symbolist Art Theories" (Ph.D. diss., University of Chicago, 1981).

93. Elmslie, "Sullivan Ornamentation," 157.

94. The idea that ornamental designs derived from botanic sources should suggest the growth of living things and not merely their visible shape also underlay the decorative art of William Morris and other theorists of this subject. See Gillian Naylor, *The Arts and Crafts Movement: A Study of Its Sources, Ideals and Influence on Design Theory* (London: Studio Vista, 1971), 106. See also John Grant Rhodes, "Ornament and Ideology: A Study in Mid-Nineteenth-Century British Design Theory" (Ph.D. diss., Harvard University, 1983).

95. Sullivan, "The Organic and the Inorganic."

96. Louis Sullivan, "Ornament in Architecture," *Engineering Magazine* 3 (August 1892):641, reprinted in *Kindergarten Chats and Other Writings*, 189.

97. Elmslie, "Sullivan Ornamentation," 157. See also Sullivan, "Ornament in Architecture," *Kindergarten Chats and Other Writings*, 188.

98. Accounts of development of ornamental forms in ancient architecture as the conventionalization of botanical forms include William M. Goodyear, "Ori-

gin of the Acanthus Motive and Egg and Dart Molding," *Architectural Record* 4 (July 1894):88–122.

99. George Grant Elmslie to Lewis Mumford, 20 April 1931, Purcell and Elmslie Collection, Northwest Architectural Archives, University of Minnesota, St. Paul, Minn. Elmslie's remark is a rebuttal to Mumford's criticism of the ornament at the base of the Schlesinger and Mayer Store in *The Brown Decades*, 156.

100. Sprague, "The Architectural Ornament of Louis Sullivan and His Chief Draftsmen," 319.

101. George Grant Elmslie to Frank Lloyd Wright, 30 October 1932, Purcell and Elmslie Collection, Northwest Architectural Archives, University of Minnesota, St. Paul, Minn.

102. Leon V. Solon, "An Architect's Signature on His Work," *Architectural Record* 48 (August 1920):173–76. Adolphe Lance (1813–1874) was also an editor of the *Encyclopédie d'Architecture*, of which Sullivan owned volumes from the first series (1851–62).

103. Specifications for the Schlesinger and Mayer Store Building, Section F, page 3.

104. Quoted in John Szarkowski, *The Idea of Louis Sullivan* (Minneapolis: University of Minnesota Press, 1956), 7.

105. "The New Schlesinger and Mayer Building, Chicago," *Brickbuilder* 12 (May 1903):101. On the character of commercial architecture see "Commercialism in Art," *Brickbuilder* 15 (November 1906):221.

106. Oscar Lovell Triggs, "Arts and Crafts," *Brush and Pencil* 1 (December 1897):47. On the Chicago Arts and Crafts Society see H. Allen Brooks, "Chicago Architecture: Its Debt to the Arts and Crafts," *Society of Architectural Historians Journal* 30 (December 1971):312–13. On the Arts and Crafts Movement in American cultural history, see T. Jackson Lears, *No Place of Grace: Antimodernism and the Transformation of American Culture 1880–1920* (New York: Pantheon Books, 1981), 66–96. On Triggs and Sullivan, see Paul, *Louis Sullivan*, 104–7.

107. Triggs, "Arts and Crafts," 47.

108. Ibid.

109. Ibid., 48.

110. Frank Lloyd Wright, "The Art and Craft of the Machine," *Catalogue of the Fourteenth Annual Exhibition of the Chicago Architectural Club* (Chicago, 1901), 17. [Page numbers in these notes for this Wright essay have been assigned as the essay was originally printed without page numbers.]

111. Sullivan records his youthful fascination with the construction of the Eads Bridge at St. Louis in *The Autobiography of an Idea*, 246–48, and his childhood enjoyment of rail travel, which continued through later life, ibid., 130–33.

112. Louis Sullivan, Kindergarten Chat XLII: "What Is an Architect?" *Kindergarten Chats and Other Writings*, 140.

113. Among Sullivan's most elegant statements of this conviction is his lecture entitled "Style," *Inland Architect and News Record* 11 (May 1888):59–60.

114. Louis Sullivan, "What is the Just Subordination, in Architectural Design,

of Details to Mass?" (1887), *Kindergarten Chats and Other Writings*, 185.

115. Louis Sullivan, Kindergarten Chat XLIX: "The Art of Expression," *Kindergarten Chats and Other Writings*, 164.

116. Frank Lloyd Wright offered this characterization of Sullivan's attitude toward materials in his tribute, "Louis H. Sullivan—His Work," *Architectural Record* 56 (July 1924):29–30.

117. Louis Sullivan, Kindergarten Chat XLII: "What Is an Architect?" *Kindergarten Chats and Other Writings*, 140.

118. Louis Gibson, "The Machine in Art," *Brush and Pencil* 1 (March 1898): 201.

119. Ibid., 201–2.

120. Ibid., 202.

121. Ibid.

122. "The New Schlesinger and Mayer Building, Chicago," 101.

123. Charles DeKay, "The Future of Metals in Decoration," *Architectural Record* 16 (July 1904):159.

124. "Decorative Iron Work," *Engineering Magazine* 8 (February 1895):1076.

125. C. Everard, "Art Iron at the Fair," *Ornamental Iron* 1 (September 1893):65.

126. "Modern Commercial Buildings," *Inland Architect and News Record* 32 (September 1898):18. The Winslow Brothers' own account of their achievement in cast and other metalwork for architecture is documented in the firm's publications, beginning with the periodical *Ornamental Iron* (1893–May 1895) and continuing through two subsequent catalogues: *Photographs and Sketches of Ornamental Iron and Bronze* (Chicago, 1901), and *Ornamental Iron and Bronze* (Chicago, 1910).

127. Wright, "The Art and Craft of the Machine," 15.

128. William R. Lethaby, "On the Use and Abuse of Cast Iron," lecture before the Arts and Crafts Exhibition Society, London; reprinted in *Architectural Review* 30 (November 1911):286.

129. Schneider's background and early involvement with Sullivan are discussed by Martin V. Reinhart in "Norwegian-Born Sculptor Kristian Schneider, His Essential Contribution to the Development of Louis Sullivan's Ornamental Style," lecture to the Symposium on the Norwegian-American Life of Chicago, the Norway Center, November 1982, Burnham Library, Art Institute of Chicago.

130. Sullivan's employment of Schneider as modeler for ornament of the Schlesinger and Mayer Store is recorded in his letter to the George A. Fuller Company, 15 October 1903; Louis H. Sullivan, Copybook of Business Letters, April 1, 1903–January 31st 1905, 194–95, Burnham Library, Art Institute of Chicago.

131. William Gray Purcell, annotations to a letter from George Grant Elmslie, undated typescript in the Purcell and Elmslie Collection, Northwest Architectural Archives, University of Minnesota, St. Paul, Minn.

132. William Gray Purcell, annotations to a letter from George Grant Elms-

lie, undated typescript in the Purcell and Elmslie Collection, Northwest Architectural Archives, University of Minnesota, St. Paul, Minn.

133. David Gebhard, *Drawings for Architectural Ornament by George Grant Elmslie, 1902–1936*, 2. Correspondence between Elmslie and Schneider is to be found in the Purcell and Elmslie Collection, Northwest Architectural Archives, University of Minnesota, St. Paul, Minn.

134. George G. Elmslie, undated response to a letter from William G. Purcell, Purcell and Elmslie Collection, Northwest Architectural Archives, University of Minnesota, St. Paul, Minn. In his response Elmslie refers to the cast iron grille designed by Sullivan and executed by the Winslow Brothers for the McCormick Residence, Chicago. The grille is illustrated in the Winslow Brothers Company, *Ornamental Iron and Bronze* (Chicago, 1910), 165.

135. Specifications for the Schlesinger and Mayer Store Building, Section F, pages 5, 2.

136. "Architecture in the Shopping District," *Inland Architect and News Record* 34 (January 1900):47.

137. William G. Purcell to Richard Nickel, 10 July 1961, Richard Nickel Committee Files, File on Carson Pirie Scott Building, Office of John Vinci, A.I.A., Chicago. The use of asphaltum as a base coat for the ornamental iron was noted during the restoration of the building in 1979. Personal conversation with Timothy Samuelson, Commission on Chicago Landmarks, 22 June 1987.

138. On Sullivan's theory of architectural polychromy, see Sprague, "The Architectural Ornament of Louis Sullivan and His Chief Draftsmen," 206–17, and David H. Crook, "Louis Sullivan and the Golden Doorway," *Society of Architectural Historians Journal* 26 (December 1967):255–58.

139. John Wanamaker, "The Evolution of Mercantile Business," *Corporations and the Public Welfare: Addresses at the Fourth Annual Meeting of the American Academy of Political and Social Science, April 19–20, 1900; Supplement to the Annals of the American Academy of Political and Social Science* (Philadelphia: American Academy of Political and Social Science, May 1900), 133.

140. David Mayer lived at 1811 Prairie Avenue in a residence still standing as part of the Prairie Avenue Historic District. Marshall Field's famous residence at 1905 Prairie Avenue, designed by Richard Morris Hunt and completed in 1873, was demolished after World War II.

141. Cleveland, "Life of Marshall Field—Chapter XI," *System* 11 (May 1907): 458–59.

142. Harry G. Selfridge, quoted in Cleveland, "Life of Marshall Field—Chapter XI," 459.

143. John Dennis, Jr., "Marshall Field," *Everybody's Magazine* 14 (March 1906):297.

144. Advertisement for Marshall Field & Co., quoted in "Short Lengths for the Ad Man," *Merchants Record and Show Window* 15 (November 1904):50.

145. Advertisement for Schlesinger and Mayer Store opening, *Chicago Record-Herald* (9 October 1903):8. The assertion that "there is nothing new under the sun" appears in Ecclesiastes 1:9.

146. The phrase "something new under the sun" appears in Sullivan's "The Tall Office Building Artistically Considered" (1896), *Kindergarten Chats and Other Writings*, 202, and in Sullivan's description of the steel frame in *The Autobiography of an Idea*, 313.

147. Wright, "The Art and Craft of the Machine," 8.

148. Ibid.

149. Advertisement for Schlesinger and Mayer Store opening, *Chicago Record-Herald* (9 October 1903):8.

150. Frank Lloyd Wright, "The Art and Craft of the Machine," 13–14. See also "Mission of the Veneer Machine," *Construction News* 22 (18 August 1906): 134. Developments in mechanized woodworking were chronicled in the Chicago trade publication *Hardwood Record* (1892–1937).

151. Ibid., 14.

152. "Window Dressing and Interior Store Decoration," *Chicago Dry Goods Reporter* 28 (1 October 1898):59. On the importance of the open plan and its design in multistory retail buildings, see John L. Mauran, "The Department Store Plan," *Brickbuilder* 17 (November 1908):252–55.

153. Sullivan, "Sub-Structure at the New Schlesinger and Mayer Store Building," *Engineering Record* 47 (21 February 1903):194.

154. A note of 31 December 1904 in Carson Pirie Scott & Co. Archives, Chicago, records the division of the total annual rent for the Schlesinger and Mayer Building in 1904 into different amounts for each floor from basement to twelfth.

155. "Large Crowds at Big New Store," *Chicago Journal* (12 October 1903):2.

156. "Fire Protection in Department Stores," *Chicago Dry Goods Reporter* 34 (14 May 1904):17.

157. "Building Ordinances of the City of Chicago," in John H. Jones and Fred A. Britten, eds., *A Half Century of Chicago Building* (Chicago, 1910), 168–72.

158. "Inside of the Store," *Chicago Dry Goods Reporter* 29 (23 December 1899):15.

159. Advertisement for Schlesinger and Mayer Store opening, *Chicago Record-Herald* (7 October 1903):8.

160. "Inside of the Store," 15.

161. Annie Marion Maclean, "Two Weeks in a Department Store," *American Journal of Sociology* 4 (May 1899):721–41.

162. Ibid., 729.

163. Advertisement for Schlesinger and Mayer Store opening, *Chicago Tribune* (10 October 1903):5. The introduction of electric lighting into the old building was noted in "The Expansion of Retail Houses," *Economist* 5 (21 February 1891):293–94. The store's lighting compares closely with Marshall Field & Co.'s innovative system for combining arc and incandescent lamps in its new store building. This system is discussed in D. H. Howard, "Progress in Store Lighting," *Merchants Record and Show Window* 12 (January 1903):4–5.

164. "Modern Store Lighting," *Chicago Dry Goods Reporter* 33 (8 August 1903):53.

165. "Modern Store Fittings," *Chicago Dry Goods Reporter* 28 (18 June 1898):17.

166. "Growth of the Big Stores," *Chicago Dry Goods Reporter* 28 (6 August 1898):25.

167. "Modern Store Fittings," 13.

168. Louis Sullivan, Kindergarten Chat V: "An Hotel," *Kindergarten Chats and Other Writings*, 27.

169. The appearance of the Chicago window and Sullivan's use of this motif in Carson Pirie Scott is discussed in Giedion, *Space, Time and Architecture*, 5th ed., revised and enlarged, 371, 377, 387–89.

170. Constitution of the Architectural League of America, quoted in George R. Dean, "A New Movement in American Architecture," *Brush and Pencil* 5 (March 1900):255. An account of the inaugural convention appears in *Inland Architect and News Record* 33 (June 1899):41–43. The league published its own account of its goals and programs in the *Architectural Annual* from 1900. On Sullivan's relationship to the league see Menocal, *Architecture as Nature*, 82–86, and Twombly, *Louis Sullivan*, 354–56, 364–69.

171. William Copeland Furber, "Commercial Architecture," *Architectural Annual* 2 (Philadelphia, 1901):91.

172. "Store Heating," *Chicago Dry Goods Reporter* 28 (17 September 1898):15.

173. On the problems of ventilating and cooling store interiors to increase shoppers' comfort, see "Hints to Retailers and State Street Observations," *Chicago Dry Goods Reporter* 28 (4 June 1898):34 and 28 (22 October 1898):45. See also "Modern Store Fittings," ibid., 28 (18 June 1898):17.

174. A description of the mechanical plant for the new Schlesinger and Mayer Store appeared in "Large Crowds at Big New Store," *Chicago Journal* (12 October 1903):2.

175. For an account of the guided tours of the newly opened Schlesinger and Mayer Store, see "New Store a Marvel," *Chicago Record-Herald* (13 October 1903):13.

176. Ibid.

177. "Large Crowds at Big New Store," 2.

178. "Palatial Store for Chicago Shoppers," *Chicago Inter Ocean* (14 October 1903):7.

179. Louis Sullivan, "The Tall Office Building Artistically Considered," *Kindergarten Chats and Other Writings*, 203.

180. Dankmar Adler, "Slow Burning and Fireproof Construction—Part II," *Inland Architect and News Record* 27 (February 1896):3–4.

181. Louis Sullivan, quoted in "Opinions on the Use of Burned Clay for Fireproofing," *Brickbuilder* 7 (September 1898):189–90.

182. "Modern Store Fittings: Suggestions from State Street," *Chicago Dry Goods Reporter* 28 (18 June 1898):17.

183. "The Needs of the Retail Quarter," *Economist* 3 (22 February 1890):200.

184. Advertisement for Schlesinger and Mayer Store opening, *Chicago Record-Herald* (7 October 1903):8.

185. The role of the department store as a women's social club is noted in Susan Porter Benson, "Palace of Consumption and Machine for Selling: The American Department Store, 1880–1940," *Radical History Review* 21 (Fall

1979):205. Interspersal of visits to downtown stores and clubs as part of the daily activity of some affluent women is noted in William R. Leach, "Transformations in a Culture of Consumption: Women and Department Stores, 1890–1925," *Journal of American History* 71 (September 1984):334.

186. Advertisement for Schlesinger and Mayer Store opening, *Chicago Record-Herald* (7 October 1903):8.

187. One early example of Sullivan's interest in woodworking as a means to architectural effect was his collaboration with craftsmen in the design of interior surfaces for the Banqueting Room of the Auditorium Building. See Edward A. Garczynski, *The Auditorium* (Chicago, 1890), 102–6.

188. William G. Purcell to Mrs. Edith Elmslie, 4 March 1953, asserted, "I sat beside George [Elmslie] when he did a lot of that Schlesinger and Mayer (C.P.S. & Co.) detailing. For example the five thickness panels for restaurant and women's rest room"; letter in Purcell and Elmslie Collection, Northwest Architectural Archives, University of Minnesota, St. Paul. A transcription survives in the Burnham Library/University of Illinois Architectural Microfilming Project, Daily Progress Records and Notes, 2 vols., I: Entry for 29 March 1951, Burnham Library, Art Institute of Chicago, which states: "Elmslie has a wooden ornamental grille about one foot square which he has hanging in his living room window. When questioned as to what it was and who designed it Elmslie said it was his design and that it was a small part of a large wall grille used as a separating element in the women's rest room at the Schlesinger and Mayer Store."

189. William G. Purcell, undated note on the Schlesinger and Mayer interiors in the correspondence file of the Sullivan Centennial Exhibition, Museum Archives, Art Institute of Chicago. Rotation of the grain in adjacent layers of the mahogany screen was noted by Timothy Samuelson, Commission on Chicago Landmarks, personal conversation, 22 June 1987.

190. Lyndon P. Smith, "The Schlesinger and Mayer Building," *Architectural Record* 16 (July 1904):60.

191. Benjamin Schlesinger, "How to Bring Visitors into the Store," *System* 9 (March 1906):292.

192. William G. Purcell, undated note on the Schlesinger and Mayer interiors in the correspondence file of the Sullivan Centennial Exhibition, Museum Archives, Art Institute of Chicago.

193. *Economist* 18 (18 September 1897):320.

194. On the restaurant of Simpson, Crawford, and Simpson, New York, see *Dry Goods Economist* 57 (24 October 1903):35.

195. Advertisement for Schlesinger and Mayer's Store opening, *Chicago Tribune* (9 October 1903):8.

196. The capacity of Chicago's department stores to amass a wide range of opulent materials was demonstrated on one occasion by Marshall Field & Co. with a window display featuring an enlarged version of the seal of the City of Chicago made entirely from imported diamonds, rubies, and sapphires. See "A Great Exposition," *Merchants Record and Show Window* 15 (November 1904):21.

197. Daily violin recitals in the restaurant of Schlesinger and Mayer were

noted in an advertisement in the *Chicago Post* (30 October 1903):2. A print of an original working drawing labeled S$_F$19A, Diagram of Musician's Stand and Railing at South End of Restaurant for Schlesinger and Mayer, dated 27 July 1903, survives in the Office of John Vinci, A.I.A., Chicago.

198. William G. Purcell to Mrs. Edith Elmslie, 4 March 1953; letter in Purcell and Elmslie Collection, Northwest Architectural Archives, University of Minnesota, St. Paul, Minn.

199. Louis Sullivan to Claude Bragdon, 8 November 1903, in Claude Bragdon, "Letters from Louis Sullivan," *Architecture* 64 (July 1931):9.

200. William Le Baron Jenney, "The Chicago Construction, or Tall Buildings on a Compressible Soil," *Inland Architect and News Record* 18 (November 1891):41.

201. Louis Sullivan, Kindergarten Chat XI: "A Department Store," *Kindergarten Chats and Other Writings*, 40—41.

202. George Grant Elmslie to Frank Lloyd Wright, 12 June 1936, reprinted in *Society of Architectural Historians Journal* 20 (October 1961):140.

203. Dimensions for a typical steel bay and the heights and widths of window openings are taken from surviving prints or blueprints of original working drawings of the Schlesinger and Mayer Store dated 1902—3 in the possession of the Architectural Collections, Chicago Historical Society, and the Office of John Vinci, A.I.A., Chicago.

204. George G. Elmslie to William G. Purcell, Labor Day [1 September] 1947, letter in Purcell and Elmslie Collection, Northwest Architectural Archives, University of Minnesota, St. Paul, Minn.

205. Louis Sullivan, Kindergarten Chat XXXVII: "The Elements of Architecture: Objective and Subjective, (I): Pier and Lintel," *Kindergarten Chats and Other Writings*, 120.

206. Ibid., 122—23.

207. Wright, "The Art and Craft of the Machine," 8.

208. Ibid., 9.

209. William Le Baron Jenney, "An Age of Steel and Clay," *Inland Architect and News Record* 16 (December 1890):75—77.

210. Dankmar Adler, "Influence of Steel Construction and Plate Glass Upon the Development of Modern Style," *Inland Architect and News Record* 28 (November 1896):36.

211. Ibid.

212. On the development of architectural terra cotta in Chicago, see Sharon F. Darling, *Chicago Ceramics and Glass: An Illustrated History from 1871—1933* (Chicago: Chicago Historical Society, 1979), 160—204.

213. George M. R. Twose, "Steel and Terra Cotta Buildings in Chicago, and Some Deductions," *Brickbuilder* 3 (January 1894):1.

214. Frank Lloyd Wright, "The Art and Craft of the Machine," 9—10.

215. Louis Sullivan, *The Autobiography of an Idea*, 258.

216. Louis Sullivan to Russell Sturgis, 6 March 1897, Purcell and Elmslie Collection, Northwest Architectural Archives, University of Minnesota, St. Paul, Minn. See also Sullivan, "Emotional Architecture as Compared with Intellectual"

(1894), in *Kindergarten Chats and Other Writings*, 194, 201.

217. Louis Sullivan, "Suggestions in Artistic Brickwork" (1910), reprinted as "Artistic Brick," *Prairie School Review* 4 (Second Quarter 1967):24.

218. Louis Sullivan, "Ornament in Architecture" (1892), *Kindergarten Chats and Other Writings*, 188.

219. On the development of this same principle in Wright's work, see Edgar Kaufmann, Jr., "Frank Lloyd Wright: Plasticity, Continuity, and Ornament," *Society of Architectural Historians Journal* 37 (March 1978):34–39.

220. William Jordy, "The Commercial Style and the 'Chicago School,'" Review of *The Chicago School of Architecture*, by Carl Condit, in *Perspectives in American History* I (1967):398–99.

221. Louis Sullivan, *Democracy: A Man-Search* (1908; Detroit: Wayne State University Press, 1961), 103–4.

222. "Architecture in the Shopping District," *Inland Architect and News Record* 34 (January 1900):47.

223. *Bayard Building, 65-67-69 Bleeker Street* (New York, n.d.), 7. Parts of the description of the Bayard Building in this real estate brochure may have been prepared by Sullivan. Sullivan elsewhere wrote of the Bayard as having a "full terra cotta front richly decorated as befits the material." Louis Sullivan to Charles F. Gunther, Esq., 3 December 1897. Manuscript Collections, Chicago Historical Society.

224. Sullivan's views were cited in George M. R. Twose, "Steel and Terra Cotta Buildings in Chicago, and Some Deductions," 1.

225. Louis Sullivan, "Ornament in Architecture" (1892), *Kindergarten Chats and Other Writings*, 189.

226. Ibid., 188.

227. Lyndon P. Smith, "The Schlesinger and Mayer Building," *Architectural Record* 16 (July 1904):59.

228. Ibid.

229. Louis Sullivan, "The Tall Office Building Artistically Considered" (1896), *Kindergarten Chats and Other Writings*, 206.

230. Ibid., 207.

231. Ibid., 208.

232. Louis Sullivan, letter to Claude Bragdon, 25 July 1904, in Claude Bragdon, "Letters from Louis Sullivan," *Architecture* 64 (July 1931):8.

233. Louis Sullivan, *Autobiography of an Idea*, 213.

234. On academic theories of architectural expression related to building type and character, see Anthony Vidler, "The Idea of Type: Transformations of an Academic Ideal, 1750–1830," *Oppositions* 8 (Spring 1977):94–115, and Donald Drew Egbert, *The Beaux-Arts Tradition in French Architecture* (Princeton, N. J.: Princeton University Press, 1980), 121–35.

235. Louis Sullivan, Kindergarten Chat V: "An Hotel," *Kindergarten Chats and Other Writings*, 27–28.

236. Louis Sullivan, Kindergarten Chat XI: "A Department Store," *Kindergarten Chats and Other Writings*, 40.

237. Ibid.

238. Louis Sullivan, "The Tall Office Building Artistically Considered," 203.

239. "Marble Building at State and Madison Streets," *Chicago Inter Ocean* (29 May 1898):20.

240. N. Max Dunning to Louis H. Sullivan, 6 December 1912. Purcell and Elmslie Collection, Northwest Architectural Archives, University of Minnesota, St. Paul, Minn.

241. Paul Cret, "The Ecole des Beaux Arts: What Its Architectural Teaching Means," *Architectural Record* 23 (May 1908):369. Cret's study in Pascal's atelier is noted in Theo B. White, *Paul Philippe Cret: Architect and Teacher* (Philadelphia: Art Alliance Press, 1973), 17, 21.

Conclusion

1. Emile Zola, quoted in Michael B. Miller, *The Bon Marché: Bourgeois Culture and the Department Store, 1869–1920* (Princeton, N.J.: Princeton University Press, 1981), 5. Zola studied the canonical Parisian department store as the setting for his novel *Au bonheur des dames* (Paris, 1883).

2. *Bayard Building, 65–67–69 Bleeker Street* (New York, n.d.), 7.

3. Louis Sullivan, "Ornament in Architecture," *Kindergarten Chats and Other Writings*, 188.

4. Louis Sullivan, "The Modern Phase of Architecture," *Inland Architect and News Record* 33 (June 1899):40. Walt Whitman was perhaps the model for Sullivan's characterization of the architect as poet of the national life of his time. On Sullivan's relationship to Whitman, see Sherman Paul, *Louis Sullivan*, 1–3, 42–45. See also Lauren S. Weingarden, "Naturalized Technology: Louis H. Sullivan's Whitmanesque Skyscrapers," *The Centennial Review* 30 (Fall 1986):480–95.

5. Louis Sullivan, quoted in "Architectural Style," *Inland Architect and News Record* 38 (September 1901):16.

6. George Grant Elmslie to Frank Lloyd Wright, 30 October 1932. Purcell and Elmslie Collection, Northwest Architectural Archives, University of Minnesota, St. Paul, Minn.

7. Louis Sullivan, Kindergarten Chat XXXIX: "On the Historic Styles" (1901), original version reprinted in *Roots of Contemporary American Architecture*, ed. Lewis Mumford (New York: Dover, 1972), 78.

8. John Wellborn Root, "Style" (1887), in Donald Hoffmann, ed., *The Meanings of Architecture: Buildings and Writings by John Wellborn Root* (New York: Horizon Press, 1967), 164.

9. "Architectural," *Chicago Times* (2 November 1878):9.

10. Claude Bragdon, "L'Art Nouveau in American Architecture," *Inland Architect and News Record* 42 (October 1903):20.

11. George M. Maher, "The Western Spirit," *Inland Architect and News Record* 47 (April 1906):39.

12. Claude Bragdon, "L'Art Nouveau in American Architecture," 19.

13. Ibid.

14. Henry W. Desmond, "The Schlesinger and Mayer Building, Another View—What Mr. Louis Sullivan Stands For," *Architectural Record* 16 (July 1904):67.

15. For assessments of Sullivan's work in relation to European architecture called Art Nouveau, see Henry-Russell Hitchcock, "Art Nouveau Architecture," in Peter Selz and Mildred Constantine, eds., *Art Nouveau: Art and Design at the Turn of the Century* (New York: Museum of Modern Art, 1959), 123–25; William Chaitkin, "Louis Sullivan" in Frank Russell, ed., *Art Nouveau Architecture* (New York: Rizzoli, 1979), 265–72; Diane Chalmers Johnson, *American Art Nouveau* (New York: Harry N. Abrams, 1979), 124–62.

16. A. W. Barker, "Louis H. Sullivan, Thinker and Architect," *Architectural Annual* 2 (Philadelphia, 1901):66.

SELECTED BIBLIOGRAPHY

Adams, Richard P. "Architecture and the Romantic Tradition: Coleridge to Wright." *American Quarterly* 9 (Spring 1957):46–62.

Adams, Samuel H. "The Conduct of Great Businesses, Part I: The Department Store." *Scribner's Magazine* 21 (July 1897):1–27.

Adler, Dankmar. "Are There Any Canons of Art?" 64th Meeting of the Sunset Club, Chicago, 7 December 1893. In *The Sunset Club, Chicago: The Meetings of 1893–94 and A List of the Members to January, 1895*, 49–61. Chicago, 1895.

———. "Influence of Steel Construction and Plate Glass Upon the Development of Modern Style." *Inland Architect and News Record* 28 (November 1896): 34–37.

———. "Slow Burning and Fireproof Construction." *Inland Architect and News Record* 26 (December 1895):60–62; 27 (February 1896):3–4.

Andreas, Alfred T. *History of Chicago*. 3 vols. 1884–86. Reprint. New York: Arno Press, 1975.

Andrew, David S. *Louis Sullivan and the Polemics of Modern Architecture: The Present Against the Past*. Urbana: University of Illinois Press, 1985.

"Architecture in the Shopping District." *Inland Architect and News Record* 34 (January 1900):46–47.

Barker, A. W. "Louis H. Sullivan, Thinker and Architect." *Architectural Annual* (Philadelphia) 2 (1901):49–66.

Barth, Gunther. *City People. The Rise of Modern City Culture in Nineteenth Century America*. New York: Oxford University Press, 1980.

Barton, Elmer E. *A Business Tour of Chicago, Depicting Fifty Years' Progress*. Chicago, 1887.

Benson, Susan Porter. "Palace of Consumption and Machine for Selling: The American Department Store, 1880–1940." *Radical History Review* 21 (Fall 1979):199–221.

Bonta, Juan P. *Architecture and Its Interpretation: A Study of Expressive Systems in Architecture.* New York: Rizzoli, 1979.

Boorstin, Daniel J. *The Americans: The Democratic Experience.* New York: Random House, 1973.

Boyer, M. Christine. *Manhattan Manners: Architecture and Style, 1850–1900.* New York: Rizzoli, 1985.

Bragdon, Claude. "An American Architect, Being an Appreciation of Louis H. Sullivan." *House and Garden* 7 (January 1905):47–55.

———. "L'Art Nouveau in American Architecture." *Inland Architect and News Record* 42 (October 1903):19–21.

Brooks, H. Allen. "Chicago Architecture: Its Debt to the Arts and Crafts." *Society of Architectural Historians Journal* 30 (December 1971):312–17.

———. "The Chicago School: Metamorphosis of a Term." *Society of Architectural Historians Journal* 25 (May 1966):115–18.

———. *The Prairie School: Frank Lloyd Wright and His Midwestern Contemporaries.* Toronto: University of Toronto Press, 1972.

Bruegmann, Robert. "Holabird & Roche and Holabird & Root: The First Two Generations." *Chicago History* 9 (Fall 1980):130–65.

Bush-Brown, Albert. *Louis Sullivan.* New York: George Braziller, 1960.

Caparn, H. A. "The Riddle of the Tall Building: Has the Skyscraper a Place in American Architecture?" *Craftsman* 10 (April 1906):477–88.

Charernbhak, Wichit. *Chicago School Architects and Their Critics.* Architecture and Urban Design, edited by Stephen C. Foster, no. 1. Ann Arbor: UMI Research Press, 1981.

Clausen, Meredith. "Frantz Jourdain and the Samaritaine of 1905." Ph.D. diss., University of California–Berkeley, 1975.

Cleveland, Harold I. "Fifty Five Years in Business: The Life of Marshall Field." *System* 9 (May 1906):455–64; (June 1906):556–66; 10 (July 1906):21–30; (August 1906):129–38; (November 1906):456–64; (December 1906):574–82; 11 (January 1907):49–56; (February 1907):123–32; (March 1907):229–37; (April 1907):361–68; (May 1907):453–63.

Commission on Chicago Historical and Architectural Landmarks. *Carson Pirie Scott & Company Building.* Chicago: City of Chicago, 1979.

Condit, Carl. "The Chicago School and the Modern Movement in Architecture." *Art in America* 36 (January 1948):19–36.

———. *The Chicago School of Architecture: A History of Commercial and Public Building in the Chicago Area, 1875–1925.* Chicago: University of Chicago Press, 1964.

———. *The Rise of the Skyscraper.* Chicago: University of Chicago Press, 1952.

Connely, Willard. *Louis Sullivan as He Lived: The Shaping of American Architecture.* New York: Horizon Press, 1960.

Crissey, Forrest. *Since Forty Years Ago: An Account of the Origin and Growth of Chicago and Its First Department Store.* Chicago: The Fair, 1915.

Crook, David H. "Louis Sullivan, The World's Columbian Exposition, and American Life." Ph.D. diss., Harvard University, 1964.

Darling, Sharon S. *Chicago Ceramics and Glass: An Illustrated History from 1871 to 1933.* Chicago: Chicago Historical Society, 1979.

David, Arthur C. "The Architecture of Ideas." *Architectural Record* 15 (April 1904):361–84.

Dean, George R. "Progress before Precedent." *Brickbuilder* 9 (May 1900):91–92.

Dennis, John, Jr. "Marshall Field: A Great Mercantile Genius." *Everybody's Magazine* 14 (March 1906):291–302.

"The Department Store in the East." *Arena* 22 (August 1899):165–86.

"The Department Store in the West." *Arena* 22 (September 1899):320–41.

Desmond, Henry W. "[The Schlesinger and Mayer Building] Another View—What Mr. Louis Sullivan Stands For." *Architectural Record* 16 (July 1904): 61–67.

Douglas, Ann. *The Feminization of American Culture.* New York: A. Knopf, 1978.

Dreiser, Theodore. *Sister Carrie.* 1900. Pennsylvania Edition. Philadelphia: University of Pennsylvania Press, 1981.

Duncan, Hugh D. *Culture and Democracy: The Struggle for Form in Society and Architecture in Chicago and the Middle West during the Life and Times of Louis H. Sullivan.* Totowa, N.J.: Bedminster Press, 1965.

Early, James. *Romanticism and American Architecture.* New York: A. S. Barnes, 1965.

Eaton, Leonard K. *American Architecture Comes of Age: European Reactions to H. H. Richardson and Louis Sullivan.* Cambridge, Mass.: M.I.T. Press, 1972.

Egbert, Donald D. *The Beaux-Arts Tradition in French Architecture.* Edited by David Van Zanten. Princeton: Princeton University Press, 1980.

————. "The Idea of Organic Expression and American Architecture." In *Evolutionary Thought in America,* edited by Stow Persons. New Haven: Yale University Press, 1950.

Elmslie, George G. Letter to Frank Lloyd Wright, 12 June 1936. *Society of Architectural Historians Journal* 20 (October 1961):140–41.

————. "Sullivan Ornamentation." *American Institute of Architects Journal* 6 (July 1946):155–58. First published in *Illinois Society of Architects Monthly Bulletin* 19–20 (June-July 1935):6.

Ferry, John W. *A History of the Department Store.* New York: Macmillan, 1960.

Fifty Photographic Views of Chicago. Chicago: Rand, McNally and Co., 1896.

Fireproof Building Construction: Prominent Buildings Erected by the George A. Fuller Company. New York and Chicago: George A. Fuller Co., 1904.

Fisker, Kay. "Louis Henry Sullivan." *Forum* (Amsterdam) Third Year, no. 12 (1948):347–55.

Flinn, John J. *Chicago: The Marvelous City of the West.* Chicago, 1892.

Gebhard, David. *Drawings for Architectural Ornament by George Grant Elmslie, 1902–1936.* Santa Barbara, Calif.: Art Gallery, University of California-Santa Barbara, 1968.

————. "Louis Sullivan and George Grant Elmslie." *Society of Architectural Historians Journal* 19 (May 1960):62–68.

————. Review of *Democracy: A Man-Search*, by Louis Sullivan; *A System of Architectural Ornament*, by Louis Sullivan; *Louis Sullivan*, by Albert Bush-Brown. *Society of Architectural Historians Journal* 21 (December 1962):194–95.

Giedion, Sigfried. *Space, Time and Architecture*. 5th ed., rev. and enl., Cambridge, Mass: Harvard University Press, 1982.

Gilbert, Paul T., and Charles L. Bryson. *Chicago and Its Makers*. Chicago: F. Mendelsohn, 1929.

Harris, Neil. "Museums, Merchandising and Popular Taste: The Struggle for Influence." In *Material Culture and the Study of American Life*, edited by Ian Quimby, 140–74. New York: W. W. Norton & Co., 1978.

Hautecoeur, Louis. *Histoire de l'architecture classique en France*. Vol. 7, *La fin de l'architecture classique, 1848–1900*. Paris: Picard, 1957.

Hendrickson, Robert. *The Grand Emporiums: The Illustrated History of America's Great Department Stores*. New York: Stein and Day, 1979.

Hilbersheimer, Ludwig. *Groszstadt Architektur*. Stuttgart: Julius Hoffmann, 1927.

Hines, Thomas S. *Burnham of Chicago, Architect and Planner*. New York: Oxford University Press, 1974.

Hitchcock, Henry-Russell. *Architecture: Nineteenth and Twentieth Centuries*. 3rd ed., Baltimore: Penguin Books, 1969.

————. "Sullivan and the Skyscraper." *Builder* 185 (7 August 1953):197–200. First published in *Journal of the Royal Institute of British Architects* 60 (July 1953):353–61.

Hoffmann, Donald. *The Architecture of John Wellborn Root*. Baltimore: Johns Hopkins University Press, 1973.

————, ed. *The Meanings of Architecture: Buildings and Writings by John Wellborn Root*. New York: Horizon Press, 1967.

Hope, Henry R. "Louis Sullivan's Architectural Ornament." *Architectural Review* (London) 102 (October 1947):111–14. First published in *Magazine of Art* 40 (March 1947):111–17.

Hower, Ralph M. *History of Macy's of New York, 1858-1919*. Cambridge, Mass.: Harvard University Press, 1943.

Hoyt, Homer N. *One Hundred Years of Land Values in Chicago, 1830–1933*. Chicago: University of Chicago Press, 1933.

Industrial Chicago. Vols. 1–2, *The Building Interests*. Chicago: Goodspeed Publishing Co., 1891.

Jenney, William Le Baron. "An Age of Steel and Clay." *Inland Architect and News Record* 16 (December 1890):75–77.

————. "The Chicago Construction, or Tall Buildings on a Compressible Soil." *Inland Architect and News Record* 18 (November 1891):41.

————. "A Few Practical Hints." *Inland Architect and News Record* 13 (February 1889):7–9.

Jodice, Romano. *L'Architettura del ferro gli stati uniti (1893–1914)*. L'Architettura del ferro, vol. 3, pt. 3. Rome: Bulzoni, 1972.

Johnson, Diane C. *American Art Nouveau*. New York: Harry N. Abrams, 1979.

Johnson, Philip. "Is Sullivan the Father of Functionalism?" *Art News* 55 (December 1956):45–46, 56–57.

Jones, John H. and Fred A. Britten, eds., *A Half Century of Chicago Building: A Practical Reference Guide*. Chicago, 1910.

Jordy, William H. *American Buildings and Their Architects: Progressive and Academic Ideals at the Turn of the Twentieth Century*. 1972. Reprint. New York: Oxford University Press, 1986.

———. "The Commercial Style and the 'Chicago School'." Review of *The Chicago School of Architecture*, by Carl Condit, in *Perspectives in American History* I (1967):390–400.

Kaufmann, Edgar, Jr., "Frank Lloyd Wright: Plasticity, Continuity, and Ornament." *Society of Architectural Historians Journal* 37 (March 1978):34–39.

———. *Louis Sullivan and the Architecture of Free Enterprise*. Chicago: Art Institute of Chicago, 1956.

Kramer, Ethel. "The Ornament of Louis Sullivan." Honors thesis, Smith College, 1960.

Leach, William R. "Transformations in a Culture of Consumption: Women and Department Stores, 1890–1925." *Journal of American History* 71 (September 1984):219–42.

Lewis, Russell. "Everything under One Roof: World's Fairs and Department Stores in Paris and Chicago." *Chicago History* 12 (Fall 1983):28–47.

Maclean, Annie M. "Two Weeks in a Department Store." *American Journal of Sociology* 4 (May 1899):721–41.

Marcus, Leonard S. *The American Store Window*. New York: Watson-Guptill, 1978.

Marrey, Bernard. *Les grands magazins: des origines à 1939*. Paris: Picard, 1979.

Mauran, John L. "The Department Store Plan." *Brickbuilder* 17 (November 1908):252–255.

Mayer, Harold M. and Richard C. Wade. *Chicago: Growth of a Metropolis*. Chicago: University of Chicago Press, 1969.

Menocal, Narciso G. *Architecture as Nature: The Transcendentalist Idea of Louis Sullivan*. Madison: University of Wisconsin Press, 1981.

Miller, Michael B. *The Bon Marché: Bourgeois Culture and the Department Store, 1869–1920*. Princeton: Princeton University Press, 1981.

Morrison, Hugh. *Louis Sullivan, Prophet of Modern Architecture*. 1935. Reprint. New York: W. W. Norton & Co., 1962.

Mumford, Lewis. *The Brown Decades: A Study of the Arts in America*. 1931. New York: Dover Publications, 1955.

———, ed., *Roots of Contemporary American Architecture*. 1952. Reprint. New York: Dover Publications, 1972.

The Museum of Modern Art. *Early Modern Architecture in Chicago, 1870–1910*. New York: Museum of Modern Art, 1933.

Museum of Science and Industry, Chicago. *A Guide to One Hundred and Fifty Years of Chicago Architecture*. Chicago: Chicago Review Press, 1985.

"Nature as an Ornamentalist." *Architectural Record* 9 (April 1900):441–49.

"The New Schlesinger and Mayer Building, Chicago." *Brickbuilder* 12 (May 1903): 101–4.

O'Gorman, James F. "The Marshall Field Wholesale Store: Materials Toward a

Monograph." *Society of Architectural Historians Journal* 37 (October 1978): 175–94.

One Year From the Fire . . . Chicago Illustrated. Chicago: J. M. Wing & Co., 1872.

Orear, George W. *Commercial and Architectural Chicago.* Chicago, 1887.

Ornamental Iron and Bronze. Chicago: Winslow Brothers Co., 1910.

Pasdermadjian, Hrant. *The Department Store: Its Origins, Evolution, and Economics.* London: Newman Books, 1954.

Paul, Sherman. *Louis Sullivan, An Architect in American Thought.* Englewood Cliffs, N.J.: Prentice-Hall, 1962.

Pevsner, Nikolaus. *A History of Building Types.* Princeton: Princeton University Press, 1976.

Pierce, Bessie L. *A History of Chicago.* 3 vols. 1940. Reprint. Chicago: University of Chicago Press, 1975.

Randall, Frank A. *History of the Development of Building Construction in Chicago.* Urbana: University of Illinois Press, 1949.

Rand McNally & Co.'s Bird's-Eye Views and Guide to Chicago. Chicago: Rand McNally & Co., 1893.

Resseguie, Harry E. "A. T. Stewart's Marble Palace—The Cradle of the Department Store." *New-York Historical Society Quarterly* 48 (April 1964): 131–62.

Rowe, Colin. "Chicago Frame." *Architectural Review* 120 (November 1956): 285–89. Reprinted in *The Mathematics of the Ideal Villa and Other Essays.* Cambridge, Mass.: M.I.T. Press, 1976, 89–117.

Schick, Louis. *Chicago and Its Environs: A Handbook for the Traveler.* Chicago, 1891.

Schuyler, Montgomery. *American Architecture and Other Writings.* 2 vols. Edited by William Jordy and Ralph Coe. Cambridge, Mass.: Harvard University Press, 1961.

———. [Franz Winkler, pseud.]. "Some Chicago Buildings Represented by the Work of Holabird and Roche." *Architectural Record* 31 (April 1912): 313–87.

Scully, Vincent. *American Architecture and Urbanism.* New York: Praeger Publishers, 1969.

———. "Louis Sullivan's Architectural Ornament: A Brief Note Concerning Humanist Design in the Age of Force." *Perspecta* 5 (1959): 73–80.

Selz, Peter and Mildred Constantine, eds. *Art Nouveau: Art and Design at the Turn of the Century.* New York: Museum of Modern Art, 1959.

Shulof, Suzanne. "An Interpretation of Louis Sullivan's Architectural Ornament Based on Its Philosophy of Organic Expression." Master's thesis, Columbia University, 1962.

Siegel, Arthur S., ed. *Chicago's Famous Buildings.* 2nd ed. Chicago: University of Chicago Press, 1969.

Siry, Joseph M. "The Carson Pirie Scott Building in Chicago." Ph.D. diss., Massachusetts Institute of Technology, 1984.

Slade, Thomas M. "A Collated Edition of Louis H. Sullivan's *Kindergarten Chats.*" Master's thesis, State University of New York at Buffalo, 1971.

Smith, Lyndon. "The Schlesinger and Mayer Building: An Attempt to Give Functional Expression to the Architecture of a Department Store." *Architectural Record* 16 (July 1904): 53–60.

Smith, Mary Ann Clegg. "John Snook and the Design for A. T. Stewart's Store." *New-York Historical Society Quarterly* 58 (January 1974): 18–33.

Sprague, Paul. "The Architectural Ornament of Louis Sullivan and His Chief Draftsmen." Ph.D. diss., Princeton University, 1968.

———. *The Drawings of Louis Henry Sullivan: A Catalogue of the Frank Lloyd Wright Collection At the Avery Architectural Library.* Princeton: Princeton University Press, 1978.

Starret, Theodore. "The Architecture of Louis H. Sullivan." *Architects' and Builders' Magazine* 44 (December 1912): 469–75.

Sullivan, Louis. "The Artistic Use of the Imagination." *Inland Architect and News Record* 14 (October 1889): 38–39.

———. *The Autobiography of an Idea.* 1924. Reprint. New York: Dover Publications, 1956.

———. *Democracy: A Man-Search.* (1907; revised 1908). Edited by Elaine Hedges. Detroit: Wayne State University Press, 1961.

———. "Emotional Architecture as Compared with Intellectual: A Study in Objective and Subjective." *Inland Architect and News Record* 24 (November 1894): 32–34. Reprinted in Athey, ed., *Kindergarten Chats,* 191–201.

———. *Kindergarten Chats and Other Writings.* Edited by Isabella Athey. 1947. Reprint. New York: Dover Publications, 1979.

———. "The Modern Phase of Architecture." *Inland Architect and News Record* 33 (June 1899): 40.

———. "Opinions on the Use of Burned Clay for Fireproofing." *Brickbuilder* 7 (September 1898): 189–90.

———. "Ornament in Architecture." *Engineering Magazine* 3 (August 1892): 633–44. Reprinted in Athey, ed., *Kindergarten Chats,* 187–90.

———. "Style." *Inland Architect and News Record* 11 (May 1888): 59–60.

———. "Sub-Structure at the New Schlesinger and Mayer Store Building." *Engineering Record* 47 (21 February 1903): 194–96.

———. "Suggestions in Artistic Brickwork." In *Artistic Brick.* St. Louis: Hydraulic Press Brick Co., c. 1910, 5–13. Reprinted as "Artistic Brick." *Prairie School Review* 4 (Second Quarter 1967): 24–26.

———. *A System of Architectural Ornament According with a Philosophy of Man's Powers.* 1924. Reprint. New York: Eakins Press, 1967.

———. "The Tall Office Building Artistically Considered." *Lippincott's Magazine* 57 (March 1896): 403–09. Reprinted in Athey, ed., *Kindergarten Chats,* 202–13.

———. "What is the Just Subordination, in Architectural Design, of Details to Mass?" *Inland Architect and News Record* 9 (April 1887): 51–54; *Building Budget* 3 (April 1887): 62–63. Reprinted in Athey, ed., *Kindergarten Chats,* 182–86.

Szarkowski, John. *The Idea of Louis Sullivan.* Minneapolis: University of Minnesota Press, 1956.

Tallmadge, Thomas E. *Architecture in Old Chicago.* Chicago: University of Chicago Press, 1941.

———. "The Chicago School." *Architectural Review* (Boston) 15 (April 1908): 69–74.

Taut, Bruno. *Die neue Baukunst in Europa und Amerika*. Stuttgart: Julius Hoffmann, 1929.

Turak, Theodore. "French and English Sources of Sullivan's Ornament and Doctrine." *Prairie School Review* 11 (Fourth Quarter 1974):5–30.

———. *William Le Baron Jenney: A Pioneer of Modern Architecture*. Architecture and
Urban Design, edited by Stephen C. Foster, no. 17. Ann Arbor: UMI Research Press, 1986.

Twombly, Robert. *Louis Sullivan. His Life and Work*. New York: Viking, Elizabeth
Sifton Books, 1986.

Twose, George M. R. "Steel and Terra Cotta Buildings in Chicago, and Some
Deductions." *Brickbuilder* 3 (January 1894):1–5.

Two Years After the Fire . . . Chicago Illustrated. Chicago: J. M. Wing & Co., 1873.

Twyman, Robert W. *History of Marshall Field & Co., 1852–1906*. Philadelphia:
University of Pennsylvania Press, 1954.

Van Ormer, Geraldine. "Louis Sullivan's Ornamentation as Exemplified in the
Carson, Pirie, Scott Building." Master's thesis, Pennsylvania State University,
1960.

Van Zanten, Ann Lorenz. "The Marshall Field Annex and the New Urban Order
of Daniel Burnham's Chicago." *Chicago History* 11 (Fall and Winter 1982):
130–41.

Veblen, Thorstein. *The Theory of the Leisure Class: A Study of Economic Institutions*.
1899. Reprint. New York: Penguin Books, 1979.

Vinci, John. "Carson Pirie Scott: 125 Years in Business." *Chicago History* 8 (Summer 1979):92–97.

Weingarden, Lauren S. "Louis H. Sullivan's Metaphysics of Architecture (1885–
1901): Sources and Correspondences with Symbolist Art Theories." Ph.D.
diss., University of Chicago, 1981.

Weisman, Winston. "Commercial Palaces of New York, 1845–1875." *Art Bulletin*
34 (December 1954):285–302.

Wendt, Lloyd and Herman Kogan. *Give the Lady What She Wants! The Story of
Marshall Field & Company*. Chicago: Rand McNally & Co., 1952.

Wiener, Alfred. *Das Warenhaus*. Berlin: Wasmuth, 1912.

Williams, Rosalind. *Dream Worlds: Mass Consumption in Late Nineteenth Century
France*. Berkeley and Los Angeles: University of California Press, 1982.

Wit, Wim de, ed. *Louis Sullivan: The Function of Ornament*. New York: W. W.
Norton & Co., 1986.

Wright, Frank Lloyd. "The Art and Craft of the Machine." In *Catalogue of the
Fourteenth Annual Exhibition of the Chicago Architectural Club*. Chicago: Chicago
Architectural Club, 1901.

———. *Genius and the Mobocracy*. 1949. 2nd ed., New York: Horizon Press, 1971.

———. "Louis H. Sullivan—His Work." *Architectural Record* 56 (July 1924):
28–32.

INDEX